# NAHUM, HABAKKUK, ZEPHANIAH

WISDOM COMMENTARY

Volume 38

# Nahum, Habakkuk, Zephaniah

Wilda C. M. Gafney

Carol J. Dempsey, OP
*Volume Editor*

Barbara E. Reid, OP
*General Editor*

A Michael Glazier Book

**LITURGICAL PRESS**
Collegeville, Minnesota

www.litpress.org

A Michael Glazier Book published by Liturgical Press

Cover design by Ann Blattner. *Chapter Letter 'W'*, *Acts of the Apostles, Chapter 4,* Donald Jackson, Copyright 2002, *The Saint John's Bible*, Saint John's University, Collegeville, Minnesota USA. Used by permission. All rights reserved.

1     2     3     4     5     6     7     8     9

**Library of Congress Cataloging-in-Publication Data**

Names: Gafney, Wilda, 1966– author.
Title: Nahum, Habakkuk, Zephaniah / Wilda C. M. Gafney ; Carol J. Dempsey, OP, volume editor ; Barbara E. Reid, OP, general editor.
Description: Collegeville, Minnesota : LITURGICAL PRESS, 2017. | Series: Wisdom commentary ; Volume 38 | "A Michael Glazier Book." | Includes bibliographical references and index.
Identifiers: LCCN 2017009640 (print) | LCCN 2017030600 (ebook) | ISBN 9780814681879 (ebook) | ISBN 9780814681626
Subjects: LCSH: Bible. Nahum—Feminist criticism. | Bible. Habakkuk—Feminist criticism. | Bible. Zephaniah—Feminist criticism.
Classification: LCC BS1625.52 (ebook) | LCC BS1625.52 .G34 2017 (print) | DDC 224/.907—dc23
LC record available at https://lccn.loc.gov/2017009640

*For my teachers, Gene Rice and Ibrahim Farajajé*

# Contents

# Abbreviations

| | |
|---|---|
| AB | Anchor Bible |
| *ABD* | *Anchor Yale Bible Dictionary*. Edited by David Noel Freeman. New Haven: Yale University Press, 1992 |
| ANE | Ancient Near East |
| AOTC | Abingdon Old Testament Commentaries |
| AYB | Anchor Yale Bible Commentary |
| BCE | Before the Common Era |
| BDAG | Danker, Frederick W., Walter Bauer, William F. Arndt, and F. Wilbur Gingrich. *Greek-English Lexicon of the New Testament and Other Early Christian Literature*. 3rd ed. Chicago: University of Chicago Press, 2000. |
| BDB | Brown, Francis, S. R. Driver, and Charles A. Briggs. *A Hebrew and English Lexicon of the Old Testament* |
| *BHS* | *Biblia Hebraica Stuttgartensia* |
| BibInt | Biblical Interpretation Series |
| *CAD* | *The Assyrian Dictionary of the Oriental Institute of the University of Chicago*. Chicago: The Oriental Institute of the University of Chicago, 1956–2006 |
| CE | Common Era |
| CEB | Common English Bible |

| | |
|---|---|
| DCH | *Dictionary of Classical Hebrew.* Edited by David J. A. Clines. 9 vols. Sheffield: Sheffield Phoenix, 1993–2014 |
| DSS | Dead Sea Scrolls |
| FCB | Feminist Companion to the Bible |
| GBS | Guides to Biblical Scholarship |
| HALOT | *The Hebrew and Aramaic Lexicon of the Old Testament.* Ludwig Koehler, Walter Baumgartner, and Johann J. Stamm. Translated and edited under the supervision of Mervyn E. J. Richardson. 4 vols. Leiden: Brill, 1994–1999 |
| HB | Hebrew Bible |
| IEJ | *Israel Exploration Journal* |
| IFT | Introductions in Feminist Theology |
| JAOS | *Journal of the American Oriental Society* |
| JFSR | *Journal of Feminist Studies in Religion* |
| JPS | Jewish Publication Society |
| JRT | *Journal of Religious Thought* |
| JSOT | *Journal for the Study of the Old Testament* |
| JSOTSup | Journal for the Study of the Old Testament Supplement Series |
| KJV | King James Version of the Bible |
| LXX | Septuagint |
| MT | Masoretic Text |
| NASB | New American Standard Bible |
| NETS | *A New English Translation of the Septuagint.* Edited by Albert Pietersma and Benjamin G. Wright. New York: Oxford University Press, 2007 |
| NIV | New International Version |
| NKJV | New King James Version |
| NRSV | New Revised Standard Version |
| OBT | Overtures to Biblical Theology |
| OtSt | *Oudtestamentische Studiën* |
| RSV | Revised Standard Version |

SBL        Society of Biblical Literature

SymS      Symposium Series

TDOT    *Theological Dictionary of the Old Testament.* Edited by
G. Johannes Botterweck and Helmer Ringgren.
Translated by John T. Willis et al. 8 vols. Grand Rapids:
Eerdmans, 1974–2006

TWOT   *Theological Wordbook of the Old Testament.* Edited by R. Laird
Harris, Gleason L. Archer Jr., and Bruce K. Waltke. 2 vols.
Chicago: Moody Press, 1980

VT         *Vetus Testamentum*

# Contributor

Rabbah Arlene Goldstein Berger serves the Olney Kehilah congregation. She is active in interfaith work for peace and understanding.

# Foreword

# *"Tell It on the Mountain"—or, "And You Shall Tell Your Daughter [as Well]"*

*Athalya Brenner-Idan*

*Universiteit van Amsterdam/Tel Aviv University*

What can Wisdom Commentary do to help, and for whom?
The commentary genre has always been privileged in biblical studies. Traditionally acclaimed commentary series, such as the International Critical Commentary, Old Testament and New Testament Library, Hermeneia, Anchor Bible, Eerdmans, and Word—to name but several—enjoy nearly automatic prestige; and the number of women authors who participate in those is relatively small by comparison to their growing number in the scholarly guild. There certainly are some volumes written by women in them, especially in recent decades. At this time, however, this does not reflect the situation on the ground. Further, size matters. In that sense, the sheer size of the Wisdom Commentary is essential. This also represents a considerable investment and the possibility of reaching a wider audience than those already "converted."

Expecting women scholars to deal especially or only with what are considered strictly "female" matters seems unwarranted. According to Audre Lorde, "The master's tools will never dismantle the master's house."[1] But this maxim is not relevant to our case. The point of this commentary is not to destroy but to attain greater participation in the interpretive dialogue about biblical texts. Women scholars may bring additional questions to the readerly agenda as well as fresh angles to existing issues. To assume that their questions are designed only to topple a certain male hegemony is not convincing.

At first I did ask myself: is this commentary series an addition to calm raw nerves, an embellishment to make upholding the old hierarchy palatable? Or is it indeed about becoming the Master? On second and third thoughts, however, I understood that becoming the Master is not what this is about. Knowledge is power. Since Foucault at the very least, this cannot be in dispute. Writing commentaries for biblical texts by women for women and for men, of confessional as well as non-confessional convictions, will sabotage (hopefully) the established hierarchy but will not topple it. This is about an attempt to integrate more fully, to introduce another viewpoint, to become. What excites me about the Wisdom Commentary is that it is not offered as just an alternative supplanting or substituting for the dominant discourse.

These commentaries on biblical books will retain nonauthoritative, pluralistic viewpoints. And yes, once again, the weight of a dedicated series, to distinguish from collections of stand-alone volumes, will prove weightier.

That such an approach is especially important in the case of the Hebrew Bible/Old Testament is beyond doubt. Women of Judaism, Christianity, and also Islam have struggled to make it their own for centuries, even more than they have fought for the New Testament and the Qur'an. Every Hebrew Bible/Old Testament volume in this project is evidence that the day has arrived: it is now possible to read *all* the Jewish canonical books as a collection, for a collection they are, with guidance conceived of with the needs of women readers (not only men) as an integral inspiration and part thereof.

In my Jewish tradition, the main motivation for reciting the Haggadah, the ritual text recited yearly on Passover, the festival of liberation from

---

1. Audre Lorde, "The Master's Tools Will Never Dismantle the Master's House," in *Sister Outsider: Essays and Speeches* (Berkeley, CA: Crossing Press, 1984, 2007), 110–14. First delivered in the Second Sex Conference in New York, 1979.

bondage, is given as "And you shall tell your son" (from Exod 13:8). The knowledge and experience of past generations is thus transferred to the next, for constructing the present and the future. The ancient maxim is, literally, limited to a male audience. This series remolds the maxim into a new inclusive shape, which is of the utmost consequence: "And you shall tell your son" is extended to "And you shall tell your daughter [as well as your son]." Or, if you want, "Tell it on the mountain," for all to hear.

This is what it's all about.

# Editor's Introduction to Wisdom Commentary

# *"She Is a Breath of the Power of God" (Wis 7:25)*

## *Barbara E. Reid, OP*

### General Editor

Wisdom Commentary is the first series to offer detailed feminist interpretation of every book of the Bible. The fruit of collaborative work by an ecumenical and interreligious team of scholars, the volumes provide serious, scholarly engagement with the whole biblical text, not only those texts that explicitly mention women. The series is intended for clergy, teachers, ministers, and all serious students of the Bible. Designed to be both accessible and informed by the various approaches of biblical scholarship, it pays particular attention to the world in front of the text, that is, how the text is heard and appropriated. At the same time, this series aims to be faithful to the ancient text and its earliest audiences; thus the volumes also explicate the worlds behind the text and within it. While issues of gender are primary in this project, the volumes also address the intersecting issues of power, authority, ethnicity, race, class, and religious belief and practice. The fifty-eight volumes include the books regarded as canonical by Jews (i.e., the Tanakh); Protestants (the "Hebrew Bible" and the New Testament); and Roman Catholic, Anglican, and Eastern

Orthodox Communions (i.e., Tobit, Judith, 1 and 2 Maccabees, Wisdom of Solomon, Sirach/Ecclesiasticus, Baruch, including the Letter of Jeremiah, the additions to Esther, and Susanna and Bel and the Dragon in Daniel).

## A Symphony of Diverse Voices

Included in the Wisdom Commentary series are voices from scholars of many different religious traditions, of diverse ages, differing sexual identities, and varying cultural, racial, ethnic, and social contexts. Some have been pioneers in feminist biblical interpretation; others are newer contributors from a younger generation. A further distinctive feature of this series is that each volume incorporates voices other than that of the lead author(s). These voices appear alongside the commentary of the lead author(s), in the grayscale inserts. At times, a contributor may offer an alternative interpretation or a critique of the position taken by the lead author(s). At other times, she or he may offer a complementary interpretation from a different cultural context or subject position. Occasionally, portions of previously published material bring in other views. The diverse voices are not intended to be contestants in a debate or a cacophony of discordant notes. The multiple voices reflect that there is no single definitive feminist interpretation of a text. In addition, they show the importance of subject position in the process of interpretation. In this regard, the Wisdom Commentary series takes inspiration from the Talmud and from *The Torah: A Women's Commentary* (ed. Tamara Cohn Eskenazi and Andrea L. Weiss; New York: Women of Reform Judaism, Federation of Temple Sisterhood, 2008), in which many voices, even conflicting ones, are included and not harmonized.

Contributors include biblical scholars, theologians, and readers of Scripture from outside the scholarly and religious guilds. At times, their comments pertain to a particular text. In some instances they address a theme or topic that arises from the text.

Another feature that highlights the collaborative nature of feminist biblical interpretation is that a number of the volumes have two lead authors who have worked in tandem from the inception of the project and whose voices interweave throughout the commentary.

## Woman Wisdom

The title, Wisdom Commentary, reflects both the importance to feminists of the figure of Woman Wisdom in the Scriptures and the distinct wisdom that feminist women and men bring to the interpretive process. In the Scriptures, Woman Wisdom appears as "a breath of the power of God, and a pure emanation of the glory of the Almighty" (Wis 7:25), who was present and active in fashioning all that exists (Prov 8:22-31; Wis 8:6). She is a spirit who pervades and penetrates all things (Wis 7:22-23), and she provides guidance and nourishment at her all-inclusive table (Prov 9:1-5). In both postexilic biblical and nonbiblical Jewish sources, Woman Wisdom is often equated with Torah, e.g., Sirach 24:23-34; Baruch 3:9–4:4; 38:2; 46:4-5; 2 Baruch 48:33, 36; 4 Ezra 5:9-10; 13:55; 14:40; 1 Enoch 42.

The New Testament frequently portrays Jesus as Wisdom incarnate. He invites his followers, "take my yoke upon you and learn from me" (Matt 11:29), just as Ben Sira advises, "put your neck under her [Wisdom's] yoke and let your souls receive instruction" (Sir 51:26). Just as Wisdom experiences rejection (Prov 1:23-25; Sir 15:7-8; Wis 10:3; Bar 3:12), so too does Jesus (Mark 8:31; John 1:10-11). Only some accept his invitation to his all-inclusive banquet (Matt 22:1-14; Luke 14:15-24; compare Prov 1:20-21; 9:3-5). Yet, "wisdom is vindicated by her deeds" (Matt 11:19, speaking of Jesus and John the Baptist; in the Lucan parallel at 7:35 they are called "wisdom's children"). There are numerous parallels between what is said of Wisdom and of the *Logos* in the Prologue of the Fourth Gospel (John 1:1-18). These are only a few of many examples. This female embodiment of divine presence and power is an apt image to guide the work of this series.

## Feminism

There are many different understandings of the term "feminism." The various meanings, aims, and methods have developed exponentially in recent decades. Feminism is a perspective and a movement that springs from a recognition of inequities toward women, and it advocates for changes in whatever structures prevent full human flourishing. Three waves of feminism in the United States are commonly recognized. The first, arising in the mid-nineteenth century and lasting into the early twentieth, was sparked by women's efforts to be involved in the public sphere and to win the right to vote. In the 1960s and 1970s, the second wave focused on civil rights and equality for women. With the third wave, from the 1980s forward, came global feminism and the emphasis on the contextual nature of interpretation. Now a fourth wave may be emerging, with a stronger emphasis on the intersectionality of women's concerns with those of other marginalized groups and the increased use of the internet as a platform for discussion and activism.[1] As feminism has matured, it has recognized that inequities based on gender are interwoven with power imbalances based on race, class, ethnicity, religion, sexual identity, physical ability, and a host of other social markers.

## Feminist Women and Men

Men who choose to identify with and partner with feminist women in the work of deconstructing systems of domination and building structures of equality are rightly regarded as feminists. Some men readily identify with experiences of women who are discriminated against on the basis of sex/gender, having themselves had comparable experiences; others who may not have faced direct discrimination or stereotyping recognize that inequity and problematic characterization still occur, and they seek correction. This series is pleased to include feminist men both as lead authors and as contributing voices.

## Feminist Biblical Interpretation

Women interpreting the Bible from the lenses of their own experience is nothing new. Throughout the ages women have recounted the biblical stories, teaching them to their children and others, all the while interpreting them afresh for their time and circumstances.[2] Following is a very brief sketch of select foremothers who laid the groundwork for contemporary feminist biblical interpretation.

One of the earliest known Christian women who challenged patriarchal interpretations of Scripture was a consecrated virgin named Helie, who lived in the second century CE. When she refused to marry, her

---

1. See Martha Rampton, "Four Waves of Feminism" (October 25, 2015), at http://www.pacificu.edu/about-us/news-events/four-waves-feminism; and Ealasaid Munro, "Feminism: A Fourth Wave?," https://www.psa.ac.uk/insight-plus/feminism-fourth-wave.

2. For fuller treatments of this history, see chap. 7, "One Thousand Years of Feminist Bible Criticism," in Gerda Lerner, *Creation of Feminist Consciousness: From the Middle Ages to Eighteen-Seventy* (New York: Oxford University Press, 1993), 138–66; Susanne Scholz, "From the 'Woman's Bible' to the 'Women's Bible,' The History of Feminist Approaches to the Hebrew Bible," in *Introducing the Women's Hebrew Bible*, IFT 13 (New York: T&T Clark, 2007), 12–32; Marion Ann Taylor and Agnes Choi, eds., *Handbook of Women Biblical Interpreters: A Historical and Biographical Guide* (Grand Rapids: Baker Academic, 2012).

parents brought her before a judge, who quoted to her Paul's admonition, "It is better to marry than to be aflame with passion" (1 Cor 7:9). In response, Helie first acknowledges that this is what Scripture says, but then she retorts, "but not for everyone, that is, not for holy virgins."[3] She is one of the first to question the notion that a text has one meaning that is applicable in all situations.

A Jewish woman who also lived in the second century CE, Beruriah, is said to have had "profound knowledge of biblical exegesis and outstanding intelligence."[4] One story preserved in the Talmud (b. Berakot 10a) tells of how she challenged her husband, Rabbi Meir, when he prayed for the destruction of a sinner. Proffering an alternate interpretation, she argued that Psalm 104:35 advocated praying for the destruction of sin, not the sinner.

In medieval times the first written commentaries on Scripture from a critical feminist point of view emerge. While others may have been produced and passed on orally, they are for the most part lost to us now. Among the earliest preserved feminist writings are those of Hildegard of Bingen (1098–1179), German writer, mystic, and abbess of a Benedictine monastery. She reinterpreted the Genesis narratives in a way that presented women and men as complementary and interdependent. She frequently wrote about feminine aspects of the Divine.[5] Along with other women mystics of the time, such as Julian of Norwich (1342–ca. 1416), she spoke authoritatively from her personal experiences of God's revelation in prayer.

In this era, women were also among the scribes who copied biblical manuscripts. Notable among them is Paula Dei Mansi of Verona, from a distinguished family of Jewish scribes. In 1288, she translated from Hebrew into Italian a collection of Bible commentaries written by her father and added her own explanations.[6]

Another pioneer, Christine de Pizan (1365–ca. 1430), was a French court writer and prolific poet. She used allegory and common sense

---

3. Madrid, Escorial MS, a II 9, f. 90 v., as cited in Lerner, *Feminist Consciousness*, 140.

4. See Judith R. Baskin, "Women and Post-Biblical Commentary," in *The Torah: A Women's Commentary*, ed. Tamara Cohn Eskenazi and Andrea L. Weiss (New York: Women of Reform Judaism, Federation of Temple Sisterhood, 2008), xlix–lv, at lii.

5. Hildegard of Bingen, *De Operatione Dei*, 1.4.100; PL 197:885bc, as cited in Lerner, *Feminist Consciousness*, 142–43. See also Barbara Newman, *Sister of Wisdom: St. Hildegard's Theology of the Feminine* (Berkeley: University of California Press, 1987).

6. Emily Taitz, Sondra Henry, Cheryl Tallan, eds., *JPS Guide to Jewish Women 600 B.C.E.–1900 C.E.* (Philadelphia: Jewish Publication Society of America, 2003), 110–11.

to subvert misogynist readings of Scripture and celebrated the accomplishments of female biblical figures to argue for women's active roles in building society.[7]

By the seventeenth century, there were women who asserted that the biblical text needs to be understood and interpreted in its historical context. For example, Rachel Speght (1597–ca. 1630), a Calvinist English poet, elaborates on the historical situation in first-century Corinth that prompted Paul to say, "It is well for a man not to touch a woman" (1 Cor 7:1). Her aim was to show that the biblical texts should not be applied in a literal fashion to all times and circumstances. Similarly, Margaret Fell (1614–1702), one of the founders of the Religious Society of Friends (Quakers) in Britain, addressed the Pauline prohibitions against women speaking in church by insisting that they do not have universal validity. Rather, they need to be understood in their historical context, as addressed to a local church in particular time-bound circumstances.[8]

Along with analyzing the historical context of the biblical writings, women in the eighteenth and nineteenth centuries began to attend to misogynistic interpretations based on faulty translations. One of the first to do so was British feminist Mary Astell (1666–1731).[9] In the United States, the Grimké sisters, Sarah (1792–1873) and Angelina (1805–1879), Quaker women from a slaveholding family in South Carolina, learned biblical Greek and Hebrew so that they could interpret the Bible for themselves. They were prompted to do so after men sought to silence them from speaking out against slavery and for women's rights by claiming that the Bible (e.g., 1 Cor 14:34) prevented women from speaking in public.[10] Another prominent abolitionist, Sojourner Truth (ca. 1797–1883), a former slave, quoted the Bible liberally in her speeches[11] and in so doing challenged cultural assumptions and biblical interpretations that undergird gender inequities.

7. See further Taylor and Choi, *Handbook of Women Biblical Interpreters*, 127–32.

8. Her major work, *Women's Speaking Justified, Proved and Allowed by the Scriptures*, published in London in 1667, gave a systematic feminist reading of all biblical texts pertaining to women.

9. Mary Astell, *Some Reflections upon Marriage* (New York: Source Book Press, 1970, reprint of the 1730 edition; earliest edition of this work is 1700), 103–4.

10. See further Sarah Grimké, *Letters on the Equality of the Sexes and the Condition of Woman* (Boston: Isaac Knapp, 1838).

11. See, for example, her most famous speech, "Ain't I a Woman?," delivered in 1851 at the Ohio Women's Rights Convention in Akron, OH; http://www.fordham.edu/halsall/mod/sojtruth-woman.asp.

Another monumental work that emerged in nineteenth-century England was that of Jewish theologian Grace Aguilar (1816–1847), *The Women of Israel*,[12] published in 1845. Aguilar's approach was to make connections between the biblical women and contemporary Jewish women's concerns. She aimed to counter the widespread notion that women were degraded in Jewish law and that only in Christianity were women's dignity and value upheld. Her intent was to help Jewish women find strength and encouragement by seeing the evidence of God's compassionate love in the history of every woman in the Bible. While not a full commentary on the Bible, Aguilar's work stands out for its comprehensive treatment of every female biblical character, including even the most obscure references.[13]

The first person to produce a full-blown feminist commentary on the Bible was Elizabeth Cady Stanton (1815–1902). A leading proponent in the United States for women's right to vote, she found that whenever women tried to make inroads into politics, education, or the work world, the Bible was quoted against them. Along with a team of like-minded women, she produced her own commentary on every text of the Bible that concerned women. Her pioneering two-volume project, *The Woman's Bible*, published in 1895 and 1898, urges women to recognize that texts that degrade women come from the men who wrote the texts, not from God, and to use their common sense to rethink what has been presented to them as sacred.

Nearly a century later, *The Women's Bible Commentary*, edited by Carol Newsom and Sharon Ringe (Louisville: Westminster John Knox, 1992), appeared. This one-volume commentary features North American feminist scholarship on each book of the Protestant canon. Like Cady Stanton's commentary, it does not contain comments on every section of the biblical text but only on those passages deemed relevant to women. It was revised and expanded in 1998 to include the Apocrypha/Deuterocanonical books, and the contributors to this new volume reflect the global face of contemporary feminist scholarship. The revisions made in the third edition, which appeared in 2012, represent the profound advances in feminist biblical scholarship and include newer voices. In both the second and third editions, *The* has been dropped from the title.

12. The full title is *The Women of Israel or Characters and Sketches from the Holy Scriptures and Jewish History Illustrative of the Past History, Present Duty, and Future Destiny of the Hebrew Females, as Based on the Word of God.*
13. See further Eskenazi and Weiss, *The Torah: A Women's Commentary*, xxxviii; Taylor and Choi, *Handbook of Women Biblical Interpreters*, 31–37.

Also appearing at the centennial of Cady Stanton's *The Woman's Bible* were two volumes edited by Elisabeth Schüssler Fiorenza with the assistance of Shelly Matthews. The first, *Searching the Scriptures: A Feminist Introduction* (New York: Crossroad, 1993), charts a comprehensive approach to feminist interpretation from ecumenical, interreligious, and multicultural perspectives. The second volume, published in 1994, provides critical feminist commentary on each book of the New Testament as well as on three books of Jewish Pseudepigrapha and eleven other early Christian writings.

In Europe, similar endeavors have been undertaken, such as the one-volume *Kompendium Feministische Bibelauslegung*, edited by Luise Schottroff and Marie-Theres Wacker (Gütersloh: Gütersloher Verlagshaus, 2007), featuring German feminist biblical interpretation of each book of the Bible, along with apocryphal books, and several extrabiblical writings. This work, now in its third edition, has recently been translated into English.[14] A multivolume project, *The Bible and Women: An Encylopaedia of Exegesis and Cultural History*, edited by Irmtraud Fischer, Adriana Valerio, Mercedes Navarro Puerto, and Christiana de Groot, is currently in production. This project presents a history of the reception of the Bible as embedded in Western cultural history and focuses particularly on gender-relevant biblical themes, biblical female characters, and women recipients of the Bible. The volumes are published in English, Spanish, Italian, and German.[15]

Another groundbreaking work is the collection The Feminist Companion to the Bible Series, edited by Athalya Brenner (Sheffield: Sheffield Academic, 1993–2015), which comprises twenty volumes of commen-

14. *Feminist Biblical Interpretation: A Compendium of Critical Commentary on the Books of the Bible and Related Literature*, trans. Lisa E. Dahill, Everett R. Kalin, Nancy Lukens, Linda M. Maloney, Barbara Rumscheidt, Martin Rumscheidt, and Tina Steiner (Grand Rapids: Eerdmans, 2012). Another notable collection is the three volumes edited by Susanne Scholz, *Feminist Interpretation of the Hebrew Bible in Retrospect*, Recent Research in Biblical Studies 7, 8, 9 (Sheffield: Sheffield Phoenix, 2013, 2014, 2016).

15. The first volume, on the Torah, appeared in Spanish in 2009, in German and Italian in 2010, and in English in 2011 (Atlanta: SBL Press). Four more volumes are now available: *Feminist Biblical Studies in the Twentieth Century*, ed. Elisabeth Schüssler Fiorenza (2014); *The Writings and Later Wisdom Books*, ed. Christl M. Maier and Nuria Calduch-Benages (2014); *Gospels: Narrative and History*, ed. Mercedes Navarro Puerto, Marinella Perroni, and Amy-Jill Levine (2015); and *The High Middle Ages*, ed. Kari Elisabeth Børresen and Adriana Valerio (2015). For further information, see http://www.bibleandwomen.org.

taries on the Old Testament. The parallel series, Feminist Companion to the New Testament and Early Christian Writings, edited by Amy-Jill Levine with Marianne Blickenstaff and Maria Mayo Robbins (Sheffield: Sheffield Academic, 2001–2009), contains thirteen volumes with one more planned. These two series are not full commentaries on the biblical books but comprise collected essays on discrete biblical texts.

Works by individual feminist biblical scholars in all parts of the world abound, and they are now too numerous to list in this introduction. Feminist biblical interpretation has reached a level of maturity that now makes possible a commentary series on every book of the Bible. In recent decades, women have had greater access to formal theological education, have been able to learn critical analytical tools, have put their own interpretations into writing, and have developed new methods of biblical interpretation. Until recent decades the work of feminist biblical interpreters was largely unknown, both to other women and to their brothers in the synagogue, church, and academy. Feminists now have taken their place in the professional world of biblical scholars, where they build on the work of their foremothers and connect with one another across the globe in ways not previously possible. In a few short decades, feminist biblical criticism has become an integral part of the academy.

## Methodologies

Feminist biblical scholars use a variety of methods and often employ a number of them together.[16] In the Wisdom Commentary series, the authors will explain their understanding of feminism and the feminist reading strategies used in their commentary. Each volume treats the biblical text in blocks of material, not an analysis verse by verse. The entire text is considered, not only those passages that feature female characters or that speak specifically about women. When women are not apparent in the narrative, feminist lenses are used to analyze the dynamics in the text between male characters, the models of power, binary ways of thinking, and dynamics of imperialism. Attention is given to how the whole text functions and how it was and is heard, both in its original context and today. Issues of particular concern to women—e.g., poverty, food, health, the environment, water—come to the fore.

16. See the seventeen essays in Caroline Vander Stichele and Todd Penner, eds., *Her Master's Tools? Feminist and Postcolonial Engagements of Historical-Critical Discourse* (Atlanta: SBL Press, 2005), which show the complementarity of various approaches.

One of the approaches used by early feminists and still popular today is to lift up the overlooked and forgotten stories of women in the Bible. Studies of women in each of the Testaments have been done, and there are also studies on women in particular biblical books.[17] Feminists recognize that the examples of biblical characters can be both empowering and problematic. The point of the feminist enterprise is not to serve as an apologetic for women; it is rather, in part, to recover women's history and literary roles in all their complexity and to learn from that recovery.

Retrieving the submerged history of biblical women is a crucial step for constructing the story of the past so as to lead to liberative possibilities for the present and future. There are, however, some pitfalls to this approach. Sometimes depictions of biblical women have been naïve and romantic. Some commentators exalt the virtues of both biblical and contemporary women and paint women as superior to men. Such reverse discrimination inhibits movement toward equality for all. In addition, some feminists challenge the idea that one can "pluck positive images out of an admittedly androcentric text, separating literary characterizations from the androcentric interests they were created to serve."[18] Still other feminists find these images to have enormous value.

One other danger with seeking the submerged history of women is the tendency for Christian feminists to paint Jesus and even Paul as liberators of women in a way that demonizes Judaism.[19] Wisdom Commentary aims to enhance understanding of Jesus as well as Paul as Jews of their day and to forge solidarity among Jewish and Christian feminists.

---

17. See, e.g., Alice Bach, ed., *Women in the Hebrew Bible: A Reader* (New York: Routledge, 1998); Tikva Frymer-Kensky, *Reading the Women of the Bible* (New York: Schocken Books, 2002); Carol Meyers, Toni Craven, and Ross S. Kraemer, *Women in Scripture* (Grand Rapids: Eerdmans, 2000); Irene Nowell, *Women in the Old Testament* (Collegeville, MN: Liturgical Press, 1997); Katharine Doob Sakenfeld, *Just Wives? Stories of Power and Survival in the Old Testament and Today* (Louisville: Westminster John Knox, 2003); Mary Ann Getty-Sullivan, *Women in the New Testament* (Collegeville, MN: Liturgical Press, 2001); Bonnie Thurston, *Women in the New Testament: Questions and Commentary*, Companions to the New Testament (New York: Crossroad, 1998).

18. Cheryl Exum, "Second Thoughts about Secondary Characters: Women in Exodus 1.8–2.10," in *A Feminist Companion to Exodus to Deuteronomy*, FCB 6, ed. Athalya Brenner (Sheffield: Sheffield Academic, 1994), 75–97, at 76.

19. See Judith Plaskow, "Anti-Judaism in Feminist Christian Interpretation," in *Searching the Scriptures: A Feminist Introduction*, ed. Elisabeth Schüssler Fiorenza (New York: Crossroad, 1993), 1:117–29; Amy-Jill Levine, "The New Testament and Anti-Judaism," in *The Misunderstood Jew: The Church and the Scandal of the Jewish Jesus* (San Francisco: HarperSanFrancisco, 2006), 87–117.

Feminist scholars who use historical-critical methods analyze the world behind the text; they seek to understand the historical context from which the text emerged and the circumstances of the communities to whom it was addressed. In bringing feminist lenses to this approach, the aim is not to impose modern expectations on ancient cultures but to unmask the ways that ideologically problematic mind-sets that produced the ancient texts are still promulgated through the text. Feminist biblical scholars aim not only to deconstruct but also to reclaim and reconstruct biblical history as women's history, in which women were central and active agents in creating religious heritage.[20] A further step is to construct meaning for contemporary women and men in a liberative movement toward transformation of social, political, economic, and religious structures.[21] In recent years, some feminists have embraced new historicism, which accents the creative role of the interpreter in any construction of history and exposes the power struggles to which the text witnesses.[22]

Literary critics analyze the world of the text: its form, language patterns, and rhetorical function.[23] They do not attempt to separate layers of tradition and redaction but focus on the text holistically, as it is in

20. See, for example, Phyllis A. Bird, *Missing Persons and Mistaken Identities: Women and Gender in Ancient Israel* (Minneapolis: Fortress, 1997); Elisabeth Schüssler Fiorenza, *In Memory of Her: A Feminist Theological Reconstruction of Christian Origins* (New York: Crossroad, 1984); Ross Shepard Kraemer and Mary Rose D'Angelo, eds., *Women and Christian Origins* (New York: Oxford University Press, 1999).

21. See, e.g., Sandra M. Schneiders, *The Revelatory Text: Interpreting the New Testament as Sacred Scripture*, rev. ed. (Collegeville, MN: Liturgical Press, 1999), whose aim is to engage in biblical interpretation not only for intellectual enlightenment but, even more important, for personal and communal transformation. Elisabeth Schüssler Fiorenza (*Wisdom Ways: Introducing Feminist Biblical Interpretation* [Maryknoll, NY: Orbis Books, 2001]) envisions the work of feminist biblical interpretation as a dance of Wisdom that consists of seven steps that interweave in spiral movements toward liberation, the final one being transformative action for change.

22. See Gina Hens-Piazza, *The New Historicism*, GBS, Old Testament Series (Minneapolis: Fortress, 2002).

23. Phyllis Trible was among the first to employ this method with texts from Genesis and Ruth in her groundbreaking book *God and the Rhetoric of Sexuality*, OBT (Philadelphia: Fortress, 1978). Another pioneer in feminist literary criticism is Mieke Bal (*Lethal Love: Feminist Literary Readings of Biblical Love Stories* [Bloomington: Indiana University Press, 1987]). For surveys of recent developments in literary methods, see Terry Eagleton, *Literary Theory: An Introduction*, 3rd ed. (Minneapolis: University of Minnesota Press, 2008); Janice Capel Anderson and Stephen D. Moore, eds., *Mark and Method: New Approaches in Biblical Studies*, 2nd ed. (Minneapolis: Fortress, 2008).

its present form. They examine how meaning is created in the interaction between the text and its reader in multiple contexts. Within the arena of literary approaches are reader-oriented approaches, narrative, rhetorical, structuralist, post-structuralist, deconstructive, ideological, autobiographical, and performance criticism.[24] Narrative critics study the interrelation among author, text, and audience through investigation of settings, both spatial and temporal; characters; plot; and narrative techniques (e.g., irony, parody, intertextual allusions). Reader-response critics attend to the impact that the text has on the reader or hearer. They recognize that when a text is detrimental toward women there is the choice either to affirm the text or to read against the grain toward a liberative end. Rhetorical criticism analyzes the style of argumentation and attends to how the author is attempting to shape the thinking or actions of the hearer. Structuralist critics analyze the complex patterns of binary oppositions in the text to derive its meaning.[25] Post-structuralist approaches challenge the notion that there are fixed meanings to any biblical text or that there is one universal truth. They engage in close readings of the text and often engage in intertextual analysis.[26] Within this approach is deconstructionist criticism, which views the text as a site of conflict, with competing narratives. The interpreter aims to expose the fault lines and overturn and reconfigure binaries by elevating the underling of a pair and foregrounding it.[27] Feminists also use other postmodern approaches, such as ideological and autobiographical criticism. The former analyzes the system of ideas that underlies the power and

24. See, e.g., J. Cheryl Exum and David J. A. Clines, eds., *The New Literary Criticism and the Hebrew Bible* (Valley Forge, PA: Trinity Press International, 1993); Edgar V. McKnight and Elizabeth Struthers Malbon, eds., *The New Literary Criticism and the New Testament* (Valley Forge, PA: Trinity Press International, 1994).

25. See, e.g., David Jobling, *The Sense of Biblical Narrative: Three Structural Analyses in the Old Testament*, JSOTSup 7 (Sheffield: University of Sheffield, 1978).

26. See, e.g., Stephen D. Moore, *Poststructuralism and the New Testament: Derrida and Foucault at the Foot of the Cross* (Minneapolis: Fortress, 1994); *The Bible in Theory: Critical and Postcritical Essays* (Atlanta: SBL Press, 2010); Yvonne Sherwood, *A Biblical Text and Its Afterlives: The Survival of Jonah in Western Culture* (Cambridge: Cambridge University Press, 2000).

27. David Penchansky, "Deconstruction," in *The Oxford Encyclopedia of Biblical Interpretation*, ed. Steven McKenzie (New York: Oxford University Press, 2013), 196–205. See, for example, Danna Nolan Fewell and David M. Gunn, *Gender, Power, and Promise: The Subject of the Bible's First Story* (Nashville: Abingdon, 1993); David Rutledge, *Reading Marginally: Feminism, Deconstruction and the Bible*, BibInt 21 (Leiden: Brill, 1996).

values concealed in the text as well as that of the interpreter.[28] The latter involves deliberate self-disclosure while reading the text as a critical exegete.[29] Performance criticism attends to how the text was passed on orally, usually in communal settings, and to the verbal and nonverbal interactions between the performer and the audience.[30]

From the beginning, feminists have understood that interpreting the Bible is an act of power. In recent decades, feminist biblical scholars have developed hermeneutical theories of the ethics and politics of biblical interpretation to challenge the claims to value neutrality of most academic biblical scholarship. Feminist biblical scholars have also turned their attention to how some biblical writings were shaped by the power of empire and how this still shapes readers' self-understandings today. They have developed hermeneutical approaches that reveal, critique, and evaluate the interactions depicted in the text against the context of empire, and they consider implications for contemporary contexts.[31] Feminists also analyze the dynamics of colonization and the mentalities of colonized peoples in the exercise of biblical interpretation. As Kwok Pui-lan explains, "A postcolonial feminist interpretation of the Bible needs to investigate the deployment of gender in the narration of identity, the negotiation of power differentials between the colonizers and the colonized, and the reinforcement of patriarchal control over spheres where these elites could exercise control."[32] Methods and models from sociology and cultural anthropology are used by feminists to investigate

28. See Tina Pippin, ed., *Ideological Criticism of Biblical Texts: Semeia* 59 (1992); Terry Eagleton, *Ideology: An Introduction* (London: Verso, 2007).

29. See, e.g., Ingrid Rose Kitzberger, ed., *Autobiographical Biblical Interpretation: Between Text and Self* (Leiden: Deo, 2002); P. J. W. Schutte, "When *They, We*, and the Passive Become *I*—Introducing Autobiographical Biblical Criticism," *HTS Teologiese Studies / Theological Studies* 61 (2005): 401–16.

30. See, e.g., Holly Hearon and Philip Ruge-Jones, eds., *The Bible in Ancient and Modern Media: Story and Performance* (Eugene, OR: Cascade, 2009).

31. E.g., Gale Yee, ed., *Judges and Method: New Approaches in Biblical Studies* (Minneapolis: Fortress, 1995); Warren Carter, *The Gospel of Matthew in Its Roman Imperial Context* (London: T&T Clark, 2005); *The Roman Empire and the New Testament: An Essential Guide* (Nashville: Abingdon, 2006); Elisabeth Schüssler Fiorenza, *The Power of the Word: Scripture and the Rhetoric of Empire* (Minneapolis: Fortress, 2007); Judith E. McKinlay, *Reframing Her: Biblical Women in Postcolonial Focus* (Sheffield: Sheffield Phoenix, 2004).

32. Kwok Pui-lan, *Postcolonial Imagination and Feminist Theology* (Louisville: Westminster John Knox, 2005), 9. See also, Musa W. Dube, ed., *Postcolonial Feminist Interpretation of the Bible* (St. Louis: Chalice, 2000); Cristl M. Maier and Carolyn J. Sharp,

women's everyday lives, their experiences of marriage, childrearing, labor, money, illness, etc.[33]

As feminists have examined the construction of gender from varying cultural perspectives, they have become ever more cognizant that the way gender roles are defined within differing cultures varies radically. As Mary Ann Tolbert observes, "Attempts to isolate some universal role that cross-culturally defines 'woman' have run into contradictory evidence at every turn."[34] Some women have coined new terms to highlight the particularities of their socio-cultural context. Many African American feminists, for example, call themselves *womanists* to draw attention to the double oppression of racism and sexism they experience.[35] Similarly, many US Hispanic feminists speak of themselves as *mujeristas* (*mujer* is Spanish for "woman").[36] Others prefer to be called "Latina feminists."[37] Both groups emphasize that the context for their theologizing is *mestizaje* and *mulatez* (racial and cultural mixture), done *en conjunto* (in community), with *lo cotidiano* (everyday lived experience) of Hispanic women as starting points for theological reflection and the encounter with the divine. Intercultural analysis has become an indispensable tool for working toward justice for women at the global level.[38]

---

*Prophecy and Power: Jeremiah in Feminist and Postcolonial Perspective* (London: Bloomsbury, 2013).

33. See, for example, Carol Meyers, *Discovering Eve: Ancient Israelite Women in Context* (New York: Oxford University Press, 1991); Luise Schottroff, *Lydia's Impatient Sisters: A Feminist Social History of Early Christianity*, trans. Barbara and Martin Rumscheidt (Louisville: Westminster John Knox, 1995); Susan Niditch, *"My Brother Esau Is a Hairy Man": Hair and Identity in Ancient Israel* (Oxford: Oxford University Press, 2008).

34. Mary Ann Tolbert, "Social, Sociological, and Anthropological Methods," in *Searching the Scriptures*, 1:255–71, at 265.

35. Alice Walker coined the term (*In Search of Our Mothers' Gardens: Womanist Prose* [New York: Harcourt Brace Jovanovich, 1967, 1983]). See also Katie G. Cannon, "The Emergence of Black Feminist Consciousness," in *Feminist Interpretation of the Bible*, ed. Letty M. Russell (Philadelphia: Westminster, 1985), 30–40; Renita Weems, *Just a Sister Away: A Womanist Vision of Women's Relationships in the Bible* (San Diego: Lura Media, 1988); Nyasha Junior, *An Introduction to Womanist Biblical Interpretation* (Louisville: Westminster John Knox, 2015).

36. Ada María Isasi-Díaz (*Mujerista Theology: A Theology for the Twenty-First Century* [Maryknoll, NY: Orbis Books, 1996]) is credited with coining the term.

37. E.g., María Pilar Aquino, Daisy L. Machado, and Jeanette Rodríguez, eds., *A Reader in Latina Feminist Theology* (Austin: University of Texas Press, 2002).

38. See, e.g., María Pilar Aquino and María José Rosado-Nunes, eds., *Feminist Intercultural Theology: Latina Explorations for a Just World*, Studies in Latino/a Catholicism (Maryknoll, NY: Orbis Books, 2007).

Some feminists are among those who have developed lesbian, gay, bisexual, and transgender (LGBT) interpretation. This approach focuses on issues of sexual identity and uses various reading strategies. Some point out the ways in which categories that emerged in recent centuries are applied anachronistically to biblical texts to make modern-day judgments. Others show how the Bible is silent on contemporary issues about sexual identity. Still others examine same-sex relationships in the Bible by figures such as Ruth and Naomi or David and Jonathan. In recent years, queer theory has emerged; it emphasizes the blurriness of boundaries not just of sexual identity but also of gender roles. Queer critics often focus on texts in which figures transgress what is traditionally considered proper gender behavior.[39]

Feminists also recognize that the struggle for women's equality and dignity is intimately connected with the struggle for respect for Earth and for the whole of the cosmos. Ecofeminists interpret Scripture in ways that highlight the link between human domination of nature and male subjugation of women. They show how anthropocentric ways of interpreting the Bible have overlooked or dismissed Earth and Earth community. They invite readers to identify not only with human characters in the biblical narrative but also with other Earth creatures and domains of nature, especially those that are the object of injustice. Some use creative imagination to retrieve the interests of Earth implicit in the narrative and enable Earth to speak.[40]

## Biblical Authority

By the late nineteenth century, some feminists, such as Elizabeth Cady Stanton, began to question openly whether the Bible could continue to be regarded as authoritative for women. They viewed the Bible itself as

---

39. See, e.g., Bernadette J. Brooten, *Love between Women: Early Christian Responses to Female Homoeroticism* (Chicago and London: University of Chicago Press, 1996); Mary Rose D'Angelo, "Women Partners in the New Testament," *JFSR* 6 (1990): 65–86; Deirdre J. Good, "Reading Strategies for Biblical Passages on Same-Sex Relations," *Theology and Sexuality* 7 (1997): 70–82; Deryn Guest, *When Deborah Met Jael: Lesbian Feminist Hermeneutics* (London: SCM, 2011); Teresa Hornsby and Ken Stone, eds., *Bible Trouble: Queer Readings at the Boundaries of Biblical Scholarship* (Atlanta: SBL Press, 2011).

40. E.g., Norman C. Habel and Peter Trudinger, *Exploring Ecological Hermeneutics*, SymS 46 (Atlanta: SBL Press, 2008); Mary Judith Ress, *Ecofeminism in Latin America*, Women from the Margins (Maryknoll, NY: Orbis Books, 2006).

the source of women's oppression, and some rejected its sacred origin and saving claims. Some decided that the Bible and the religious traditions that enshrine it are too thoroughly saturated with androcentrism and patriarchy to be redeemable.[41]

In the Wisdom Commentary series, questions such as these may be raised, but the aim of this series is not to lead readers to reject the authority of the biblical text. Rather, the aim is to promote better understanding of the contexts from which the text arose and of the rhetorical effects it has on women and men in contemporary contexts. Such understanding can lead to a deepening of faith, with the Bible serving as an aid to bring flourishing of life.

## Language for God

Because of the ways in which the term "God" has been used to symbolize the divine in predominantly male, patriarchal, and monarchical modes, feminists have designed new ways of speaking of the divine. Some have called attention to the inadequacy of the term God by trying to visually destabilize our ways of thinking and speaking of the divine. Rosemary Radford Ruether proposed *God/ess*, as an unpronounceable term pointing to the unnameable understanding of the divine that transcends patriarchal limitations.[42] Some have followed traditional Jewish practice, writing *G-d*. Elisabeth Schüssler Fiorenza has adopted *G\*d*.[43] Others draw on the biblical tradition to mine female and non-gender-specific metaphors and symbols.[44] In Wisdom Commentary, there is not one standard way of expressing the divine; each author will use her or his preferred ways. The one exception is that when the Tetragrammaton, YHWH, the name revealed to Moses in Exodus 3:14, is used, it will be without vowels, respecting the Jewish custom of avoiding pronouncing the divine name out of reverence.

---

41. E.g., Mary Daly, *Beyond God the Father: A Philosophy of Women's Liberation* (Boston: Beacon, 1973).

42. Rosemary Radford Ruether, *Sexism and God-Talk: Toward a Feminist Theology* (Boston: Beacon, 1983).

43. Elisabeth Schüssler Fiorenza, *Jesus: Miriam's Child, Sophia's Prophet; Critical Issues in Feminist Christology* (New York: Continuum, 1994), 191 n. 3.

44. E.g., Sallie McFague, *Models of God: Theology for an Ecological, Nuclear Age* (Philadelphia: Fortress, 1987); Catherine LaCugna, *God for Us: The Trinity and Christian Life* (San Francisco: Harper Collins, 1991); Elizabeth A. Johnson, *She Who Is: The Mystery of God in Feminist Theological Discourse* (New York: Crossroad, 1992). See further Elizabeth A. Johnson, "God," in *Dictionary of Feminist Theologies*, 128–30.

## Nomenclature for the Two Testaments

In recent decades, some biblical scholars have begun to call the two Testaments of the Bible by names other than the traditional nomenclature: Old and New Testament. Some regard "Old" as derogatory, implying that it is no longer relevant or that it has been superseded. Consequently, terms like Hebrew Bible, First Testament, and Jewish Scriptures and, correspondingly, Christian Scriptures or Second Testament have come into use. There are a number of difficulties with these designations. The term "Hebrew Bible" does not take into account that parts of the Old Testament are written not in Hebrew but in Aramaic.[45] Moreover, for Roman Catholics and Eastern Orthodox believers, the Old Testament includes books written in Greek—the Deuterocanonical books, considered Apocrypha by Protestants.[46] The term "Jewish Scriptures" is inadequate because these books are also sacred to Christians. Conversely, "Christian Scriptures" is not an accurate designation for the New Testament, since the Old Testament is also part of the Christian Scriptures. Using "First and Second Testament" also has difficulties, in that it can imply a hierarchy and a value judgment.[47] Jews generally use the term Tanakh, an acronym for Torah (Pentateuch), Nevi'im (Prophets), and Ketuvim (Writings).

In Wisdom Commentary, if authors choose to use a designation other than Tanakh, Old Testament, and New Testament, they will explain how they mean the term.

## Translation

Modern feminist scholars recognize the complexities connected with biblical translation, as they have delved into questions about philosophy of language, how meanings are produced, and how they are culturally situated. Today it is evident that simply translating into gender-neutral formulations cannot address all the challenges presented by androcentric texts. Efforts at feminist translation must also deal with issues around authority and canonicity.[48]

---

45. Gen 31:47; Jer 10:11; Ezra 4:7–6:18; 7:12-26; Dan 2:4–7:28.

46. Representing the *via media* between Catholic and reformed, Anglicans generally consider the Apocrypha to be profitable, if not canonical, and utilize Wisdom texts liturgically.

47. See Levine, *The Misunderstood Jew*, 193–99.

48. Elizabeth Castelli, *"Les Belles Infidèles*/Fidelity or Feminism? The Meanings of Feminist Biblical Translation," in *Searching the Scriptures*, 1:189–204, here 190.

Because of these complexities, the editors of Wisdom Commentary series have chosen to use an existing translation, the New Revised Standard Version (NRSV), which is provided for easy reference at the top of each page of commentary. The NRSV was produced by a team of ecumenical and interreligious scholars, is a fairly literal translation, and uses inclusive language for human beings. Brief discussions about problematic translations appear in the inserts labeled "Translation Matters." When more detailed discussions are available, these will be indicated in footnotes. In the commentary, wherever Hebrew or Greek words are used, English translation is provided. In cases where a wordplay is involved, transliteration is provided to enable understanding.

## Art and Poetry

Artistic expression in poetry, music, sculpture, painting, and various other modes is very important to feminist interpretation. Where possible, art and poetry are included in the print volumes of the series. In a number of instances, these are original works created for this project. Regrettably, copyright and production costs prohibit the inclusion of color photographs and other artistic work. It is our hope that the web version will allow a greater collection of such resources.

## Glossary

Because there are a number of excellent readily available resources that provide definitions and concise explanations of terms used in feminist theological and biblical studies, this series will not include a glossary. We refer you to works such as *Dictionary of Feminist Theologies*, edited by Letty M. Russell with J. Shannon Clarkson (Louisville: Westminster John Knox, 1996), and volume 1 of *Searching the Scriptures*, edited by Elisabeth Schüssler Fiorenza with the assistance of Shelly Matthews (New York: Crossroad, 1992). Individual authors in the Wisdom Commentary series will define the way they are using terms that may be unfamiliar.

## Bibliography

Because bibliographies are quickly outdated and because the space is limited, only a list of Works Cited is included in the print volumes. A comprehensive bibliography for each volume is posted on a dedicated website and is updated regularly. The link for this volume can be found at wisdomcommentary.org.

## A Concluding Word

In just a few short decades, feminist biblical studies have grown exponentially, both in the methods that have been developed and in the number of scholars who have embraced them. We realize that this series is limited and will soon need to be revised and updated. It is our hope that Wisdom Commentary, by making the best of current feminist biblical scholarship available in an accessible format to ministers, preachers, teachers, scholars, and students, will aid all readers in their advancement toward God's vision of dignity, equality, and justice for all.

———•◆•———

## Acknowledgments

There are a great many people who have made this series possible: first, Peter Dwyer, director of Liturgical Press, and Hans Christoffersen, publisher of the academic market at Liturgical Press, who have believed in this project and have shepherded it since it was conceived in 2008. Editorial consultants Athalya Brenner-Idan and Elisabeth Schüssler Fiorenza have not only been an inspiration with their pioneering work but have encouraged us all along the way with their personal involvement. Volume editors Mary Ann Beavis, Carol J. Dempsey, Amy-Jill Levine, Linda M. Maloney, Ahida Pilarski, Sarah Tanzer, Lauress Wilkins Lawrence, and Seung Ai Yang have lent their extraordinary wisdom to the shaping of the series, have used their extensive networks of relationships to secure authors and contributors, and have worked tirelessly to guide their work to completion. Two others who contributed greatly to the shaping of the project at the outset were Linda M. Day and Mignon Jacobs, as well as Barbara E. Bowe of blessed memory (d. 2010). Editorial and research assistant Susan M. Hickman has provided invaluable support with administrative details and arrangements. I am grateful to Brian Eisenschenk and Christine Henderson who have assisted Susan Hickman with the Wiki. There are countless others at Liturgical Press whose daily work makes the production possible. I am especially thankful to Lauren L. Murphy and Justin Howell for their work in copyediting, Colleen Stiller, Production Manager, Stephanie Nix, Production Assistant, and Tara Durheim, Associate Publisher for Academic and Monastic Markets.

# Nahum

## Author's Introduction

# *Nahum's Troubling God: When God Is Not Worthy*

The proclamations of Nahum are the prophecies of a violently angry, bloodthirsty[1] God,[2] "words of hatred, abuse and delight in divine retribution."[3] The presentation of God is as troubling as is the reality of readers, interpreters, and preachers reading the description of God in Nahum literally. The text of Nahum is a literary composition that describes itself as being produced as a ספר, "book" or "scroll," in Nahum 1:1.[4] This characterization distinguishes the text of Nahum from other prophetic collections and points to the writing of Nahum as a prophetic

---

1. Valerie Bridgeman, "Nahum," in *Africana Bible*, ed. Hugh Page Jr., et al. (Minneapolis: Fortress, 2010), 194.

2. I am using "God" to render YHWH rather than "Lord," as does the NRSV, to resist explicitly gendering the deity. In places where I quote the biblical text I will use "God" in large-and-small caps as is the convention for rendering the Tetragrammaton.

3. Michael Carden, "The Book of the Twelve Minor Prophets," in *The Queer Bible Commentary*, ed. Deryn Guest (London: SCM, 2006), 472.

4. None of the other prophetic texts are described as a book or scroll in their superscription. The text of Jeremiah is called a book/scroll in Jer 25:13; 30:2. Isaiah (30:8; 34:16) and Malachi (3:16) also mention scrolls.

activity.[5] Nahum is a multilayered text woven into its final form by an unknown person or persons. Among those layers are traditions, perhaps including archived sayings, of an ancestral prophet Nahum in whose mouth the written text of Nahum is placed. Nahum is also a character in the text, the speaker-prophet, and, to some degree, the creation of its author and final redactor. The relative anonymity of Nahum in the text—his one descriptor, "the Elqoshi" in 1:1, is obscure—and the admission that the work was crafted as a written work facilitate a literary reading of Nahum. The writing prophet is also a "Nahum," a poet-prophet communicating a prophetic vision.[6] Each Nahum in the layers of text and tradition is in his or her way prophetic.[7]

Like the recalcitrant Jonah, Nahum's prophetic gaze is set on Nineveh, the "city of blood" whose king is perpetually wicked.[8] Targum Jonathan explicitly links Jonah (prophet and book) with Nahum by positioning Nahum's prophecy as a response to Nineveh's return to her[9] sinful ways after a brief period of repentance due to Jonah's preaching (1:1). Unlike Jonah, Nahum has no reprieve for Nineveh. Nahum's proclamations are not dispassionate judgment or justice; they are vengeful. Nahum offers extreme examples of standard prophetic categories: proclamations against other nations and proclamations of judgment and doom and, buried within raging rhetoric, a word of comfort for Judah, a traditional salvation proclamation in 1:12-13 with additional words of comfort in 1:15 (2:1 MT).

In the book of Nahum, Judah is the Southern Monarchy, still standing after the fall of the Northern Monarchy to the Assyrians in 723 BCE. The fall of Samaria and the North is religiously, culturally, politically, and economically devastating. The Assyrians deport a significant portion of

5. The superscription identifies the text of Nahum as a חזון, a prophetic vision of Nahum (but not surprisingly of God). The identity of the written text as a prophecy presents Nahum in its final form as a prophetic production and thereby establishes its author, the poet, as a prophet.
6. Carol Dempsey considers this vision to have been "an intuitive experience." Carol J. Dempsey, *Amos, Hosea, Micah, Nahum, Zephaniah, Habakkuk,* New Collegeville Biblical Commentary (Collegeville, MN: Liturgical Press, 2013), 108.
7. There is no way to identify this poet's gender. I prefer the masculine pronoun because of the ways in which the Nahums blend into each other and because the notion of a woman writing these vicious, sexually violent lyrics is particularly jarring.
8. Contra NRSV "city of bloodshed" in 3:1 and the king's "endless cruelty" in 3:19.
9. Cities in the ancient Israel and the Afro-Asian confluence of the ancient Near East were often portrayed as female. The gender designation was often a function of grammar or cultural understanding with the city as mother, protectress, or the charge of a particular deity.

the population of ten[10] tribes (2 Kgs 17:18-23). Second Kings describes the resettlement of the land of Israel (the Northern Monarchy) by foreigners deported by Assyria from other conquered lands (2 Kgs 17:24). Under the shadow of Assyria and its capital Nineveh, Judah is nominally independent, self-governing but paying heavy tribute to the Assyrians, and subject to harassment and invasion with little or no provocation.

From a literary perspective Nineveh is the subject[11] of these proclamations, but the Ninevites cannot be expected to have heard them or to have read them. Neither Nahum the character nor his purported ancestral antecedent has been sent to Nineveh like Jonah. It is certainly possible the proclamation in part or whole would have made its way to Nineveh, perhaps provoking alarm at the possibility of the threat from another people's god. Reading from the perspective of Nahum the character, it may be the judgment of God against Nineveh is final and determinative, so it matters not whether Nineveh has heard these words. Yet portions of the text are composed as though there is an audience present other than its target. Judah is the intended audience for the prophet Nahum's message in the setting of the book.

The book itself speaks to a wider audience than seventh-century Judah (with or without Nineveh), encompasses a broader time period than its 663 to 612 BCE setting, and is shaped by hands other than those of a prophet called Nahum. Duane L. Christensen collates the scholarship and proffers six periods in which the book of Nahum as it now stands could have been finalized:

1. soon after the fall of Thebes to Ashurbanipal in 663 BCE

2. around the time of Ashurbanipal's death (ca. 630 BCE)

3. just before the fall of Nineveh in 612 BCE

4. shortly after the fall of Assyria

5. after the fall of Assyria in the exilic and/or postexilic period

6. the Maccabean period (ca. 175–165 BCE)[12]

---

10. Counting each of the half-tribes of Manasseh and Naphtali separately; they are the descendants of Joseph and rarely reckoned as a tribe along with the descendants of his brothers. Levi never received an allotment of land and Simeon is located in the interior of Judah.

11. I use the term "subject" to describe the contents of the proclamation and the term "target" to refer to the addressee.

12. Duane L. Christensen, *Nahum: A New Translation with Introduction and Commentary*, AYB (New Haven: Yale University Press, 2009), 54.

What is certain is Thebes has fallen prior to the finalization of the book and its composition, if Nahum 3:8 is original to the book. If the book is finalized and promulgated prior to the fall of Nineveh, it interprets the signs of Assyria's decline and predicts its inevitable fall. If early, Nahum's rhetoric could have been used to encourage and support rebellion either when Assyria seemed invincible or when the behemoth began to totter. Christensen himself dates the redaction of Nahum to the Babylonian exile, arguing for its production as a "numerical and musical" composition, noting the inability to identify any Nahum text independent of the Book of the Twelve.[13] Whether reading/hearing Nahum in light of the internal Josian context, on the cusp of its decline or in the aftermath of its fall, Nineveh's fate is an object lesson in God's power and concern for Judah, both of which were subject to questioning in light of the Assyrian subjugation of Judah. As is the case with much of the biblical, especially prophetic, literature, Nahum's proclamations can be reinterpreted with regard to the Babylonians and other subsequent foes.

Women as well as men would hear these proclamations and perhaps read them, yet their target audience is male, as is the case for the Hebrew Scriptures writ large. Since women's bodies supply the imagery for Nineveh's plunder and rapine, I join Renita Weems in wondering "what did it do to ancient Hebrew women to hear and be subjected to such ranting of prophets in the squares and market places" and, I add, in sacred spaces, given Nahum's likely address to Judah in the Jerusalem temple complex?[14]

The language of the text is vengeful and wrathful (1:2), portraying God as raw power (1:3-5) and as fulfilling Torah: Nahum 1:3 reproduces the opening words of Numbers 14:18, יהוה ארך אפים, "GOD is slow to anger," but omits the intermediate lines about divine love and forgiveness then moves to execute judgment with another direct quote from the verse, ונקה לא ינקה, "by no means clearing (the guilty)." Nahum does not reproduce the latter portion of Numbers 14:18. According to the internal logic of the book, the venomously vitriolic proclamations of Nahum are an *apologia* for the well-deserved fate of Nineveh the dispossessor of cities, most notably Samaria and the entire Northern Israelite monarchy (2 Kgs 15:29-31; 17:3-6, 24; 18:9-12). This reading recognizes and rejects that rationale, refusing to grant legitimacy to language and imagery built on the savaging of a woman's body—even a metaphorical one.

---

13. Ibid., 4–17, 54–55. He begins his commentary with a lengthy "Logoprosodic" analysis of the text to demonstrate its structure as a numerical composition.

14. Renita Weems, *Battered Love: Marriage, Sex, and Violence in the Hebrew Prophets* (Minneapolis: Fortress, 1995), 8; see also the discussion on 41–42 and 66–67.

The rhetoric of Nahum is gendered; using the limited categories[15] of biblical Hebrew in which cities are grammatically feminine, Nahum portrays Nineveh as a hybridized city-woman, common in the Scriptures and across the broader ancient Near East (ANE) where cities were not just feminine but often female, regularly conflated with goddesses in close, often intimate, relationships with their human king. The city-as-woman metaphor shapes and is shaped by Israelite gender constructions of women and men.[16] It plays on cultural stereotypes and reinforces existing stereotypes,[17] but contrary to the dominant pattern in the Hebrew Scriptures in which cities are regularly castigated, ANE city-women were not disparaged in their literature.[18] In Nahum, Nineveh,[19] Thebes,[20] and Judah[21] are all configured as female using feminine grammar. Put, Nubia (Ethiopia), Egypt, and Libya mentioned briefly in the same context should be understood in the same way.

While not named, Ishtar, the principle deity[22] of Assyria and all Mesopotamia and protectress of and resident in Nineveh, lurks behind the scenes of Nahum. As Ishtar is sovereign over war and sexual desire,[23] the Sargonoid monarchs understood themselves to be beloved by Ishtar and under her benefaction.[24] An attack on Nineveh is an attack on Ishtar, since gods were as closely associated with their cities as they were with

---

15. In biblical Hebrew and other Semitic languages, every noun, whether animate or not, is either feminine or masculine. In some cases, i.e., people and animals, grammatical gender is directly linked to biological sex.

16. Julia M. O'Brien, *Nahum*, Readings: A New Biblical Commentary (London: Black, 2002), 92.

17. Weems, *Battered Love*, 23, 79, 107.

18. Ibid., 45.

19. Nineveh's gendering is clear given its portrayal as woman; Nah 3:4 and 7 make Nineveh's feminine gender explicit.

20. Nahum 3:8 communicates Thebes's gendering with the third-person feminine singular pronoun לה, "her."

21. Judah's feminine gender is clear in Nah 1:15 (2:1 MT) when reading in Hebrew; it is not obvious in English.

22. Simo Parpola argues Ishtar is the "mother aspect" of Asshur, the male deity for which Assyria is named, one with him and distinct from him at the same time, Simo Parpola, *Assyrian Prophecies*, State Archives of Assyria, vol. 9 (Helsinki: Helsinki University Press, 1997), xxxvi.

23. Laurel Lanner, *"Who Will Lament Her?" The Feminine and the Fantastic in the Book of Nahum*, vol. 11 (New York: T & T Clark, 2006), 37, 60–61.

24. Tikva Frymer-Kensky, *In the Wake of the Goddesses: Women, Culture, and the Biblical Transformation of Pagan Myth* (New York: Free Press, 1992), 63–64.

their temples.[25] Moreover, Nahum specifically targeted Nineveh's gods though he did not name them (Nah 1:14).

Judah is the audience of the book but not its target; thus, Nahum offers no prophetic delineation of sin designed to bring about repentance. Nahum targets Nineveh with the rhetoric of sexualized violence other prophets direct toward Israel and Judah, usually to bring about their repentance.[26] Neither God nor Nahum, however, provide opportunity for repentance because none will be accepted. The traditional vocabulary[27] for sin is entirely lacking along with means of redress, though Nineveh is briefly identified as counseling and executing "evil" and "wickedness" (Nah 1:11, 15 [2:1 MT]). The rationale for deploying punitive sexual violence against Nineveh is not the same as it is for Judah. Nineveh is not the wife[28] of God whom God has a particular right to discipline with violence for adultery and betrayal. God has the power to do so and punishes her anyway.

Without the marital metaphor as its underpinning, the divine violence against Nineveh can be constructed as an indication of God's universal sovereignty and/or revenge for the Assyrian imperial violence against Israel/Judah, i.e., the siege of Jerusalem in 701 BCE and the fall of the Northern Monarchy in 723/22 BCE. From the perspective of Nineveh the violence enacted by Israelite warriors might have been experienced as a rebellion or uprising in one of its provinces. The sexual violence would not have been particularly shocking to Nineveh or Israel as it commonly accompanied the waging of war in the ancient world; sexual violence

25. Lanner, *Who Will Lament Her?*, 57–79. Additionally, Lanner posits one or more Israelite/Canaanite goddess Asherah or Astarte influenced by and/or partially conflated with Ishtar, including as the Queen of Heaven may lie underneath the text of Nahum (74–79).

26. Though Jeremiah pessimistically deems Judah as likely "to do good" as Nubians are to change their skin in Jer 13:23, he nevertheless holds out the possibility of repentance, asking how long until Judah is restored from her transgression. Ezekiel's rationalization implies the possibility of, and failure to, repent in Ezek 23:8-9, specifying that because Samaria (called Oholah) did not give up her "whorings" she was subjected to violence. The transgressions of and retaliations against Samaria (Oholah) and Jerusalem (Oholibah) are expressed in violent pornotropic language.

27. The Hebrew words for "sin," "transgression," "iniquity," etc., are lacking.

28. I normally eschew the language of marriage with reference to the Hebrew Scriptures, given the variety of conjugal configurations that do not correspond readily to contemporary notions and forms of marriage. The relationship of God and Israel in the Scriptures is, however, cast as a male-female hierarchal conjugal union.

continues to be deployed in the prosecution of a war, simultaneously condemned as a war crime.[29]

In addition, unlike when sexually violent language is deployed against Israel or Judah, there will be no reconciliation after the assault.[30] I am using the language of rape and sexual assault in the modern sense to indicate a lack of consent given by the women (predominantly here) for sexual contact even though the hearers and readers of Nahum may not have regarded the events in the same light. One major difference between Israelite and contemporary understandings of rape is in the Hebrew Scriptures rape was a crime against a man in a patriarchal system[31]—a husband, fiancé, or father—and not a crime against the woman herself.

Even though Nineveh was inhabited by human persons and her fate is the fate of those persons, the rhetoric that personifies Nineveh can make it easy to regard the city abstractly and to lose focus of her people. Assyria is, in the eyes of Israel and the redactors of the Hebrew Bible, an "evil empire."[32] The reader/hearer is supposed to believe Assyria and her people deserve what happens to them. The text keeps the reader/hearer focused on the circumstances of Nineveh's people by describing the fate of select individuals and groups with no expectation of sympathy. The people of Nineveh are very much present in Nahum and represented by enslaved women beating their breasts and moaning like doves (2:7 [2:8 MT]), the Assyrian people as a whole or perhaps just the military

29. Gerlinde Baumann, "Nahum: The Just God as Sexual Predator," in *Feminist Biblical Interpretation: A Compendium of Critical Commentary on the Books of the Bible and Related Literature*, ed. Luise Schottroff and Marie-Theres Wacker (Grand Rapids: Eerdmans, 2012), 433–42, at 438.

30. See Hos 2:14, 19-20; 14:4-7 for the language of reconciliation and even honey-mooning alternating with cycles of violence in the book.

31. While the entire social and religious culture of ancient Israel cannot be simply categorized as patriarchal, the term does describe the system in which the rape of a woman or girl is a crime against men.

32. Ronald Reagan infamously uttered the words "evil empire" when describing the former Soviet Union to the National Association of Evangelicals in Orlando, Florida, March 9, 1983. Empire as much as the persons and nations that are constitutive of it dominate, oppress, subjugate, enslave, rape, exploit, and dispossess. See Mitri Raheb's characterization of empire as "demonic" and resistance to empire as "an act of faith" in Mitri Raheb, *Faith in the Face of Empire: The Bible through Palestinian Eyes* (New York: Orbis Books, 2014), 100. From a womanist perspective, empire is an evil that opposes the well-being of the beloved community. Empire can be reckoned as a self-perpetuating organism, mechanism, or entity that transcends historical social-political exemplars.

derided as [being like] women (3:13), and heaps of unmourned, unburied bodies in the streets (3:3).[33] The dignitaries of Thebes bound in fetters are present in 3:10, along with an untold number of infants who are subject to a grisly death. The mothers whose babies were smashed at every street corner are absent. In contrast, the people of Judah, the undifferentiated charge of their vengeful divine protector and arguable audience for the diatribe that is Nahum, are only minimally present.[34]

The text reveals little of the person of Nahum, no lineage, no royal affiliation, but does provide in 1:1 a possible hometown, Elkosh, which is otherwise unknown (the Targum reads Beth Qoshi). No discernable link exists between Elkosh and the Galilean town Capernaum, כפר נחם, traditionally understood to be the home, *caper*, "town," of Nahum. Nahum's prophecies would seem to be somewhat at odds with his name; the stem נחם means "comfort" or, perhaps more contextually appropriate, "relent." Nineveh's repentance in response to Jonah's preaching is styled as "God relented," וינחם, and did not bring destruction on them in Jonah 3:10.

Nahum's proclamations must certainly postdate Assyrian colonization and incorporation of Samaria in 723/22 BCE. They can be read as either predating and predicting the fall of Nineveh in August 612 BCE or as postdating Nineveh's fall, as a response to its demise, an act of interpretation prophecy. The text may well straddle the fall of Nineveh. The verbs range from imperfect to perfect and include participles that transcend time. A single dating indicator is present in the text: the fall of Thebes[35] in 663 BCE (3:8) has already happened, so the text would have been composed between then and (or just shortly after) 612 BCE.[36]

While not making an argument about the unity of the corpus or authorship, I am taking Nahum as a literary whole. In general I resist emend-

---

33. In 3:7, Nahum, or perhaps God, asks who will mourn for fallen Nineveh. No answer is given. Why would anyone lament the fall of Nineveh? Who indeed would do such a thing?

34. Judah appears once in 1:15 (2:1 MT). Israel does not appear at all; Jacob signifying Israel appears only in 2:1 (2:2 MT).

35. I will take up the identification of Thebes in the commentary on 3:8.

36. For the possibilities of even later dating, see Christensen, *Nahum*, 54–56. See also Ehud Ben Zvi who offers four contexts and periods in which the fifteen prophetic books of the Hebrew Scriptures could have been produced, ranging from "neo-Babylonian Judah" in 586–538 BCE to the breadth of the diaspora, 586–332 BCE. Ehud Ben Zvi, "The Concept of Prophetic Books and Its Historical Setting," in *The Production of Prophecy: Constructing Prophecy and Prophets in Yehud*, ed. Diana V. Edelman and Ehud Ben Zvi (London: Equinox, 2009), 73–95, esp. 79–80.

ing the text beyond the scribal corrections in the Masoretic Text (MT). The Hebrew of Nahum is vivid, sonorous, and complex, characterized by dizzying shifts in pronouns.[37] In order to make sense of them I have divided Nahum's proclamations into four prophecies[38] following the superscription, breaking the text at each Masoretic subdivision indicated by ס or פ:[39]

I. Superscription, 1:1

II. Prophecy 1, 1:2-11, a hymn of praise to God

III. Prophecy 2, 1:12-13, a brief address to Judah

IV. Prophecy 3, 1:14–2:13 (1:14–2:14 MT), proclamations to multiple subjects

   a. proclamation to and against Nineveh and/or her king in 1:14

   b. proclamation to Judah as an aside in 1:15

   c. proclamation to and against Nineveh and/or her king in 2:1

   d. second proclamation to Judah as an aside 2:2 (2:1, 3 MT)

V. Prophecy 4, 3:1-19, "woe"[40] prophecy, escalation of violent rhetoric against Nineveh to sexual assault

---

37. See the discussions of the specific proclamations for the range of gender identifications through pronoun use.

38. I am using "proclamations" to describe the content of Nahum's prophetic discourse broadly and "prophecies" to describe discrete units within that block. An oracle, a prophetic utterance, is the technical description of prophecy represented by משא, the description of the contents of Nahum in 1:1; משא is the first word of the book. Since the text of Nahum is by its own description a book, the oracular language is a literary construction.

39. In the MT individual passages are delineated with a soft break marked with a ס and a hard break indicated by a פ, most often at the end of a verse. The content of what I have labeled prophecy 3 is the most difficult to define. I read the third prophecy as beginning in 1:14, signaled by וצוה עליך יהוה, indicating a new proclamation parallel to כה אמר יהוה, which begins prophecy 2 in 1:12. The negative proclamation of Nah 1:14 can function as a standalone proclamation since it is closed by a major Masoretic break. Given that the following verses switch from Nineveh to Judah as the addressee and back again Nah 1:14 can also be read as introducing a collection of alternating addresses bundled together as a single oracular proclamation.

40. A "woe" oracle or prophecy is a specialized subgenre of prophecy characterized by the word "woe," הוי, generally as the first word.

Inasmuch as the book of Nahum is a response to Assyrian imperial domination, the text is postcolonial literature. As the Babylonian Empire replaced the Assyrian Empire and successive waves of oppression and occupation followed in their wake, Nahum's rhetoric remained serviceable, meriting a commentary by the Qumran community in *Pesher Nahum* (on Nah 1:3-6 and 2:11–3:14) and an address by Josephus in *Antiquities*.[41] There were also multiple manuscripts and fragments of the Twelve dispersed among different sites.[42]

Nahum has been studied in whole and in part by feminists owing largely to the female personification of Nineveh and her sexual assault by God. This womanist and feminist reading of Nahum will: (1) examine the use of gender in Nahum, (2) attempt to identify underlying female characters, and (3) pay particular attention to the ways in which actual and metaphorical female bodies are subject to human and divine violence. That violence occurs in prophetic and divine rhetoric. This volume will also consider the implications of that rhetoric for contemporary readers for whom Nahum is Scripture.

41. O'Brien, *Nahum*, 14, 40.

42. 4QXII$^g$ (Nah 1:7-9; 2:9-11; 3:1-3, 17); the Greek manuscript of the Twelve, 8HevXIIgr, contains Nah 1:13-14; 2:5-10, 14; 3:3, 6-17. There is also a catena on the end times in 4QMidr Eschat$^b$ incorporating Nah 2:11; Nah 3:8-10 is present in the pseudo-Ezekiel text 4QpsEzek, and Nah 1:2 is in the A manuscript of the Damascus Document.

# Nahum 1:1-11

# *Nahum's God Is Not the God of My Ancestors*

## Superscription (Nah 1:1)

The first word of Nahum is מַשָּׂא. The book presents itself as a technical form of prophecy, an "oracle" or "prophetic utterance." Yet those prophetic proclamations are no longer oracular—if they were ever spoken before being written. The text joins other prophetic works in the Hebrew Bible in being styled as a collection of prophecies that were once delivered orally.

According to the editor or narrator, Nahum practices two well-attested forms of prophecy: his מַשָּׂא, "prophecy," derives from a חָזוֹן, "vision."[1] The superscription proclaims the vision of Nahum has been transcribed; it is the only prophetic work called a "book"[2] in its superscription.[3] Unlike

---

1. Prophetic books described as oracles or prophetic utterances include Isaiah, Ezekiel, Habakkuk, Zechariah, and Malachi and, in Proverbs, Agur ben Jakeh (Prov 30:1) and the mother of King Lemuel (Prov 31:1). Prophets who are presented as experiencing visions include Isaiah, Ezekiel, Obadiah, Habakkuk, and Nathan in 1 Chr 17:15. The books of Samuel (1 Sam 3:1), Hosea (12:10), Micah (3:6), Psalms (89:19), Proverbs (29:18), Lamentations (2:9), and the breadth of Daniel describe visions as a normative prophetic or other revelatory experience.

2. A סֵפֶר is a "scroll." Books did not exist in the Iron Age. The common translation, "book," is anachronistic.

3. Julia M. O'Brien, *Nahum*, Readings: A New Biblical Commentary (London: Black, 2002), 41, 46, 65.

13

### Nahum 1:1

¹:¹An oracle concerning Nineveh.
The book of the vision of Nahum of
Elkosh.

other prophetic texts described as prophetic utterances, the intimation is that Nahum's author chose a literary rather than oral medium for the work; that suggestion is likely a literary strategy of the poet-prophet who adapted earlier traditions.[4] The framing with which Nahum as a literary work is presented is based on the superscription is of a prophet who wrote his prophecies out for dissemination and preservation. As a result, some regard the work as an epistle.[5]

Nineveh is named before naming Nahum, establishing the text's priorities from the beginning. Nineveh is mentioned by name three times throughout the work as the object of the proclamation.[6] Nineveh, its people, armies, monarchs, and gods are objects of God's vengeance proclaimed in the work that bears Nahum's name. Nahum, the literary character and the prophet who is invoked in and signified by this collection of oracular material, is not called a prophet.[7] The prophethood of Nahum is assumed. The poet who has woven the threads of a Nahum tradition with threads of his own weaving, thus crafting the work as it exists is, I argue, a prophet in his own right.

Nineveh was the capital of the Neo-Assyrian[8] Empire that decimated the Northern Monarchy, leaving a tithe of the people who were once

---

4. I consider that there are at least three Nahums intertwined: (1) an oracular prophet whose authority is conjured by the invocation of the name Nahum who may be entirely a literary creation, (2) a poet-prophet responsible for crafting the book in part or whole who may not be an individual but a school or guild like the Deuteronomist, and (3) the character of Nahum in the text.

5. Adam S. Van der Woude, "The Book of Nahum: A Letter Written In Exile," *OtSt* 20 (1977): 124.

6. Nah 1:1; 2:8 (2:9 MT); 3:7.

7. The only prophets with canonized works who are identified as prophets in the introductions to their prophetic collections are Haggai (1:1) and Zechariah (1:1). Amos famously rejects the mantel of a professional prophet in 7:14.

8. The Late (or Neo-)Assyrian Empire flourished from the mid-eighth century BCE until the fall of Nineveh in 612 BCE. Subduing Egypt and Philistia while incorporating Babylonia, Assyria was without rival at its peak strength. The strength of the empire in this period is attributed to the strength and ferocity of its ruling dynasty that began

known as Israel. The final capital of the empire and one of its four major cosmopolitan centers,[9] Nineveh represents the Assyrian Empire, the enemies of God and Judah, and every foreign threat, all of which keeps the rhetoric of Nahum alive beyond its originating context(s). Nineveh is wholly "other," with reference to Israel. Its otherness is indicated by its founding narrative, which highlights its architect, Nimrod, and his Hamite identity in Genesis 10:8-10 and Micah 5:6.[10]

---

### TRANSLATION MATTERS

Within the first proclamation there is a partial and broken acrostic in Nahum 1:1-8.[11] Because the key letters are present at such varying intervals, ranging from one to three lines apart, no clarity exists as to whether these letters are intentional. It is possible a later hand attempted to identify, craft, or complete the acrostic but failed or gave up. Only half of the alphabet can be located in this tenuous structure. For this study, such details pertaining to the acrostic are irrelevant.

---

The Assyrian Empire dates from the mid-fourteenth century BCE, when it coalesced into what would become the Middle Assyrian Empire, then it waxed and waned until its fall. The fall of Assyria to the Babylonian Empire was more of an assimilation furthered by an internecine war in the mid-seventh century. The strength of Assyria was its dreaded army, a brutally efficient, ruthlessly competent, and highly organized infantry

---

with Tiglath-Pileser III (744–727 BCE) known as "Pul" in the Hebrew Bible (2 Kgs 15:19; 1 Chr 5:26). His successor, Shalmaneser V (726–722 BCE) was killed, and then Sargon II (722–701 BCE) seized the throne in the same year the empire conquered Samaria. As a result it is nearly impossible to know who to credit for the demise of the Israelite Northern Monarchy. The prominence of Sargon was such that all of these kings are called "Sargonoid."

9. The four major cities in Assyria were Arbela, Asshur, Calah, and Nineveh.

10. O'Brien, *Nahum*, 39.

11. The acrostic is partial or defective in the following ways: (1) The key words are not in the same position; e.g., א begins the first word of 1:2 but ב is either בעל in the middle of v. 2 or בסופה, "whirlpool," in v. 3. This is true for other letters. (2) The fourth letter, ד, is missing. (3) The acrostic breaks off after ה, which begins v. 5. The next letter, ו, is so ubiquitous as the primary conjunction it is not clear whether ותשא, which begins the second half of v. 5, is intended to be part of a larger pattern. At this point letter patterns are in the eye of the beholder; ל (לא, first word second phrase) and מ (מה, first word) are inverted in v. 9 and ס in v. 11, which must be taken from the section break, is followed by ר, רבים, in the middle of the first clause of v. 12.

and chariot corps.[12] The empire was characterized in its own time and for posterity by ruthless violence against the peoples it subjugated. Assyrian imperial violence was legendary, its images preserved for posterity in *bas reliefs* such as those documenting the infamous siege of Lachish.

Images of the siege preserved for posterity include prisoners stripped naked and impaled on sharp sticks, others with their skin flayed off and flesh cut away to the bone. Fallen monarchs could look forward to being put on display in a cage with the heads of recently executed sovereigns hung around their necks as reminders of their ultimate fate.[13]

Assyrian domination did not end in Israel with the fall of the Northern Monarchy. Judah paid significant tribute—"rent"—to Assyria to retain its throne. At one point Hezekiah (716–686 BCE) even peeled the gold off the Jerusalem temple doors when the silver in its treasury was insufficient to slake their demands (2 Kgs 18:15-16).[14] Though Judah miraculously sur-

---

12. Albert Kirk Grayson, "History and Culture of Assyria," *ABD* 4:732–55.

13. Duane L. Christensen, *Nahum: A New Translation with Introduction and Commentary*, AYB (New Haven: Yale University Press, 2009), 336.

14. The account of Hezekiah's submission can be found in 2 Kgs 18:13-16. Sennacherib's account includes the exact amount of silver recorded in the biblical text, along with a much larger tribute, including women from the royal household, some of whom are identified as Hezekiah's daughters. William W. Hallo and K. Lawson Younger Jr., eds., *The Context of Scripture*, vol. 2: *Monumental Inscriptions from the Biblical World* (Leiden: Brill, 2003), 303.

vived an (unexpectedly interrupted) Assyrian siege in 701 BCE, the miracle did not include liberation from Assyrian subjugation.[15] Judah's relative stability under Hezekiah and his much maligned son Manasseh (696–642 BCE) was likely due to the stability of the Assyrian Empire and Judah's submission to Assyria, however reluctant. The transition from Manasseh through Amon (643–640 BCE) to Josiah (641–609 BCE) accompanied the decline of the empire and coincides with the putative frame of the contents Nahum, from the fall of Thebes (663 BCE) to the fall of Nineveh (612 BCE).

## Prophecy 1 (Nah 1:2-11)

> *A God jealous and vengeful (is) The Divine Warrior,[16]*
> *vengeful is the Divine Warrior and Lord[17] of Wrath.*
> *The Divine Warrior takes vengeance.[18]*

The opening proclamation of Nahum is a hymn of praise to a devastatingly powerful God who will wield cosmic power against any and all enemies. This proclamation could also be classified as a psalm and may have come to function as a liturgy commemorating the fall of Nineveh.[19] The Divine Warrior will prosecute a holy war[20] that will encapsulate natural and supernatural forces against Nineveh.[21] God's empyrean power couples with the will and desire to destroy God's enemies embodied in

15. The biblical text provides two explanations for the miracle: (1) a senior military and administrative official (the Rabshakeh) heard a rumor that the Nubian pharaoh Tirhakah was moving against him (2 Kgs 19:7-9), and (2) God smote 185,000 Assyrians, resulting in their king, Sennacherib, returning home to be assassinated (2 Kgs 19:35-37). These accounts are duplicated in Isa 37:1-37.

16. I am using the imagery and theme of the subunit to flesh out *qere* readings of YHWH following the example of Joel Rosenberg, who supplies the translations in David A. Teutsch and Betsy Platkin Teutsch, *Kol Haneshemah: Shabbat Vehagim*, 3rd ed. (Elkins Park, PA: Reconstructionist Press, 2000).

17. The text has בעל here, hence the lack of large-and-small caps. Baal, which I translate as "Lord" here, intentionally overlaps with Lord, the traditional *qere* for YHWH. Whether there are one, two, or three deities in the first verse is neither clear nor, perhaps, supposed to be clear.

18. The translations of Scripture texts in the body of this commentary are mine; the NRSV text is, however, used for the sections of Scripture at the beginning of each chapter.

19. Laurel Lanner, *"Who Will Lament Her?" The Feminine and the Fantastic in the Book of Nahum*, vol. 11 (New York: T & T Clark, 2006), 7.

20. Arguably all sanctioned war in the Hebrew Scriptures is holy war. See Susan Thistlethwaite, " 'You May Enjoy the Spoil of Your Enemies': Rape as a Biblical Metaphor for War," *Semeia* 61 (1993): 61, 67.

21. Lanner, *Who Will Lament Her?*, 26.

*Nahum 1:2-11*

2A jealous and avenging God is
the Lord,
the Lord is avenging and
wrathful;
the Lord takes vengeance on his
adversaries
and rages against his enemies.
3The Lord is slow to anger but
great in power,
and the Lord will by no means
clear the guilty.

His way is in whirlwind and storm,
and the clouds are the dust of
his feet.

4He rebukes the sea and makes
it dry,
and he dries up all the rivers;
Bashan and Carmel wither,
and the bloom of Lebanon
fades.
5The mountains quake before him,
and the hills melt;
the earth heaves before him,
the world and all who live in it.

6Who can stand before his
indignation?
Who can endure the heat of
his anger?

Nineveh down to the soil on which they stand. Nineveh cannot stand in the face of God's rage. The very rocks on which she was founded will be ruptured and will buckle underneath her, taking her down with them.

God's motivation is ancient and familiar: God is jealous and vengeful. The description is primal and emotional: God is *exceptionally* jealous. God's jealousy is proclaimed repeatedly in the Torah, primarily to explain the prohibition against worshiping other gods and to explain the rage such worship engenders.[22] Exodus 34:14 goes so far as to say God's name is קנא, Jealous. Similarly, vengeance is a divine prerogative, one God occasionally grants humans to execute in God's name.[23] Rather than the familiar קנא, expressing jealousy in passages such as Exodus 20:5,[24] the text of Nahum has a form found otherwise only in Joshua 24:19, קנוא.[25] In the Joshua text God is holy, jealous, and unforgiving. The use of קנוא here signifies the lack of forgiveness demonstrated by the citation of Numbers 14:18, altered to remove the description of God as forgiving (and loving) in Nahum 1:3. In both of those passages jealousy is characteristic of a

22. Exod 20:5; 34:14; Num 5:30; 11:29; Deut 4:24; 5:9; 6:15; 32:19.
23. Gen 4:15; Lev 19:18; Isa 34:8; 35:4; 61:2; Jer 51:36; Ezek 25:12-17.
24. See also Exod 34:14; Deut 4:24; 5:9; 6:15.
25. *Brown-Driver-Briggs* (BDB), *The Hebrew and Aramaic Lexicon of the Old Testament* (*HALOT*), and the *Dictionary of Classical Hebrew* (*DCH*) regard קנוא as an adjective. Gesenius and *The Theological Wordbook of the Old Testament* (*TWOT*) regard קנוא as a noun derived from a Piel form.

His wrath is poured out like fire,
and by him the rocks are
broken in pieces.
[7]The LORD is good,
a stronghold in a day of trouble;
he protects those who take refuge
in him,
[8]even in a rushing flood.
He will make a full end of his
adversaries,
and will pursue his enemies
into darkness.

[9]Why do you plot against the
LORD?
He will make an end;
no adversary will rise up twice.
[10]Like thorns they are entangled,
like drunkards they are drunk;
they are consumed like dry
straw.
[11]From you one has gone out
who plots evil against the
LORD,
one who counsels wickedness.

possessive male spouse and includes the right to shame and humiliate sexually and nonsexually, beat, injure, maim, and/or kill his woman for infidelity as well as to hold her down for others to use sexually and punitively. He is also entitled to inflict physical (though generally not sexual) violence on his rival and kill him as well.[26]

Divine jealousy is traditionally aroused when God's wife services other gods, interpreted as adultery without regard to actual sex-based religious practices.[27] In Nahum Nineveh is exclusively female but is not God's adulterous wife—though she will be treated as such. Furthermore, Nineveh is neither God's cuckolding rival—her gender notwithstanding—nor is there a claim Judah was seduced away or went astray, lusting or whoring after either Ishtar, Nineveh's goddess, or even her Semitic counterpart, Astarte. In fact, there are no goddesses either named or mentioned in Nahum, which is surprising since Nineveh's "gods" are mentioned in 1:14; all of the divine language, names, terminology, and rhetoric in Nahum is masculine. Nahum's author(s) and audience would have known Ishtar was Nineveh's preeminent deity.[28] (On the one hand, it would seem to be an overreach to read an intentional androcentric or

26. Renita J. Weems, *Battered Love: Marriage, Sex, and Violence in the Hebrew Prophets* (Minneapolis: Fortress, 1995), 18–22, 25–34.

27. Ezekiel 16 and 23 are among the most notorious examples of retributive sexual violence in the Hebrew Bible. In the Ezekiel texts God hands Samaria and Judah over to their assailants (16:39; 23:28). See also Jer 13:26; Hos 2:3, 10 and Isa 47:1-3 direct similar rhetoric toward Babylon.

28. The inclusion of Baal by name in particular would seem to signal no discomfort with naming and taming non-Israelite deities so the omission of Ishtar's name and

patriarchal slight there. On the other hand, a conflation of Ishtar with Nineveh allows for her savaging and humiliation without acknowledging her as a goddess.)

## TRANSLATION MATTERS

Belial or "worthless/ness," בְּלִיַּעַל, is a euphemistic expression that communicates lack of value, particularly scruples. Persons are described as a daughter[29] or son(s),[30] and occasionally men of Belial to indicate their low regard. More rare, the term stands alone as in Nahum 1:11 and 1:15.[31] It will come to function as a proper name for the personification of evil—Satan—as seen in the Dead Sea *War Scroll*, *Zadokite Document*, and numerous other texts and fragments and, with a modified spelling, in the Christian Testament, 2 Corinthians 6:15 and 2 Thessalonians 2:3.

In the Hebrew Scriptures God is not only jealous *of* but also jealous *for*. God is jealous for God's holy name (Ezek 39:35), for God's land (Joel 2:18), and for Jerusalem and Zion (Zech 1:14 and 8:2). The naming of Judah in Nahum 1:15 (2:1 MT) indicates the divine jealousy is on behalf of God's beloved Zion and provides the rationale for God's fury in Nahum. At the same time, God is vengeful, נקם; this Hebrew root describes sevenfold vengeance against anyone who would take it upon him- or herself to kill Cain (Gen 4:15). Lamech[32] uses the same root for his self-articulation: he should be avenged seventyfold if Cain merits seven (Gen 4:24). In Deuteronomy vengeance is a divine prerogative.[33] God's exercise of vengeance is, to say the least, extravagant in the Hebrew Scriptures. In Numbers 31 divine vengeance manifested

---

conflation of her with one or more unnamed deities is curious and surprising. See Lanner, *Who Will Lament Her?*, 53.

29. Hannah asks Eli not to think of her as a בַּת־בְּלִיַּעַל, a woman of no worth, in 1 Sam 1:16 when he accuses her of wandering around the shrine drunk.

30. Deut 13:13; Judg 19:22; 23:13; 1 Sam 2:12; 10:27; 25:17; 1 Kgs 21:13.

31. The use of Belial in the psalms is distinct. It stands alone but modifies abstract and concrete threats: Pss 18:4; 41:8; 101:3. In Job 34:18 Belial is a slur.

32. Lamech's introduction to the text is a series of one-upmanships. He becomes the father of polygamy, taking two women when all before him took (or were given) only one. He also proclaims he has killed someone for merely striking him and makes a claim about sevenfold vengeance.

33. Deut 32:35, 41, 43.

in the sexual enslavement of thirty-two thousand Midianite virginal and prepubescent girls to the Israelites along with the extermination of men and boys on the most specious of false pretenses.[34] This vengeance is a blunt instrument; no one in the text is concerned about casualties or collateral damage. The target of God's vengeance is Nineveh from the first line of the book (1:1; 2:8; 3:7) and Assyria (3:18) by name and the king of Assyria by title in the penultimate verse in the book (3:18). The text does not delineate Assyria's specific transgressions; rather, the text seems to appeal to broad knowledge of Assyrian conduct.

In crafting a portrait of God, Nahum draws on a familiar confession in verse 3, God is "slow to anger," but the confession has a significant twist. With the exception of Nahum 1:2, in every text where God is proclaimed to be "slow to anger," the next phrase is "abounding in steadfast love."[35] In Jonah 4:2 and Joel 2:13 these attributes are also linked with divine tenderness: God is "gracious and mother-loving," חנון ורחום, expressed in "relenting," נחם,[36] from inflicting the well-deserved punishment. There is no love articulated, human or divine, in the book of Nahum—though God's love for Judah may be read into the good news to her. Instead of love, Nahum's God offers "power," כח—great power—expressed in whirlwind and storm (1:3 and in v. 8, the flood). These experiences are more than a traditional theophany or the dust under the soles of the divine feet (1:3) of Nahum's anthropomorphic God. Cloud and storm are the provenance of Baal, who is God's long-standing rival. "Cloud-Rider" is one of Baal's primary appellations in numerous Ugaritic texts.[37]

The opening words of the first proclamation subordinate the gods of Canaan to the God of Israel. Those words are a sign of things to come for the gods of Nineveh. Here, God not only dominates Baal's realm but

---

34. Num 31:1-3, 7-9, 35. Numbers 31:16 makes the false claim that Midianite women seduced Israelite men at Baal Peor at Balaam's instigation even though the text makes clear there were no Midianites present at the site of the offense in Num 25:1-5. Verse 1 specifies the involvement of Moabite women, a completely different community, but the vengeful deity is not concerned with the specifics. This false claim also resulted in the slaughter of the newlywed Midianite Cozbi bat Zur and her groom, the Israelite Zimri ben Salu (but curiously not Moses and his Midianite wife) in Num 25:6-17. In the text God approves of this slaughter and rewards the executioner.

35. Exod 34:6; Num 14:18; Neh 9:17; Ps 86:15; 103:8; 145:8; Joel 2:13; Jonah 4:2.

36. נחם, *n-ḥ-m* is the root of Nahum's name.

37. See the Balu Myth in William W. Hallo and K. Lawson Younger Jr., *The Context of Scripture*, vol. 1: *Canonical Compositions from the Biblical World* (Leiden: Brill, 2003), 248–49, 251–52, 258, 261, 266.

takes Baal's name/title too, repurposing it as "Lord of Wrath," בעל חמה, in 1:2 just as El, named first in the verse, has long been equated with or assimilated into YHWH. In so doing, Nahum yokes the three regional gods and thus elevates YHWH at the expense of the Canaanite gods. Building on the creation traditions of Baal and YHWH, Nahum continues to establish God's *bona fides* in Nahum 1:4; God wields the power to devastate and desiccate lush food-producing land symbolized by Bashan and Carmel.[38]

Having identified the hybridized God (El/YHWH/Baal) within the scope of the cosmos, Nahum turns to terrestrial affairs. He begins by assuring God is beneficent and protective of undisclosed beneficiaries.[39] In verse 7 God is good "in the day of trouble." The phrase "in the day of trouble" is a common expression, but "trouble" here, צרה, can also be a female "adversary," and in this context, the word could refer to Nineveh. Verse 8 supports this reading and states that God will make an end to "her place," a reading JPS preserves.[40] Similarly in verse 9, she— "trouble"—will not rise up twice.[41] Nineveh is going to be put down, once and for all. Nineveh is not the only candidate for God's female adversary. Some scholars read the subject as Ishtar rather than Nineveh.[42]

Abruptly the female subject disappears for a moment, replaced in verse 10 by an indeterminable "they" in a nearly impenetrable alliterative prosaic phrase, כי עד־סירים סבכים וכסבאם סבואים, *ki ad-sirim s'vukim uk'sov'om s'vuim*: "just as thorns are entangled and like drunkards are drunken," the unidentified "they" will be completely consumed. If the feminine subject of the previous text were Nineveh, then the plural subject could be her occupants. More expansive readings of verse 10 find either the subject is all of Assyria or all of Israel's enemies and therefore a warning to Judah herself.[43] The ambiguity is in keeping with the broader text that is periodically vague in order to preserve its utility beyond the fall of Nineveh. The short-lived shift to the third-person inclusive plural, "they

38. Isaiah 33:9 and Jer 50:19 present Bashan and Carmel as already desolate. Nahum and Isaiah name the pair in the same sequence; Jeremiah inverts them.

39. The JPS Tanakh adds the pious phrase "to those who hope in Him" to complete the phrase.

40. The word choice "adversaries" used in the NRSV unnecessarily changes the number from singular to plural. God's single foe is Nineveh.

41. Now "adversary" appears as singular in the NRSV.

42. Lanner, *Who Will Lament Her?*, 20, 87. The lexeme can also mean "rival" as in "rival wife" used in 1 Sam 1:6 and Sir 37:11 (Ms B) in the Cairo Geniza cache.

43. Lanner, *Nahum*, 88.

are entangled," is puzzling. Verse 11 returns to the feminine singular, this time in the second person; Nineveh is addressed directly: "From you [fem. sing., i.e., Nineveh] has gone out one [masc. sing.] who has plotted wickedness against God." The masculine verb is possibly a veiled reference to Sennacherib, architect of the aborted siege of Jerusalem in 701 BCE or even a military commander.[44] Again the lack of specificity makes the text applicable to any Assyrian campaign.

By not naming an Assyrian king, the passage can be read as a proclamation against all kings, particularly in the period from the fall of Samaria (723/722 BCE) to the fall of Nineveh (613 BCE) that has proven so fertile for Nahum's invective. The most significant Assyrian kings of this period with regard to the biblical text include Shalmaneser (727–722 BCE), who was credited with the conquest of Samaria in the biblical text;[45] his successor Sargon II (722–705 BCE), called the subduer of Judah in the Nimrud Inscription;[46] Sennacherib (705–681 BCE), believed to have besieged Jerusalem;[47] Esarhaddon (681–669 BCE), reported to have taken Judean king Manasseh to Babylon as a hostage;[48] Ashurbanipal (668–627 BCE), responsible for the fall of Thebes mentioned in Nahum 3:8; and Sin-sar-iskun (623–612 BCE), who died in Nineveh when it fell.

The anonymous plotter against God in verse 11, whether monarch, adviser, or warrior, who gave the "worthless" (בליעל, lit. "Belial") counsel to attack Judah and Jerusalem, would seem to have brought Nineveh's fate down upon her. Nineveh's fate has been sealed. She will be put to an end, verse 8, and her worthless counselor will be cut off.

44. Alternately, the reference to the "one who has gone out" may refer to the commander of the action, for example, the Rabshekeh who taunts Hezekiah and his officials, mocking God in 2 Kgs 17–18. The episode is duplicated is Isa 36–37.

45. 2 Kgs 17:3-6.

46. 2 Kgs 17:24-27; Hallo and Younger, *Monumental Inscriptions*, 2:298.

47. It is also possible Sargon II led the siege but it is not possible to verify either possibility.

48. 2 Chr 33:11-13; see also 2 Kgs 19:35-37 and Ezra 4:1-2.

# Nahum 1:12–2:13[14]

# *Good News to Judah, Devastating News to Nineveh*

## Prophecy 2 (Nah 1:12-13)

The second proclamation, a scant two verses, is addressed to a single feminine recipient, but, in my judgment, that recipient is not Nineveh. There is no vengeful or punitive rhetoric indicating Nineveh. Instead, there are words of remission and liberation that are standard prophetic fare for Israel and Judah. Surprisingly, Jerusalem is not named here or elsewhere in Nahum.[1] The Targum corrects this omission and names Jerusalem in verse 12. If this address is to Judah then Judith Sanderson's presupposition that Nahum's proclamations were delivered in Jerusalem is more than reasonable.[2] The address speaks to Judah and about a second unnamed subject in the third-person plural: "They will be mown (down like grass)." "They" who will be mown down are Assyrians, *en toto*, or perhaps just the military. The ambiguity

---

1. Laurel Lanner, *"Who Will Lament Her?" The Feminine and the Fantastic in the Book of Nahum*, 11 (New York: T & T Clark, 2006), 2, 25. Zion and the Jerusalem temple are also absent.

2. Judith Sanderson, "Nahum," in *The Women's Bible Commentary*, ed. Carol A. Newsom and Sharon H. Ringe (London: SPCK, 1992), 232–36, at 232.

| | |
|---|---|
| [12]Thus says the LORD, | I will afflict you no more. |
| "Though they are at full strength and many, | [13]And now I will break off his yoke from you |
| they will be cut off and pass away. | and snap the bonds that bind you." |
| Though I have afflicted you, | |

in verse 12 echoes 1:10 in which "they" who will be entangled also represent the Assyrians.

Unlike the first prophecy, 1:2-11, the second one begins with a proper prophetic formula, כה אמר יהוה, "So says GOD." The first letters of the four words that follow the formula form an acrostic that conveniently spells *ashur*, "Assyria," confirming they are the ones who will be mowed down. The God whose sovereignty was just articulated with awe-inspiring rhetoric tells Judah not to worry about "their" numbers. The message is consistent with the broader theology of the Hebrew Bible, Deuteronomistic theology: though God has "afflicted" Judah in the past, God will not afflict them ever again. This line of thought was that God brought about good and evil, the latter often as punishment. The language echoes Deuteronomy 8:2, 16, where God "afflicts" Israel in order to test the nation. The language also evokes other prophetic texts, such as Isaiah 40:2 in which Judah's suffering is sufficient, i.e., proportionate to her sin, and thus at an end. Whatever penalty Judah has owed has been paid. The poet-prophet is careful to interpret the oppression Israel and Judah have experienced at the hands of Assyria as the choice of the sovereign God to punish God's people. Because the poet is ultimately composing for the Judean people who have legitimate questions about why they have been subjected to Assyrian oppression, it is important to maintain that God is in control and making deliberative choices, especially in light of the uncomfortable similarities between Judah's experience and Nineveh's fate. Conversely, the poet-prophet will frame Nineveh's fall as the failure of Nineveh's goddess[3]

---

3. The poet and/or final redactor have subsumed Ishtar, Nineveh's patron, into Nineveh's "gods" in Nah 1:14.

and monarch to protect their dependents.[4] The final word of Prophecy 2 is emancipation. Judah's bonds—a pole-yoke and its fetters—will be shattered and ripped off (both in Piel) in verse 13.

## Prophecy 3 (Nah 1:14–2:13 [1:14–2:14 MT])

Beginning with Nahum 1:14, the sorting out of the characters, subjects, and objects of the proclamations becomes increasingly difficult. The division of the proclamations in this commentary is but one of multiple options greatly facilitated by Laurel Lanner's incredibly helpful translation with gendered subtitles.[5] Prophecy 3 moves from royal and divine figures and then alternates between Judah and Nineveh. Nahum, the prophetic character in the text, speaks for God to and about all of these entities. In the process, the person and number of the addressees change so frequently the poet-prophet supplies the speaker-prophet with the appropriate names, Judah, Jacob, and Israel, to help the reader follow the rhetoric. The rhetoric is also variable, at turns maleficent and beneficent. There are also portions to a wider public that would function well as dramatic asides to an audience in a theatrical or other public performance. That wider public is also Judah, named in 1:15 (2:1 MT) and implied in 2:2 (2:3 MT). My suggestions for navigating the shifts in Prophecy 3 follow:

1:14 to king/monarchy

1:15 (2:1 MT) to wider public, Judah (by name)

2:1 (2:2 MT) to Nineveh

2:2 (2:3 MT) to wider public, mentions Jacob/Israel

2:3-12 (2:4-13 MT) to wider public, mentions Nineveh (2:8 [2:9 MT])

2:13 (2:14 MT) to Nineveh

---

4. Julia O'Brien reads the interpretation of the fall of Nineveh as "male anxiety" through Judith Butler's *Bodies That Matter: On the Discursive Limits of "Sex"* (New York: Routledge, 1993), 95.

5. Lanner, *Who Will Lament Her?*, 80–85. Since the addressees include human persons as well as Nineveh and Judah personified, I prefer to identify the subjects as "feminine" and "male" rather than "women" and "men" as does Lanner.

¹⁴The LORD has commanded
concerning you:
"Your name shall be
perpetuated no longer;
from the house of your gods I will
cut off
the carved image and the cast
image.
I will make your grave, for you are
worthless."

¹⁵Look! On the mountains the feet
of one
who brings good tidings,
who proclaims peace!
Celebrate your festivals, O Judah,
fulfill your vows,
for never again shall the wicked
invade you;
they are utterly cut off.

²:¹A shatterer has come up against
you.
Guard the ramparts;
watch the road;
gird your loins;
collect all your strength.

²(For the LORD is restoring the
majesty of Jacob,
as well as the majesty of Israel,
though ravagers have ravaged
them
and ruined their branches.)

³The shields of his warriors are red;
his soldiers are clothed in
crimson.
The metal on the chariots flashes
on the day when he musters
them;
the chargers prance.
⁴The chariots race madly through
the streets,
they rush to and fro through
the squares;
their appearance is like torches,
they dart like lightning.

In 1:14 Nahum addresses a new masculine subject in the second-person singular. Now words of emancipation replace words of extirpation. The focus has clearly shifted from grammatically feminine Judah to a male or at least masculine adversary. The verse could stand alone, though I am considering it as part of a third proclamation, one characterized by multiple shifts in the proclamation's target, including gender. It is possible but unlikely the prophet is now using the masculine gender for Nineveh, the city he has previously prophesied to as a feminine entity. Each gender shift, however, seems to identify a shift in the proclamation's target. I contend this is the case here. With the Targum, I read the subject of Nahum 1:14 as the king of Assyria, either an individual monarch or the monarchy personified.[6]

---

6. Duane L. Christensen, *Nahum: A New Translation with Introduction and Commentary*, AYB (New Haven: Yale University Press, 2009), 242.

⁵He calls his officers;
  they stumble as they come
    forward;
they hasten to the wall,
  and the mantelet is set up.
⁶The river gates are opened,
  the palace trembles.
⁷It is decreed that the city be exiled,
  its slave women led away,
moaning like doves
  and beating their breasts.
⁸Nineveh is like a pool
  whose waters run away.
"Halt! Halt!"—
  but no one turns back.
⁹"Plunder the silver,
  plunder the gold!
There is no end of treasure!
An abundance of every
    precious thing!"

¹⁰Devastation, desolation, and
    destruction!

Hearts faint and knees
    tremble,
all loins quake,
all faces grow pale!
¹¹What became of the lions' den,
  the cave of the young lions,
where the lion goes,
  and the lion's cubs, with no
    one to disturb them?
¹²The lion has torn enough for his
    whelps
  and strangled prey for his
    lionesses;
he has filled his caves with prey
  and his dens with torn flesh.

¹³See, I am against you, says the LORD of hosts, and I will burn your chariots in smoke, and the sword shall devour your young lions; I will cut off your prey from the earth, and the voice of your messengers shall be heard no more.

The prophesied fate of the monarch or monarchy is dynastic dissolution. The speaker-prophet prophesies the end of the monarch's name and fame—שם means both. The prophet in the text specifies that the dynastic portion of the prophesy in verse 14 came directly at the command of God. The poet-prophet supplies the speaker-prophet with a pun; God says the king's name will not be "implanted," "sown," or "perpetuated" using the agricultural verb, זרע. The king of Assyria will have no son-kings to follow in his line even though he may have fathered sons. He will impregnate no more women with his seed. Instead, God will plant *him*. God will dig, "make," his grave. The verse concludes with the charge that the king is "worthless." What comes to mind here is the taunt proclaimed by the Assyrian military official, the Rabshakeh, against Judah and its God in 2 Kings 18:28-35.[7]

_____

7. "Do not listen to Hezekiah when he misleads you by saying, YHWH will deliver us. Has any of the gods of the nations ever delivered its land out of the hand of the

Closely linked with the king's name and fame is the standing, reputa-
tion, and physical presence of his goddesses-and-gods,[8] whether "carved-
stone," פסל, or "cast-metal," מסכה. Speaking through the prophet in the
first person, God declares God will personally cut off the goddesses-
and-gods of Assyria/Nineveh and their images from within their own
temples or houses. Curiously the text names neither Ishtar nor Nabu.
Both of these gods were worshiped in Nineveh. The absence of Ishtar,
the major deity, is especially surprising since other biblical texts do not
shy away from condemning foreign gods by name. As noted previously,
El and Baal have both been named.[9] Despite the glaring omission of her
name, it is likely Ishtar was understood to be evoked in the personification of Nineveh. Therefore it is possible, and I would argue likely, that
the physical and sexual assaults on Nineveh should be understood as
the subjugation and sexual humiliation of Ishtar. The presentation of
Nineveh as personified as a hybridized city-woman, particularly in
Nahum 3:5-7, supports this reading.[10]

Ishtar was the dominant goddess of Mesopotamia. She was known
as Inanna to the Sumerians, Ishtar to the Assyrians, and Astarte to the
Canaanites in Canaan. The name was likely corrupted to Ashtoreth in
the Hebrew Bible. Her portfolio included aspects mortal women were
not expected to imitate. She was, in Tikva Frymer-Kensky's assessment,
"undomesticated."[11] She would come to be called Mulissu in Nineveh
in the seventh century. Simo Parpola notes the fluidity of identity between Ishtar and the Assyrian national god, Asshur, which meant that
to invoke Ishtar was to invoke Asshur.[12] Further, the preferable or at

---

king of Assyria? . . . Who among all the gods of the countries have delivered their
countries out of my hand, that YHWH should deliver Jerusalem out of my hand?"
(2 Kgs 18:32b-33, 35; NRSV, modified).

8. As a plural form, אלהים includes both genders.

9. Alternately, Frymer-Kensky notes that in the Prophets God does not triumph
over other gods when defeating foreign cities and nations, and deference to monotheistic sensitivities may account for the absence of Ishtar's name in Nahum. See
Tikva Frymer-Kensky, *In the Wake of the Goddesses: Women, Culture, and the Biblical
Transformation of Pagan Myth* (New York: Free Press, 1992), 172.

10. Francisco O. García-Treto, "Nahum," in *The New Interpreter's Bible: General Articles and Introduction, Commentary, and Reflections for Each Book of the Bible, Including
the Apocryphal/Deuterocanonical Books* (Nashville: Abingdon, 1994), 614.

11. Frymer-Kensky, *In the Wake*, 25.

12. Simo Parpola, *Assyrian Prophecies*, State Archives of Assyria, vol. 9 (Helsinki:
Helsinki University Press, 1997), xx.

least dominant mode of divine interaction was through Ishtar and not Asshur, as amply demonstrated by extant Assyrian prophecies. The conflation of divinity extends, in at least one other case, to Nabu and Marduk (generally called Bel).[13] Ishtar and Nabu were the patrons of wisdom and writing, respectively. They were worshiped in temples on the same mound in Nineveh, Kuyunjik.[14] A revival in Nabu's worship is credited to Sammuramat, the wife of Assyrian Shamshi-Adad (823–811 BCE) and mother of Adad-Nirari III (810–783 BCE).[15] This devotion led to the erection of his temple adjacent to the already two-millennia-old temple of Ishtar.[16] In my reading of the text, the prophecies of Nahum are as much an attack on Ishtar (and Nabu) as they are on Nineveh, its monarchy, and its people.

Exegetes have long wrestled with the division between Nahum 1 and 2. Gentile translations such as the NRSV, on which this commentary series is based, identify verse 15 as the final verse of Nahum 1. In Jewish texts, Nahum 2 begins with what is Nahum 1:15 in Christian Bibles; the LXX follows the MT in ending chapter 1 with the fourteenth verse. Nahum 1:15 marks a dramatic shift in tone; it is a call to celebration and shares resonances (in italics below) with Isaiah 40.

13. Ibid., xviii. Parpola goes further and argues that Assyrian religion is actually monotheistic (xxi, xxv) and draws parallels between Ishtar and the Holy Spirit (xxvi). While acknowledging Inanna is not generally known as a mother herself, Parpola identifies Ishtar as the "mother aspect" of Asshur (xxvi). See also Frymer-Kensky, *In the Wake*, 27.

14. Julian Reade, "The Evolution of Assyrian Imperial Architecture: Political Implications and Uncertainties," in *Mesopotamia: rivista di archeologia, epigrafia e storia orientale antica* 46 (2011): 112.

15. Rivkah Harris, "Women: Royal Women," *ABD*, 6:950. Sammuramat was memorialized on a stela, a carved or engraved stone pillar. Inscriptions are uncommonly rare for women, even royal ones. Her monument reads: *Stela of Sammuramat (Semiramis), the royal lady of Shamshi-Adad, king of the universe, king of Assyria, mother of Adad-nirari, king of the universe, king of Assyria, daughter-in-law of Shalmaneser, king of the four quarters*. (William W. Hallo and K. Lawson Younger Jr., *The Context of Scripture*, vol. 2: *Monumental Inscriptions* [Leiden: Brill, 2003], 277. There is significant scholarly debate over how to translate *segallu*; "consort" and "palace-lady" are other options in the literature.) She is also listed on a stela belonging to her son in which she is described as crossing the Euphrates with him to go to war (ibid., 2:273).

16. Reade, "Evolution," 111–12.

| Nahum 1:15 | Isaiah 40:9 |
|---|---|
| *Look!* On the *mountains* the *feet* of one | Onto a high *mountain* go-up |
| *who proclaims good news* | Zion *proclaimer of good news*[17] |
| who makes peace known! | raise—with power—your voice |
| Celebrate your festivals Judah | Jerusalem *proclaimer of good news* |
| perform your vows | raise (it up), fear not |
| for never again shall the wicked pass through you | say to the cities of Judah |
| they are completely cut off. | *Look!* "Here is your God!" |

For the first time in the book the prophet addresses Judah directly by name in Nahum 1:15 (2:1 MT). Here Judah is feminine, in keeping with the common personification of cities as women in biblical prophetic literature and throughout the ANE. When the biblical text does not personify Judah it generally takes masculine pronouns evoking the person and patriarch Judah.[18] The cry in Nahum 1:15 (2:1 MT) to the wider Judean public is celebratory and seemingly at odds with the rest of the proclamation and the book as a whole. The phrases "good news" and "peace" are traditional tidings of joy. The cause of this joy in the book's framing and the impending doom of Nineveh links this passage with the

17. The proclaimers of good news, preachers, in Isa 40:9, are identified with Zion/ Jerusalem; the parallel language refers to the one city. In the rhetoric placed in the mouth of Nahum in the text the preachers are either the city personified as a woman proclaiming the good news or a human woman, perhaps a prophet, sent to proclaim good news to the city. Androcentric scholarship has often resisted the later reading because such scholarship doubts a second grammatically feminine actor. I read the text as a woman prophet preaching in and to Jerusalem, particularly since the book of Isaiah already includes at least one woman prophet (see Isa 8:1-4). For more on women as proclaimers of good news, see the Translation Matters section on p. 33, regarding Nah 1:14–2:13. For more on the configuration of cities as women and personified inhabitants, see the expressions בתולת ישראל, "Virgin Israel" (Jer 18:13; 31:4, 21); בת עמי, "My Daughter-People" (Isa 22:4; Jer 8:19; Lam 2:11; etc.); בת ציון, "Daughter Zion" (2 Kgs 19:21; Ps 9:14; Isa 1:8); יושבת ציון, "she-who-dwells (in) Zion" (Isa 10:24; 12:6; Jer 51:35; Ps 9:11). See also Frymer-Kensky, *In the Wake*, 168–78.

18. Cp: Isa 7:6; Jer 3:7-11; 13:19; 14:2; and Joel 4:20 with Isa 3:8; 11:13; Hos 10:11; and 11:12, Julia O'Brien, *Nahum*, Readings: A New Biblical Commentary (London: Black, 2002), 58.

larger collection of proclamations. The use of participles allows the text to be read in the present tense and to anticipate the promised liberation.[19] The identity of the one who proclaims the good news is not given; it is not important in the proclamation. Those who bear the tidings of victory are often anonymous in the Hebrew Bible.[20]

## TRANSLATION MATTERS

The "one-who-bears-good-news," מבשׂר, in Nahum 1:15 (2:1 MT) is part of a larger cultural practice enjoined by women and men; the title is used for heralds and messengers both literal and metaphorical. In Psalm 68:11 (68:12 MT), המבשׂרות, those who proclaim the good news are women who form a great army. In the LXX מבשׂר is most often translated by εὐαγγελίζω, the primary verb for proclaiming the gospel in the Christian Testament. The gospels and epistles scrupulously avoid having women proclaim the gospel using this vocabulary (instead, Mary Magdalene "announces" the resurrection to the apostles using ἀγγέλλω in John 20:18). Nonetheless, in the Christian Testament women do proclaim the good news of Jesus in spite of the lexical limitations placed on them: the woman at the well in John 4:28-30, Priscilla in Acts 18:26, the apostle Junia in Romans 16:7, and Paul's female co-workers Tryphena and Tryphosa in Romans 16:12, and perhaps others.

This single verse, Nahum 1:15 (2:1 MT), proclaims the good news of Judah's deliverance and what will come to be called "gospel"[21] in other contexts. The prophecy is that Judah will be liberated and her people can return to their way of life framed by the festivals that mark the passage of time in Israel's cosmos. The return to festival observances and fulfillment of vows pledged signal full restoration of worship at the Jerusalem temple and the economy it generates as in Psalm 51:18-19. The call to return to festival celebration may be in response to an actual or perceived drop in pilgrimages to the Jerusalem temple after the 701 BCE siege or another conflict. The reference to Jerusalem and its temple is apparent without explicit mention of either. As the remainder of the prophecy makes clear, Judah's salvation will be purchased with the blood of Nineveh's people, which is not good news for the Ninevites.

---

19. Carol J. Dempsey, *Amos, Hosea, Micah, Nahum, Zephaniah, Habakkuk*, New Collegeville Bible Commentary 15 (Collegeville, MN: Liturgical Press, 2013), 110–11.

20. 1 Sam 4:17; 2 Sam 4:10; 18:26.

21. The LXX uses εὐαγγελιζομένου here; the verb εὐαγγελίζω is the basis of the root "evangel."

The final line of the celebratory verse is the declaration that the "worth-less" (בליעל, Belial, see Nah 1:11) will never "pass through" her (Judah) again.[22] It is not clear whether this refers to Assyria or any subsequent foreign power. The passage resonates with Zion theology common in the psalms proclaiming the inviolability of Zion (see Pss 48:4-8; 125:1; 132:13-18; etc.).

The beginning of a new verse, 2:1 (2:2 MT), introduces another shift in grammar. Retaining the feminine singular grammar but changing the antecedent, Nahum 2:1 (2:2 MT) shifts from Judah to Nineveh, indicated by threat language: "one-who-scatters" (cities) is coming against you ("against your face," על פניך). Since Judah was just comforted with the promise that she would not be further afflicted (1:13) or invaded (1:15 [2:1 MT]), it does not make sense that she is now subject to a forced diaspora. That would be inconsistent with the good news of salvation/deliverance. The female recipient of this threat, whom I read as Nineveh, is also told to prepare for a siege. In the same verse, a male recipient is told to "strengthen loins" and "fortify power." Both verbs in 2:1 (2:2 MT), "strengthen," חזק, and "fortify," אמן, are masculine singular imperatives, but each object lacks a gender-revealing possessive pronoun. Lanner reads the verse as a continued reference to the previous female recipient, Nineveh.[23]

While it makes sense that Nineveh is the one told to strengthen her loins, Nahum appears invested in portraying Nineveh exclusively as female and therefore available for sexual violation. Attributing "male-loins," מתנים, to Nineveh would seem to muddy the metaphor since the term generally applies to males in the canon.[24] The normative association of "loins" with male subjects may explain the shift to a male recipient and the lack of a gendered possessive pronoun, i.e., "strengthen loins" rather than "strengthen your loins."[25] In this reading the one strengthening his loins would be the king or city commander responsible for Nineveh's fortifications and defense. The male figure is an extension and repre-sentative of Nineveh. Ultimately, the actions of this unidentified male figure will be futile; there will be "anguish in all loins" (v. 10 [v. 11 MT]).

Nahum 2:2 (2:3 MT) is an apologia for God's actions against Nineveh. The verse is not addressed to anyone in particular; rather, it functions

---

22. See the discussion of Belial, בליעל, in Translation Matters for prophecy 1.

23. Lanner, *Nahum*, 82.

24. The warrior-hearted woman of Prov 31:17 is the sole exception; however, she is intentionally characterized in military terms that normally apply to men.

25. The only mention of explicitly female loins is חלצים in Isa 32:11; however, חלצים is used for male loins in its other occurrences.

like a theatrical aside in which a narrator provides contextual information to the audience. The prophet is explaining to his audience, Judah, the purpose of his prophecies: the restoration of the גאון, "pride/glory/ magnificence" of Jacob. Jacob is not the person here but rather a synonym for the remnant of Israel, Judah. As a result of the previous catastrophic wave of Assyrian violence in 723 BCE Judah is all that is left of the double monarchy and their predecessor twelve tribes.[26]

*Weaving Hope Into and Out of Unwelcome Scripture*

As a woman, a mother, and a Jew, I had great difficulty recognizing Nahum as prophecy. The prophetic stories I am used to reading, *haftarot*, are carefully crafted selections of the Prophets that always hold out the possibility of hope and redemption. Nahum is full of physical and sexual violence, of imagery I would rather not let into my consciousness. There is no redemption offered. I don't recognize my God in this book, in this message. Nahum, however, is part of the Jewish canon, and as a rabbah (a contemporary feminine Hebrew term for a rabbi) I had to find some way to interpret and own this book.

I found myself drawn to the ending of verse 2:3 (2:4 MT).

"The shields of his mighty men are dyed red; the men of the army are in crimson; the chariots are in the fire of torches on the day of his preparation, and the cypresses are 'enwrapped,' והברשים הרעלו."[27] We meet soldiers readying for battle with language that uses colorful, manly images. At the end of these images we find a cypress tree. What is the image of a cypress tree doing there? These Hebrew words are translated various ways: the cypresses are "enwrapped," the spears of pine are "brandished,"[28] the juniper arrows are "poisoned,"[29] among others. The image of a cypress enwrapped spoke to me. Although the Hebrew is masculine, the image brought to mind traits that are often identified with women—

26. It is useful for readers of the Hebrew Bible to keep track of the differing ways in which Jacob/Israel is used in different texts: the patriarch, the people descended from the patriarch, the united monarchy, the Northern Monarchy, and the Judean remnant of the larger Israel.

27. The translation is from A. J. Rosenberg, *Twelve Prophets: A New English Translation*, vol. 1 (New York: Judaica Press, 1991). והברשים are "cypresses," rendered "chargers" in the NRSV.

28. Frank E. Gaebelein, *The Expositor's Bible Commentary: Daniel, Minor Prophets*, vol. 7 (Grand Rapids: Zondervan, 1985).

29. Christensen, *Nahum.*

timelessness, strength, and the backbone of a family. It reminded me of the ancient Jewish tradition found in the Talmud of planting a cypress tree when a girl is born, a cedar for a boy.

I visualized a cypress tree enwrapped in hope. Thus, for me, this cypress tree is strong, stands straight, points heavenward, and bends and bows in times of sorrow or struggle, providing protection and structure. And most important, trees have longevity on their side. They can live for centuries, withstand the good and the bad, and propagate to ensure the existence of future generations. That future cannot be built without women, nor without hope.

The cypresses, like the women and children who are the most vulnerable to violence throughout time, are enwrapped with protection. If we look to Nahum 1:7 we fleetingly see a God of compassion and refuge, "God is good, a refuge in times of trouble. He knows those who have faith in Him" (my translation). I see the cypress as the mother wrapped in and around her children, protecting the present, ensuring the future. She relates to this God of compassion and refuge. And while I rebuke the violent message of the text with the image of the cypresses enwrapped, I can cling to verse 7 as the possibility of a God who comforts. The mother-cypress is an ember of light amid the destruction and violence afflicting those around it. She is a symbol of survival.

Reading the book of Nahum is difficult enough without the curse of being able to visualize the storyline being replicated in the senseless violence of today's world. That is why it is so important to remember the one thing that we all share. We are *all* created, כדמותנו בצלמנו, in God's image: woman, man, Jew, Muslim, and Christian. To survive as a society, we must believe that there is a glimmer of redemption even in the most evil of people. Thus, even in the face of the ancient prophecy in Nahum, even in the face of the world today, there is hope.

*Rabbah Arlene Goldstein Berger*

Nahum 2:3-13 (2:4-14 MT) is a lengthier prophetic discourse that ostensibly describes Nineveh, named in verse 8 (9 MT). Verses 3-13 also seem to address an audience as does verse 2. Rather than narrate key background or contextual information, these verses read like an extended soliloquy addressed to an audience. These theatrical elements are a function of the shift from speaking to Judah and Nineveh in the previous unit to a descriptive address in the third person (see 1:15 and 2:1). The Hebrew of this section is difficult; I commend Laurel Lanner's translation.[30] Verses 3-10 (4-11 MT) describe the fall and sack of Nineveh, an event Nahum will continue to describe with even more detail in chapter 3. The march to Nineveh's destruction begins with its[31] warriors, in verse 3 (4 MT). At first the Assyrian army is impressive—crimson uniforms and gleaming chariots (vv. 3-4 [4-5 MT])[32]—but then they fall apart (v. 5 [6 MT]), impotent to stop the breach of the city (vv. 6-9 [7-10 MT]). That the red-garbed army will soon be awash in its own red blood is left unsaid. In spite of the defense perimeter erected in verse 5 (6 MT), the city will be washed away. The "river-gates" of verse 7 (8 MT) reflect the topography of Nineveh, which is situated on the east bank of the Tigris River. There was an extensive system of dams, canals, and sluice gates in and around Nineveh. Nahum envisions God opening the gates and flooding the city, an action that causes the palace (or temple) to shudder.[33] The palace or temple in verse 6 (7 MT) is symbolic of all of Nineveh's monumental architecture that will be swept away. In spite of her feats of engineering, Nineveh is as insubstantial as "a pool of water" whose waters "flee." The poetic rhetoric is not necessarily intended to convey a prediction or interpret a historical event. The fall of Nineveh was not due to an inundation. Rather, the poet-prophet portrays Nineveh as an insubstantial and chaotic element over which God has complete mastery, as God has demonstrated earlier (Nah 1:4 [5]).

Nahum 2:7 (2:8 MT) recounts the exile of fallen Nineveh with a nearly untranslatable word, והצב,[34] followed by two rhythmic verbs. My solution follows the NRSV; reading הצב as "it has been established" portrays the fall of Nineveh as divinely orchestrated. The second and third verbs of verse 7 (8 MT), גלתה העלתה, form a mellifluous pair, *gulletah hoalatah*. Together the two verbs decree Nineveh's immediate fate, "to go into exile" and "to go up [into exile]."

---

30. Lanner, *Who Will Lament Her?*, 80–85.

31. Literally "his," i.e., the king's warriors.

32. An alternate reading is that the impressively kitted out forces in 2:3-4 (2:4-5 MT) are the divine host, "chariots of fire" (Christensen, *Nahum*, 273). Christensen too finds the stumbling, inept army in v. 5 [6] is Assyria's.

33. A היכל can be either a "temple" or a "palace." In actuality, more than one palace and temple existed in Nineveh.

34. See the Translation Matters section for the discussion. The passive voice of the Hophal obscures the one who has established the fate of Nineveh, God, which accounts for the masculine singular verb. In my reading, Ishtar is identified with Nineveh; her temple is there, the city is under her protection, the king is her beloved, and the body of the city-woman in Nahum's metaphor is her body. The enslaved women are her servants in the broadest sense, whether or not they serve her temple.

## TRANSLATION MATTERS

The NRSV, Dead Sea Scrolls Bible, CEB, NASB, NIV, and NKJV read והצב as the masculine singular Hophal of נצב, i.e., "it is decreed" (lit. "was made to stand") that Nineveh be "exiled"; גלתה, the next verb, is feminine singular. The KJV, JPS, Geneva, and Bishop's Bibles transliterate "Huzzab," which (who) they understand to be a queen, Assyrian if human, or Ishtar if heavenly (hence the RSV's "mistress"). It is rare, but not impossible, for a biblical Hebrew noun to precede its verb; however, the word does not make sense as an Assyrian royal woman's name. It bears no resemblance to the names of the most likely referents, Naqia (Zakutu in Akkadian) and Tashmetum-sharrat.[35] Given that the poet-prophet does not name the king of Assyria, though the prophet in the text addresses him directly repeatedly, it would be odd for the text to name one of the Assyrian queens. It also seems unlikely the poet-prophet or subsequent redactors would preserve the name of a foreign woman who is not exercising authority over or against Judah. If הצב is a name it does not, as is common, provide etymology and/ or a pun relating to the queen, her actions, or how she is viewed in the text, i.e., Miriam as "bitter" and "water" reflecting slavery and exodus. Hebrew biblical names can be quite scornful, like Zeruah, mother of Jeroboam whose name seems to mean "diseased woman," not necessarily as a diagnosis, but likely as a slur on his origins. The Targum reads the verse as pertaining to the queen but omits the difficult word and has instead מלכתא, "the queen," being carried out on her litter to exile accompanied by the enslaved women of 2:8.[36] Judith Sanderson reads the text as the account of Ishtar's exile fulfilling Nahum 1:14, while Aron Pinker finds a reference to Ishtar and her Descent myth in the disputed line.[37] If the text is about Ishtar being exiled then the women-servants would likely be her cultic functionaries.[38] The reading of NRSV that the fall of Nineveh is the referent also includes Ishtar and her women-servants as Nineveh is her city and the home of her temple.

The rhetoric of exile in biblical Hebrew is inherently sexualized because גלה, "to go into exile," is also "to uncover," including "to strip [naked]." The third verb in verse 7 (8 MT), העלתה, "that she be brought up," is not explicitly translated separately in the NRSV. Lanner's translation of the pair, "she is exposed [גלתה], she is offered up [העלתה]," expresses the

---

35. See the discussion of 2:11-12 (2:12-13 MT) for more on the Assyrian royal women.

36. The LXX and Vulgate present entirely different traditions here. LXX reads: "The structure, ὑπόστασις, has been uncovered and continued to rise"; the Vulgate reads: *miles captivus abductus est*, "The soldier is led away."

37. Sanderson, "Nahum," 232, and Aron Pinker, "Descent of the Goddess Ishtar to the Netherworld and Nahum II 8," *VT* 55 (2005): 89–100.

38. Lanner, *Who Will Lament Her?*, 17.

sexualized nuances of the conquest of the feminine Nineveh and accounts for both verbs.[39] I propose: "It has been established that she be exiled/ exposed and be offered up [for rapine]" for the opening of Nahum 2:7 (2:8 MT). Behind the three passive verbs that open verse 7 (8 MT) is the Babylonian army who does the exiling, exposing, and offering up. That army will become more visible as the passage continues. In the poet's articulation, God is the power behind the destruction and dishonoring of Nineveh. In his hermeneutic Cyaxeres of Media and Nabopolasser, father of Nebuchadnezzar, are God's proxies. God's use of a foreign monarch is not unprecedented in Israel's Scriptures; Cyrus of Persia is called God's shepherd (Isa 44:28), messiah (Isa 45:1), and fulfillment of prophecy (2 Chr 36:22-23; Ezra 1:1-4). The sexualized exile/exposure of Nineveh is coupled with the cries of her (now) enslaved women[40] beating their breasts and crying like doves (v. 7 [8 MT]).[41] Who are these women? Were they temple functionaries in the service of Ishtar? Are they women who were already enslaved in Nineveh, or are all of Nineveh's women and girls now enslaved and being exiled?

Nahum names Nineveh for the second time in 2:8 (2:9 MT); she cannot hold back the tide of her losses. A disembodied voice orders the unseen troops to plunder and pillage. There is silver, gold, and no end of delectable items, including women and girls—the spoils of war—available

---

39. עלה is used of offering sacrifices and is the etymological root of "holocaust," a burnt offering.

40. I find it disingenuous to translate אמה here and שפחה and עבד elsewhere as "servants." A womanist reading of this text can neither ignore the human bondage in the text nor its amelioration in translation. JPS and Lanner refer to the women as "handmaids" and "maidservants," respectively, which I find unnecessarily softens the human trafficking that pervades the Scriptures and the worlds from which they emerge. The absolute control and unquestioned right to use the bodies of slaves however lord (אדון), master (בעל), and mistress (גבירה) saw fit is one indicator that slavery rather than servitude is being described in these texts. The possibility of manumission after a designated period does not negate the total control of the bodies of the enslaved exercised by those who held them in thrall. Even if the women in Nah 2:7 (2:8 MT) are temple-slaves representing a voluntary or even honorary enslavement, the enslavement of the vanquished is abject; these women are now the chattel of men and women, not gods and goddesses. The biblical text makes clear enslaved women could expect sexual violation as a matter of course; the text generally avoids discussion of male sexual victimization.

41. מנהגות is either the fem. pl. Piel participle of נהג II, "lament," or the corresponding Pual participle of נהג I, "(to be) led away." The word choice may reflect an intentional double entendre from the pen of a skilled poet.

for the taking. The specific mention of enslaved women at the bottom of Nineveh's hierarchy gives way to sweeping generalizations of Ninevites without clear gender or class indicators: "hearts melt, knees knock, loins[42] are anguished and faces blanch."

The proclamation moves to Nineveh's experience of her subjugation in verse 10 (11 MT). She is devastated. The NRSV captures the alliteration of the Hebrew here: "Devastation, desolation, and destruction!"[43] Now the proclamation becomes a taunt in 2:11-12 (2:12-13 MT):

> *Where is the abode of lions?*
> *And the grasslands of the young lions?*
> *The lion used to roam there*
> *the lioness[44] and cubs were there and no one disturbed them.*
> *A lion tears enough prey for his cubs*
> *and strangles for his lioness.*
> *He has filled his caves with prey*
> *and his abodes with shredded flesh.*

On the heels of Nineveh's fall in the preceding verses, before the dust settles, the prophet asks jeeringly, where Nineveh's lion's den is, the palace of her king.[45] Where are their grasslands where the cubs used to romp, the royal gardens and parks? The prophet mocks that there used to be such a place where the lionesses and their cubs, the royal family, napped like cats in the sun. Now the prophet instructs the lion-king on the art of being a lion: What a real lion does is to provide for his lionesses and cubs. Where are your stores of food and provisions for your family? The answer to the prophet's sarcastic questions is the rubble of the fallen city and its contents. What little the lion has left is being carried off.

Neither poet-prophet nor speaker-prophet Nahum identifies the lion or the lioness and their cubs. The prophecy targets the Assyrian monarchy writ large but at the same time makes reference to an individual king who schemed against God (Nah 1:9, 11), tentatively identified as

---

42. מתנים is only used of male loins and is lacking a gendered possessive pronoun here.

43. בוקה ומבוקה ומבלקה, *buqah umvuqah umvulaqah.*

44. I am following Lanner in reading לביא as "lioness" here in opposition to "lion" in NRSV and JPS; see also Gen 49:9; Num 23:24; 24:9; Job 4:11; Isa 30:6; Ezek 19:2; Joel 1:6 for לביא as "lioness." Additionally, in v. 12 (13 MT) masculine אריה pairs with feminine לבאתיו, "his lionesses." Also see the following Translation Matters section for more on the vocabulary for lions in the Hebrew Scriptures.

45. The Targum omits the metaphor specifying "kings" and "princes" and "their wives and children" in 2:12-13 (Eng vv. 11-12).

Sennacherib. Sennacherib was most likely responsible for the 701 BCE siege of Jerusalem in response to Hezekiah's rebellion. Additionally, Sennacherib had no less than three palaces in Nineveh with women's quarters. Portions of these palaces and some of their associated women's quarters have been excavated.[46] It is not impossible Nahum would have had some idea of the luxury in which Assyrian kings in general or a particular monarch lived.

## TRANSLATION MATTERS

Biblical Hebrew has a rich vocabulary for lions. There are at least five lexical roots: (1) ארי and אריה represent the vast majority of citations, thirty-five and fifty-seven times, respectively. Ten occurrences of אריה are Aramaic. In their singular forms, ארי and אריה represent only male lions; there is no feminine singular or plural form. Both plural forms of אריות and אריים, which occur only once, are traditionally parsed as masculine plural—though like all such nouns they should be regarded as an inclusive plural. אריה and אריות occur in Nahum 2:11 (2:12 MT); אריה occurs again in verse 12 (13 MT). (2) Similarly, כפיר occurs in masculine singular and plural with no feminine forms; it occurs as a plural in Nahum 2:11 (2:12 MT). It has been understood specifically as a young lion and occurs some thirty-one times in the canon. (3) The only feminine forms occur with the stem לביא, which is pointed to differentiate between masculine, *lavi'*, and feminine, *laviyya'*; the MT provides the masculine singular form in Nahum 2:12 which I read as feminine based on its use in there. (See the discussion of prophecy 3.) The feminine plural form with a masculine singular possessive suffix לבאתיו occurs in Nahum 2:12 (2:13 MT). It occurs fourteen times in the canon; לבא, which may be an alternate or misspelling, accounts for one of those fourteen occurrences. The final two terms do not occur in Nahum. (4) ליש occurs a scant three times and only in the masculine singular. (5) שחל, occurring twice, also appears solely in the masculine singular.

If Sennacherib is a particular subject of Nahum's invective then one of his lionesses would be Naqia,[47] who held a prominent political role. Literate, Naqia conducted official royal correspondence, received reports on military matters and those of state religion, and initiated and oversaw construction of a palace.[48] Like many monarchs, Naqia was

---

46. Sarah C. Melville, "Neo-Assyrian Royal Women and Male Identity: Status as a Social Tool," *JAOS* 124 (2004): 37–38.

47. Naqia is an Aramaic name; she was also known as Zakutu in Akkadian.

48. Conversely, Melville reads her role as merely "symbolic"; ibid., 53.

commemorated in stone and bronze.[49] As the conjugal partner of Sennacherib, Naqia was the queen mother, *ummi sharri*, of their son Esarhaddon (681–669 BCE) and functioned in the same capacity for her grandson Ashurbanipal (668–627 BCE), a role similar to a Judean גבירה or "queen mother."

Sennacherib's other "lioness" would be Tashmetum-sharrat who may have been the mother of his firstborn son, Asshur-nadin-sumi. Sennacherib engraved his appreciation of her "perfect features above all other women" on a bull colossus at the entrance to the women's quarters of one of his palaces in Nineveh.[50] On the same inscription Sennacherib called Tashmetum-sharrat his "beloved wife." Sennacherib's "cubs" would include his daughter Shadditu, whose mother may have been Naqia, in addition to the better-known Esarhaddon. Esarhaddon's "cubs" would also include a daughter, Sherua-etirat, with his consort, Esharra-hamat. If the lion were Ashurbanipal, his lioness would be Libali-sharrat with no known offspring.[51]

In Judah, which is Nahum's real audience for the diatribe directed toward Nineveh, the lion motif would be a familiar one used throughout the wider ANE. The lion was a symbol for royalty throughout the region, including in Israel and Judah. In the material culture of Assyria, carvings and statues of lions represented the Assyrian monarch as well as the goddess Ishtar. The Assyrian royal lion, his lionesses, and their cubs would have analogues in the Judean monarchy. From a Judean perspective, the lioness in the royal family was more likely to be the queen mother than the king's wife.[52] The Hebrew Scriptures employ the lioness metaphor for a royal woman in a poignant lament for the last queen mother in the waning days of the Judean monarchy. Ezekiel's lament (19:1-9) for the fallen cub-princes of Israel and their lioness-mother communicates the struggle and ultimately the sorrow of Queen Mother Hamutal, the mother of not one but two kings—Jehoahaz and Zedekiah—in the dying monarchy: "What was your mother? A lioness among lions!"

Because Judean royal women are well represented in the royal annals of Judah, specifically, some sixteen Judean queen mothers compared

49. Albert Kirk Grayson, "History and Culture of Assyria," *ABD* 4:746.

50. Melville, "Neo-Assyrian Royal Women," 51–52.

51. Ibid., 42–45.

52. Royal wives in Judah did not take the title "queen." The feminine מלכה corresponding to מלך, "king," in the Hebrew Scriptures is used only for foreign queens like the Queen of Sheba and Esther in a foreign country. Similarly, Assyrian royal wives were not generally known as *sharratu*, "queen," though foreign queens were (ibid., 43).

with three Israelite queens,[53] it is possible to identify the Judean coun-terparts of the major Assyrian royal women. During the period most closely associated with the content of Nahum, Judean queen mothers Abijah (or Abi) bat Zechariah, mother of Hezekiah; Hephzibah, mother of Manasseh; Meshullemeth bat Haroz, mother of Amon; and Jedidah, mother of Josiah are presented with their sons' enthronement narra-tives.[54] Due to the minor age of Josiah who was eight years old upon his ascension to the throne, Jedidah likely ruled in his stead for some time. Hephzibah and Meshullemeth would have been Naqia's contemporaries. In her compilation of extant women's seals, Hennie J. Marsman offers the seal of one משלמת, Meshullemeth, without further description of the person.[55] Should the owner of the seal indeed have been the Judean queen mother—by no means demonstrable—it would be an extremely rare extrabiblical artifact pertaining to the material world of Israelite or Judean royal women who have no surviving monuments like their As-syrian counterparts. Furthermore, the seal and others like it[56] point to the literacy of elite women in Judah, which when combined with that of their Assyrian contemporaries points to a broader tradition of women's literacy in royal contexts in the ANE.

Nahum's mocking taunt against Nineveh's pride of lions gives way to a formal prophetic pronouncement at the end of the third proclama-tion in 2:13. Invoking the formulae הנני אליך, "I am against you,"[57] and

---

53. English translations are notoriously misleading on titles of Israelite and Judean royal women. The NRSV uses the word "queen" or a derivative to translate a variety of words: בת נדיב, "noble daughter" (Song 7:1); שגל, "captive/consort" (Neh 2:6; Ps 45:9); שרה, "princess" (Isa 49:23); and גבירה, "queen mother" (1 Kgs 11:19; 15:13; 2 Kgs 10:13; 2 Chr 15:16; Jer 13:18; 29:2).

54. 2 Kgs 18:2; 21:1, 19; 22:1.

55. Hennie J. Marsman, *Women in Ugarit and Israel: Their Social and Religious Position in the Context of the Ancient Near East* (Leiden: Brill, 2003), 656–57.

56. Literacy among royal women in the wider ANE and ancient Israel has been amply demonstrated in the archaeological record by royal seals, seal impressions called bullae, and preserved correspondence. See ibid., and André Lemaire, "Educa-tion: Ancient Israel," *ABD*, 2:311. For the literacy of royal women in Assyria, especially Eshardaddon's daughter Sherua-ethirat, see Melville, "Neo-Assyrian Royal Women," 42. I have also collected a list of twenty-five female scribes active in the ANE, including in the service of Hammurabi; see Wilda Gafney, *Daughters of Miriam: Women Prophets in Ancient Israel* (Minneapolis: Fortress, 2007), 123–24.

57. The formula is adaptable depending on the gender of its object or audience. Nineveh (Nah 2:13; 3:5), Tyre and Sidon (Ezek 26:3; 28:22), and the personified inhab-itants of a valley (Jer 21:13) are feminine; the prophets of Ezek 13:17 are female, and the rest are masculine (Jer 29:3, 10; 35:3; 38:3; 39:1; 50:31; 51:25). Gerlinde Baumann

נאם יהוה צבאות, "an utterance of GOD of Celestial-Warriors," the prophet in the text announces the systematic dismantlement and destruction of Nineveh and its conquest infrastructure. God who has been El, Baal, and YHWH at the opening of the book (Nah 1:2) and YHWH throughout, is now and until its end, the Commander of Heaven's Armies.[58] The double prophetic formula is repeated exactly in Nahum 3:5. The God who orders the stars of heaven into battle array and commands both heavenly beings and heavenly bodies will burn the chariots with which Assyria has conquered and maintained its empire. God will personally send them up in smoke in 2:13 (2:14 MT).[59] Next, the young lions who would otherwise grow up to reestablish and avenge the empire will be cut down. Should any escape, they will be cut off from their prey. Finally, Assyria's "emissaries," מלאככה,[60] will announce no more invasions or annexations. The prophecies of Nahum over Nineveh could well come to an end with this verse, but Nahum has a flair for the lurid and the grotesque. The final proclamation will recount the fall of Nineveh in disturbingly violent vivid detail.

---

translates Nah 2:13 as "See, I will come over you," making the sexualized nature of the attack explicit in "Nahum: The Just God as Sexual Predator," in *Feminist Biblical Interpretation: A Compendium of Critical Commentary on the Books of the Bible and Related Literature*, ed. Luise Schottroff and Marie-Theres Wacker (Grand Rapids: Eerdmans, 2012), 435.

58. The antiquated traditional phrase "Lord of Hosts" does not always convey the sense of a celestial army in battle formation evoked by יהוה צבאות.

59. הבערתי, "I will [cause to] burn," Hiphil.

60. According to Wilhelm Gesenius the suffix on מלאך is irregular, "wholly abnormal." I concur with both his assessment of the form and remedy, namely, reading the suffix as a dittography of the following ה (see Gesenius, *Gesenius' Hebrew Grammar*, ed. E. Kautzsch and A. E. Cowley [Oxford: Clarendon, 1910], § 91*l*). The text is also a reminder that the primary definition of מלאך is "messenger" or "emissary." Some of those messengers display supernatural characteristics in the text and are appropriately known by its secondary meaning, "angel." To wit, מלאך can always be translated as "messenger" but not always as "angel."

# Nahum 3:1-19

# *The Rape of Nineveh:*
# *A Girl Child Ain't Safe*

## Prophecy 4 (Nah 3:1-19)

The fourth proclamation in Nahum, which comprises the third chapter of the book, is a taunt song over the metaphorical body of the fallen city-woman, Nineveh. The song begins with a traditional prophetic interjection: "Woe!" Nahum excoriates Nineveh: "city of bloodshed" and "utterly duplicitous" (3:1). The judgment rendered in that description makes all she has available for the taking, and Nineveh's possessions are substantial. She is overflowing with booty[1] and ripe for predation. Assyria's chariots are legendary but no match for the celestial forces. To be clear, no certainty exists as to whether or not the infantry and chariots in Nahum 3:2-3 belong to Assyria or to God. This lack of clarity is unimportant and does not affect the outcome of God's judgment or its consequences. The slaughter is epic—piles and piles of the dead bogging down the warriors (v. 3). Nahum does not specify whether the fallen are all Nineveh's warriors or include her civilians as well.

---

1. I am using the sexualized "booty" to translate טרף, "prey," to signal the sexual plunder of human—primarily women's—bodies. "Booty" means both "plunder" and "buttocks," which represent human bodies available for sexual plunder.

45

*Nahum 3:1-19*

3:1Ah! City of bloodshed,
 utterly deceitful, full of booty—
 no end to the plunder!
2The crack of whip and rumble of
 wheel,
 galloping horse and bounding
 chariot!
3Horsemen charging,
 flashing sword and glittering
 spear,
piles of dead,
 heaps of corpses,
dead bodies without end—
 they stumble over the bodies!
4Because of the countless
 debaucheries of the
 prostitute,
 gracefully alluring, mistress of
 sorcery,
who enslaves nations through her
 debaucheries,
 and peoples through her
 sorcery,

5I am against you,
 says the LORD of hosts,
 and will lift up your skirts over
 your face;
and I will let nations look on your
 nakedness
 and kingdoms on your
 shame.
6I will throw filth at you
 and treat you with contempt,
 and make you a spectacle.
7Then all who see you will shrink
 from you and say,
"Nineveh is devastated; who will
 bemoan her?"
 Where shall I seek comforters
 for you?

8Are you better than Thebes
 that sat by the Nile,
with water around her,
 her rampart a sea,
 water her wall?

In verses 4-7 the taunt becomes sexually explicit and violent. Nineveh is a whore whose whoredoms are beyond counting. She is not only an abundantly graceful whore[2] who sells nations through her whoredoms but also a master[3] sorcerer who sells families through her sorceries.

---

2. Gerlinde Baumann translates זונה טובות as "beautiful whore," in "Nahum: The Just God as Sexual Predator," in *Feminist Biblical Interpretation: A Compendium of Critical Commentary on the Books of the Bible and Related Literature*, ed. Luise Schottroff and Marie-Theres Wacker (Grand Rapids: Eerdmans, 2012), 435, as do Pamela Gordon and Harold Washington in "Rape as a Military Metaphor in the Hebrew Bible," in *A Feminist Companion to the Latter Prophets*, ed. Athalya Brenner, FCB 8 (Sheffield: Sheffield Academic, 1995), 308–25, at 319–20. Identifying Nineveh as a desirable whore is a way of blaming her for attracting men to her, including those who will abuse and rape her. However, טובת חן is a new clause set off with *merchah* and *tifchah*; since טובת modifies חן, not זונה, Nineveh's "gracefulness" is abundant, not her whorings.

3. Literally "mistress of sorcery," although mistress means "extramarital sexual partner" as much as it does "woman with power/authority over X." Unlike "master," "mistress" does not generally connote "expert in X." I use "master" to signal her sorcerous prowess.

⁹Ethiopia was her strength,
    Egypt too, and that without
        limit;
    Put and the Libyans were her
        helpers.

¹⁰Yet she became an exile,
    she went into captivity;
even her infants were dashed in
        pieces
    at the head of every street;
lots were cast for her nobles,
    all her dignitaries were bound
        in fetters.
¹¹You also will be drunken,
    you will go into hiding;
you will seek
    a refuge from the enemy.
¹²All your fortresses are like fig
        trees
    with first-ripe figs—
if shaken they fall

into the mouth of the eater.
¹³Look at your troops:
    they are women in your midst.
The gates of your land
    are wide open to your foes;
fire has devoured the bars of
        your gates.

¹⁴Draw water for the siege,
    strengthen your forts;
trample the clay,
    tread the mortar,
    take hold of the brick mold!
¹⁵There the fire will devour you,
    the sword will cut you off.
It will devour you like the
        locust.
Multiply yourselves like the locust,
    multiply like the grasshopper!
¹⁶You increased your merchants
    more than the stars of the
        heavens.

Presumably she sells both nations and families into slavery (v. 4). While זונה literally means "prostitute," it does not always refer to sex work. In the Israelite context women who violated, or were accused of violating, sexual norms could be labeled a זונה, which also functioned as a slur, equivalent to the word "whore." For sex workers the term conveyed both meanings, "prostitute" and "whore."[4] The charges of whoring and adultery are distinct but regularly linked. The prophets infamously charge Israel and Judah with whoredom using graphic sexually explicit language for religious infidelity that did not include any sexual activity, though the charge could also be brought against anyone who intermarried.[5] The personification of Israel, Judah, and Jerusalem as women meant their sins were styled as adultery. The charge of adultery is an easy

4. Contra Judith Sanderson ("Nahum," in *The Women's Bible Commentary*, ed. Carol A. Newsom and Sharon H. Ringe [London: SPCK, 1992], 233), to understand the semantic range of the term one must look beyond discussions of prostitution in ancient Israel.

5. See Prov 23:27; Isa 57:3; Jer 3:8-9; 5:7; 13:27; and Hos 4:13-14.

*Nahum 3:1-19 (cont.)*

The locust sheds its skin and
flies away.
[17]Your guards are like
grasshoppers,
your scribes like swarms of
locusts
settling on the fences
on a cold day—
when the sun rises, they fly away;
no one knows where they have
gone.
[18]Your shepherds are asleep,
O king of Assyria;
your nobles slumber.
Your people are scattered on the
mountains
with no one to gather them.
[19]There is no assuaging your
hurt,
your wound is mortal.
All who hear the news about you
clap their hands over you.
For who has ever escaped
your endless cruelty?

fit when the claim was that the Israelites and Judeans were unfaithful to God with another god. The metaphor rested on the understanding that sexual betrayal—primarily of a husband, secondarily of a father—was the worst thing a woman could do. The author of Nahum may have been aware of Ishtar's identity as prostitute and association with sex workers and intentionally conflated Nineveh with her goddess.[6]

According to the text, two activities provide the means by which Nineveh/Assyria has enslaved the peoples her empire has conquered: sex and sorcery. Those conquered peoples include the fallen Northern Monarchy, seduced, bewitched, or both. Rather than credit the male monarch with successful statecraft, Nahum charges that female Nineveh has become ascendant through illicit, sexualized means. She has seduced nations into submission through her whoredoms as the Hebrew root זנה indicates. The poet layers the word whore in (3:4): זנוני זונה . . . בזנוניה, the "whorings of the whore" and "her whorings." While labeling Nineveh a whore, Nahum contrives sexual transgressions for her. Nineveh is presented as sexually active in order to condemn her for that sexual activity. That condemnation in turn justifies the punitive sexual violence that will be deployed against Nineveh.

Nahum's rhetoric also provides an explanation for the theological problem resulting from Assyria's domination of Israel and Judah. Assyria could not have legitimately triumphed over Judah. The only way Assyria

6. Tikva Frymer-Kensky, *In the Wake of the Goddesses: Women, Culture, and the Biblical Transformation of Pagan Myth* (New York: Free Press, 1992), 28–29.

could have accomplished all it did, including the domination of Israel, was through immoral means. Nineveh's prosperity stems not from the success of Assyria in expanding its empire but from unfettered female sexuality of the worst kind, foreign. The characterization of Nineveh as a whore is rooted in misogyny and xenophobia. Nineveh, personified as a woman, is a whore because she is foreign; all non-Israelite women are treated with suspicion if not outright hostility in the Hebrew Bible. The most common charge against foreign women is that they seduce Israelite men into apostasy, a transgression configured as adultery. The poet-prophet is counting on his readers and hearers sharing or at least recognizing the view that women's sexuality is threatening and it should be constrained, i.e., placed under male control. Nineveh is also a whore because the patriarchal palette is limited, and Nahum paints with only one end of that small spectrum.

In biblical and contemporary contexts the label "whore" is a tool of slut-shaming. The words "slut" and "whore" and the rape metaphor employed by Nahum depend on extremely negative[7] views of women rejected by womanists and feminists. The charge has literal and non-literal components. The charge is also irrational. Israel and Judah can be charged with adultery for abandoning their covenant with God, but Nineveh is not God's spouse or partner. Indeed, Nineveh has not betrayed her divine spouse. The Hebrew Bible does not otherwise use the language of whoring to articulate the relationship between non-Israelite peoples and their deities, and the poet-prophet never explains why Nineveh is a whore for worshiping her own goddess.

Nahum multiplies the accusations in 3:4: Nineveh is a sorceress as well as a seductress. The combination evokes Jezebel, the woman of the "many whoredoms and sorceries" in 2 Kings 9:22, the only other text where the two words appear. Though the name-calling has an air of pettiness about it, being called a "whore" or a "sorceress" was potentially lethal for women. Sorcery, כשפים, was not permitted within ancient Israel (Deut 18:10).[8] Sorcery was only explicitly lethal for female practitioners

7. Carol J. Dempsey, *Amos, Hosea, Micah, Nahum, Zephaniah, Habakkuk*, New College-ville Bible Commentary 15 (Collegeville, MN: Liturgical Press, 2013), 113.

8. Deuteronomy 18:10 prohibits sorcery for both genders: "There shall not be found among you one who makes son or daughter pass through fire, divines divinations, is a cloud-caster, an omen-reader or a sorcerer." Nevertheless, no death penalty is imposed in the Deuteronomy passage.

(Exod 22:18).[9] No corresponding statute exists for male sorcerers. Nahum condemns Nineveh for practicing sorcery as though she were a recipient of Torah. The Targum takes the notion Nineveh is somehow subject to Torah further and reminds listeners and readers that God forgives those who return to Torah but will not forgive those who will not return (1:3). The Targum applies Torah standards to Nineveh explicitly.[10] Repeating the opening line of Nahum 2:13 (2:14 MT) in 3:5, Nahum pronounces another sentence on Nineveh justified by *lex talionis* reasoning in 3:4. Nineveh has behaved like a whore, and God shall treat her like one.[11] The words of God and Nahum are fused in the first person eight times in verses 5-6:

> See Me! I come upon you!
> An utterance of GOD of Celestial-Warriors.
> I will roll your skirts up over your face
> and I will let nations look at your pudenda[12]
> and kingdoms your shame.
> I will hurl on you abominable-images
> I will dishonor you
> and I will make you a spectacle.

The assault is simultaneously physical and sexual. The woman is snatched and imprisoned. There is no escape. She is publically stripped. The poet-prophet does not describe her being held down, struggling, screaming, crying, praying, or begging. The cuts, scrapes, bruises, and blows she receives in the first stage of the attack are not recorded in the text. The reader/hearer must supply the details. Twisted over her face, her clothing chokes and strangles her and muffles her voice. Her body is truncated because of the covering of her face and head. She is reduced

---

9. Exodus 22:18 (22:17 MT) pronounces a death sentence only for women who perform sorcery: "A woman-sorcerer [מכשפה] shall not live."

10. Isaiah treats Babylon as though she were also God's covenant partner in chap. 47, addressing her as "virgin daughter Babylon" and "daughter Chaldea" just as Judah is called both "daughter" and "virgin daughter." Material in the two books is interrelated, but the sequence and nature of the relationship is impossible to sort out.

11. Nineveh is also guilty of enslaving nations. Her punishment reflects the offense in 2:7 (2:8 MT) and 3:10.

12. My translation here follows Rashi, who interprets מערך as עריה־בשת from Mic 1:11, where it means "bared-shame" or "exposed genitalia." The Vulgate supports this reading with *pudenda tua*, as does Lanner, who renders "I will reveal your genitals up to your face" (*"Who Will Lament Her?" The Feminine and the Fantastic in the Book of Nahum*, vol. 11 [New York: T & T Clark, 2006], 84). The Targum is more circumspect in its translation: "I will reveal your sins."

to her vagina, sexually accessible and vulnerable. A parallel couplet in the second half of 3:5 suggests those holding her may have spread her legs to make it easier for those around her to see her vulva, called her "shame," קלון. The physical assault escalates with the throwing of religious artifacts, "abominable-images," שקצים, at the captive woman; she is being stoned with her own sancta. If the שקצים are images of Ishtar, then her goddess not only does not help Nineveh but also wounds her. Verse 6 describes a public sexual assault. Following Gerlinde Baumann, I contend נבל, "dishonor," as used in verse 6 is a euphemism for rape, which is the most extreme example of dishonoring a woman in the Israelite cultural context.[13] That the most common vocabulary for rape is absent may reflect some limits in the poet's rhetoric about his own God.[14] Though the poet stops short of using the specific Hebrew biblical vocabulary for rape, it is not difficult to imagine his ancient hearers knew full well that dishonoring women in war and conquest meant rape more often than not. All of these things are happening in public before a jeering crowd, intimated in verse 7, who may also be participating in other ways. After the rape the crowd retreats into a horrified silence. No one will look her in the eyes. No one will care for her. She has survived her rape, but no one will comfort her. The poet moves away from the city-woman's body at this point.

13. Baumann prefers "violate" to "dishonor" ("Nahum: The Just God as Sexual Predator," 436). One might question how God accomplishes this act when there is no literary depiction of male genitalia in the Scriptures. (Even the conception of Jesus as portrayed by the gospels is accomplished without a divine penis.) In this passage the woman is held down and stripped; her genitalia is exposed, and she is dishonored. The whole experience is a sexual assault whether or not she was penetrated with a human or divine penis, or object. I believe reticence to articulate the assault on Nineveh as a rape angles dangerously close to the problematic concept of what is "legitimately" rape.

14. ענה, "rape/abuse/violate," is the most significant Hebrew lexeme for rape (Gen 34:2; 2 Sam 13:14; Judg 20:5; Lam 5:11). The word ענה can also refer to the imposition of physical violence, "oppress" or "afflict" used for both Sarah's violence against Hagar (Gen 16:6, 9), and Egyptian violence against enslaved Israelites. I contend the two meanings overlap. The language of "force," חזק, usually in the Hiphil, appears intermittently (Deut 22:25; 2 Sam 13:11). More rare are the terms שגל, "seize/violate/ravish" (Zech 14:2), and עלל, "glean/scrape" (made more devastating with the preposition בה, "inside her" in Judg 19:25). In other cases the regular language of sexual intercourse is used: גלה ערוה, "uncovering nakedness"; ידע, "to know" (Judg 19:25); and שכב, "to lie with." In the case of the latter, a preposition may be present but may not indicate consent, i.e., Gen 34:2; Deut 22:25. Alternately the preposition may be absent, augmenting the rhetorical force of the charge, i.e., Reuben's rape of Bilhah in Gen 35:22 or David's rape of Bathsheba in 2 Sam 11:4.

The presentation of God as a sexual assailant is part of what makes this passage in Nahum so troubling for many of its religious readers and hearers.[15] These words describing God instigating a sexual assault and calling others to join in are attributed to God and spoken in the first person by God in the text. This passage, perhaps more than others, raises the question of the function and authority of Nahum as Scripture and the relationship of Nahum's god to the God of the wider biblical tradition. In other texts God offers city-women up for punitive physical and sexual violence at the hands of others but does not participate, e.g., Samaria (Ezek 23:4, 9-10), Jerusalem (Ezek 16:37-41), and Babylon (Isa 47:1-3). The authors of those texts drew the line at God participating in what was often a gang rape. Yet the author of Nahum is not unique in presenting God as participating in sexual assault. In Jeremiah 13:22, 25-26 and Hosea 2:3, 10 God is portrayed as enacting sexualized violence against Judah personally. The punishment God inflicts on Nineveh in Nahum is like that inflicted on Judah in other texts. God's outrage at Nineveh's proclivities is expressed in the same idiom God uses for Israel, Judah, and Jerusalem, the whoredom of an unfaithful wife.

There are a number of parallels between Jeremiah 13:20-27 and Nahum 3:1-7. In both, God is the attacker; in both, God strips the city-woman and exposes her vulva. It is God[16] who says to Jerusalem in Jeremiah 13:26: "I will snatch your skirts over your face and your shame will be seen."[17] Both Jeremiah 13:26 and Nahum 3:5 use "shame," קלון, to signify the woman's vulva. As is the case for Nineveh, Jerusalem's malfeasance, described as iniquity, leads to her exposure and violation, articulated as "violence," חמס, against her in Jeremiah 13:22. In Jeremiah 13:27 Jerusalem is charged with multiple offenses: possession of the same abominable-images hurled at Nineveh in Nahum 3:6, adultery, neighing-like-a-horse (in sexual ecstasy?), and wicked whoredom. Her crime was forgetting God; she committed whoredom and adultery (Jer 13:25, 27). Nineveh (Nah 3:6), like Jerusalem (Jer 13:27), has detestable religious artifacts,

---

15. Baumann's title, "The Just God as Sexual Predator," gives voice to the dissonance many experience in identifying Nahum's god as the God of the biblical tradition, let alone as their God.

16. It is important to remember a significant portion of religious readers read the words attributed to God in Scripture as being God's words even when they bring a variety of interpretive practices to the text. As I read Nahum and prepare this manuscript I am cognizant of a wide range of pieties related to the biblical text and am particularly aware of literalist readings.

17. Compare with God's address to Nineveh in Nah 3:5: "I will roll your skirts up over your face and I will let nations look at your pudenda and kingdoms your shame."

"abominable-images," שקצים. The Jerusalem prophecy ends with a "woe" while the Nineveh prophecy begins with one. The most significant difference comes at the end of Jeremiah 13:27 where the prophet holds out the possibility of reform for Jerusalem. There is none for Nineveh.

The most graphic depiction of God using sexual assault as retribution occurs in Ezekiel 16, particularly in verse 37, which targets Jerusalem. After a lengthy recitation of all God has done for her, how she came from nothing, and how nobody wanted her, God accuses Jerusalem of whoring with anyone who passes by. The outraged God names the Egyptians, Assyrians, and Babylonians, claiming Jerusalem whores to such an extent that Philistine women were scandalized (vv. 25-29). The claim that Jerusalem's whoring scandalized even Philistine women was a cut against both Jerusalem and Philistia, for surely the reader/hearer knew just how depraved one had to be to shock a Philistine woman. God continues, unrelenting: Jerusalem even refused to take payment like a good whore. These accusations read like verbal and emotional violence.

God will use these indictments to justify a punitive sexual assault on Jerusalem in Ezekiel 16:37: "I will gather all your lovers, those to whom you were so sweet and all those you love and all those you hate; I will gather them against you and surround you and I will uncover your nakedness to them and they shall see every bit of your nakedness." The "uncovering" of "nakedness" is a euphemism for intimate access that can include sexual contact.[18] The text suggests more than her exposure and may intimate her rape as well. The mob that comes "upon" her in verse 40 may also hint at rape. It may well be that the ambiguity is intentional, inviting the reader to imagine the worst. Ezekiel 16:38 explains this assault is the judgment for a woman who commits adultery. In verse 39 God delivers her into the hands of her former lovers for whatever abuse they wish to inflict on her—stripping (v. 39), stoning and hacked with swords (v. 40), and public burning[19]—to teach other women what may

---

18. The passage in Lev 18:6-19 prohibiting the uncovering of the nakedness of specific relatives is framed in terms of "seeing" and includes taking a woman as a rival to her sister (v. 18) and "approaching" a menstruating woman (v. 19), strongly suggesting intercourse. Leviticus 20:11 equates having intercourse with one's father's wife as uncovering the father's nakedness. Some suggest the issue with the exposure of Noah's nakedness to Ham was sexual contact; see Frederick W. Bassett, "Noah's Nakedness and the Curse of Canaan: A Case of Incest?" *VT* 21 (1971): 232–37, and Bradley Embry, "The 'Naked Narrative' from Noah to Leviticus: Reassessing Voyeurism in the Account of Noah's Nakedness in Genesis 9.22-24," *JSOT* 35 (2011): 417–33.

19. The homes that are burnt are part of the "body" of the city-woman.

happen to them if they commit adultery against their husbands (v. 41). This is an Iron Age honor killing.

The overlapping verbal, physical, and sexual violence in these texts is most often justified within the framework of a patriarchal conjugal union.[20] In Jeremiah 13 and Ezekiel 16, Jerusalem is God's wife, and God punishes her as any Iron Age man would punish a cheating wife, with violence that included stripping her publically and holding her down for others to violate sexually. Whether spouse-initiated gang rape actually occurred in ancient Israel is moot; the rhetoric presumes the hearers accept the premise as valid. Yet the marriage metaphor cannot apply to Nineveh because she is not God's wife; God has no wife other than Israel/Judah/Jerusalem. Nineveh's assault is not justified because she is an adulterous wife. Her sexual violation is justified because she is an enemy woman in a captured city; systematic violation of enemy women is well documented in Israel's Scriptures.[21] Nineveh's fate is comparable to Judah's subsequently at the hand of the Babylonians. In Lamentations 1:10 Jerusalem is the raped and ravaged city-woman: her infants die in their mothers' arms (Lam 2:11-12; 4:4), then women contemplate and apparently eat their infants (Lam 2:20; 4:10); bodies are piled in the streets (Lam 2:21); women are raped (Lam 5:11); and a litany of further indignities follow.

God takes vengeance on the body of the city-woman for her offenses and those of her king. Just as the metaphor of the abused (punished, adulterous) wife depends on recognizable underlying experiences and concepts—betrayal, infidelity, anger, outrage, justification of punitive domestic abuse[22]—so too the rhetoric of sexual conquest has recognizable corollaries in the experience of war and its aftermath. The rhetorical treatment of the subjugated Nineveh is a portrait of the sack of women's bodies that accompanied the sack of enemy territory. Metaphors are exercises in truth-telling.[23] The rape of Nineveh makes visible the rapes of Canaanite and other women in Israel's military victories. This is significant because rape is broadly missing from the Hebrew Bible's account of

---

20. Baumann, "Nahum: The Just God as Sexual Predator," 437.

21. For the taking of non-Israelite women, see Num 31:9, 35; Deut 21:10-14; 1 Sam 30:1-2. For Israelites taking Israelite women captive, see Judg 21 and 2 Chr 28:8-15.

22. Prov 6:34: "For the fury of a husband is jealousy, and in the day of his vengeance he shows no pity."

23. Susan Thistlethwaite, " 'You May Enjoy the Spoil of Your Enemies': Rape as a Biblical Metaphor for War," *Semeia* 61 (1993): 60.

Israel's conquests, apart from a few narratives detailing forced marriages to captive girls and women.

When Nineveh is assaulted, her people are assaulted. The women of Nineveh whose bodies and culturally cued experiences form the framework for the city-woman metaphor are specifically targeted from the enslaved women of 2:7 (2:8 MT) to the royal lion-women in 2:11-12 (2:12-13 MT). Both groups of women and all of those not mentioned are subject to the consequences of Nineveh's fall, including potentially lethal physical and sexual violence resulting in their bodies piled in the streets (3:3). As a hybrid entity, the city-woman retains her identity as the city and continues to represent the Assyrian Empire. The ravishing of the city is an affront to the honor of Nineveh's king charged with protecting her.[24] The specific taunting of the Assyrian lion-king makes clear his honor is at stake in both sexual and verbal assaults on Nineveh. Nahum's premodern readers and hearers would have differentiated the sexual use of captured women as part of the spoils of war to which victorious combatants were entitled from rape as the Israelites understood it—theft of sexual property from a husband, fiancé, or father.[25] While biblical tradents and their early interpreters may not have considered the sexual use of Nineveh's captive women to be rape, they would have understood the loss of city, women, warriors, offspring, and honor as devastating.[26] The savaging of Nineveh represents the practices of systematically plundering the bodies of women and girls as acts of war and vengeance,[27] which would be instantly recognizable to Nahum's hearers and readers. Furthermore, since this diatribe was articulated in and for Judah, the treatment of Nineveh serves as a reminder for Israel that they are potentially subject to the same punishment.[28]

---

24. Baumann, "Nahum: The Just God as Sexual Predator," 438.

25. Thistlethwaite, "Rape as a Biblical Metaphor," 59, 62–63.

26. F. Rachel Magdalene cautions against applying contemporary definitions of rape, i.e.," a violation of a woman's body" (336) to the ancient world. Instead she proposes: "the sexual violation of one man's property by another man, . . . the means by which one group of men demonstrated their control of or authority over another group of men by forced sexual access to the human female property of the weak." See "Ancient Near Eastern Treaty-Curses and the Ultimate Texts of Terror: A Study of the Language of Divine Sexual Abuse in the Prophetic Corpus," in *A Feminist Companion to the Latter Prophets*, ed. Athalya Brenner, FCB 8 (Sheffield: Sheffield Academic, 1995), 336, 338–39.

27. See the rapine of Midianite girls in Num 31:1, 15-18 as an act of vengeance.

28. Valerie Bridgeman, "Nahum," in *Africana Bible*, ed. Hugh Page Jr., et al. (Minneapolis: Fortress, 2010), 195.

In Nahum 3:7 Nineveh's name appears for the third and final time. After she has been publically humiliated, stripped, beaten, bloodied, and possibly raped and left for dead, her body becomes an object lesson that engenders no compassion. Those who see her bloody ruin shrink from it in horror, saying in verse 7, "Nineveh is devastated." The prophet cannot scrape up anyone to so much as "shake their heads (in sympathy)," נוד, let alone mourn her or give her a decent burial.[29] Jeremiah 15:5 asks the same question on behalf of Jerusalem: "Who will pity you Jerusalem and who will shake-their-head-in-grief for you?"

As the prophet gloats[30] over the fallen city-woman, whether or not she is alive or dead does not matter. Were she alive and capable of forming a response she would have no answers to his questions. Arguably knowing full well Ashurbanipal conquered Thebes in 663 BCE, Nahum asks, "Are you better than Thebes?" (3:8).[31] Thebes was defended by water: the Nile to her west, the Red Sea a hundred miles east. The path to the sea was fully under her control. Water, however, is no defense against God who rebukes the sea and drains it and then empties the rivers of their waters (Nah 1:4). Moreover, Egypt, symbolized by Thebes, had one of the most formidable armies of the period. The ascent of the twenty-fifth dynasty brought their Kushite[32] military prowess to the Egypt they now ruled along with the strength of their African allies, Put and Libya (3:9). Put here is likely Punt (Egyptian *pun.t*), which at the time would correspond with Somalia. As a result of their expansion Kushite Egypt stretched from North Africa to East Africa. Notwithstanding, the legendary warriors[33] who held and defended that territory were insufficient to prevent the fall of Thebes. Even though Nineveh is technically mightier than the defeated Thebes, Nineveh will not be able to stand against God who is mightier than all. Nineveh will fall just as Thebes fell.

---

29. The verb נוד, "shake (one's head) in grief," is common in Jeremiah; see Jer 16:5; 18:16; 22:10; 48:17.

30. I envision the recitation of this proclamation as a performance piece.

31. See the identification of Thebes in the following Translation Matters section.

32. The territory of Kush, כוש, extended from Egypt's southern border to parts of Central Africa, including portions of contemporary Sudan and Ethiopia, and was later known as Nubia.

33. Perhaps the most renowned Kushite or Nubian warrior in the Hebrew Scriptures is Tarharqa (alt. Tirhakah) whose very name caused Sennacherib to break off his siege of Jerusalem (see 2 Kgs 19:9).

## TRANSLATION MATTERS

In Nahum 3:8 Thebes is represented by נא אמון, a Hebrew phonetic rendering of the Egyptian name for Thebes, "No-Amon," "the city of Amon," whose worship became ascendant in the eighteenth dynasty and was particularly vibrant in Thebes.[34] The LXX preserves "Amon" but the phrase "Are you better than No-Amon" is instead "Tune a chord, prepare a portion, O Amon" (NETS). The MurXII scroll includes the otherwise unattested phrase, "[whose] wall was a rampart from the sea was her wall" in verse 8. In the Targum the Egyptian city is אלכסנדרא, Alexandria, founded more than three hundred years after the fall of Nineveh (and Thebes).

As Nahum describes the fall of Thebes, he is describing Assyrian atrocities since Assyria conquered Thebes under Ashurbanipal. Assyrians exiled Thebes; Assyrians divvied up the former nobles of Thebes on street corners as human plunder hauled off in chains; and Assyrians smashed the skulls of her infants on the pavement of every street in town in 3:10. The metaphorical and rhetorical sexual violence against Nineveh also has an antecedent in Assyrian sexual assault of Theban women.

The passive voice in Nahum 3:10, עלליה יוטשו, "her babies were smashed/ shattered," keeps the focus on the children and their fate rather than on the soldiers who are killing them. Beyond functioning as a terrorist propaganda, the practice served to rid the victors of unwanted children who would impede them in transporting and managing the captive women they had just seized and enslaved. This recurring brutality was performed and/or justified by Israelites and their enemies alike and was occasionally accompanied by the gutting of pregnant women.[35] Brutal violence was an inevitable part of war, a barbarism with which they

34. Theodore J. Lewis "Amon (Deity)," *ABD*, 1:197.
35. In 2 Kgs 8:12 Elijah weeps as he prophesies Hazael will smash babies and rip open the bellies of pregnant women when he becomes king of Aram. In Isa 13:16 Isaiah prophesies the infants of Babylon will be smashed before the eyes of their people and their women raped. Hosea cites an otherwise unknown incident in which mothers and their children were smashed (Hos 10:14) while prophesying the same fate for the Northern sanctuary, Beth-El. In a rare episode in 2 Chr 25:11-12, the people of Judah sent ten thousand Edomites to their deaths, forcing them over a cliff, smashing them against the rocks below. Their ages are not given but the victims seem to represent a random sample of the defeated community. Perhaps the most well-known example of this rhetoric is Ps 137:9, in which the psalmist celebrates the anticipated smashing of Babylonian babies against rocks.

had become accustomed and one they wished to see visited upon their enemies, particularly those who had committed such acts against them.

In 3:11 Nahum addresses Nineveh the hybridized city-woman directly again. Here the prophet prophesies Nineveh's response to the trauma that will be inflicted on her. She will self-medicate with alcohol and seek a hiding place in vain. The fortresses that would offer refuge will be taken as easily as first-ripened figs plucked from a tree (v. 12). No men remain for the city-woman to turn to for protection. Either they have all been killed or the survivors have been completely emasculated and demoralized; verse 13 derides Nineveh's men as being women.[36] The language play here is multilayered. Nineveh is female; her people ("troops" in NRSV), עַמֵּךְ, are technically grammatically inclusive. Because of the terror God has brought on Nineveh's people, they are (like) women. In this context, being women means being vulnerable to rape by the invaders. In the same way, the invasion of the city is also a rape. Nineveh's now-feminized men are as vulnerable to rape as are her women and Nineveh herself. In the poet's oratory the "gates" of Nineveh's men and women are "wide open" for their enemies to enter as easily as their enemies enter their city gates. In the poet's metaphor the gates of the city-woman are analogous to a woman's vagina and buttocks.[37]

In verse 14, Nahum tells the city-woman to prepare to be besieged and gives specific instructions to stockpile water and reinforce the walls of the fortresses he had ridiculed earlier in verse 12. Having extended to Nineveh what might seem like hope for survival, Nahum then snatches it away (v. 15). Nahum tells Nineveh that her preparations will be futile. She will be devoured by fire, cut down (lit. "off"), by sword. Nineveh is doomed. There is no escape. There is no strength in her numbers, but Nahum encourages her to futilely multiply herself like hordes of locusts.[38] It is gallows humor at her expense. There is no time for Nineveh to give birth to more citizens or to commission more troops. The troops she has, who approximate a locust horde, flee as quickly as the insects. In what might be called snark, Nahum points out the nearly endless numbers of Assyria's merchants, scribes, and officials in verses 16-17 (15-16 MT);[39]

36. Julia M. O'Brien, *Nahum*, Readings: A New Biblical Commentary (London: Black, 2002), 70.

37. See F. Rachel Magdalene's translation of Jer 12:22 and Isa 3:17-26 and her discussion of Nahum in "Ancient Near Eastern Treaty-Curses," 328–29, 332–33.

38. יֶלֶק and אַרְבֶּה are two different kinds of locust or perhaps locusts at different stages of development.

39. See מְנֻזָּר in Translation Matters: Prophecy 4.

they are all equally useless. The merchants were cultural emissaries who would have direct contact with the peoples Assyria subjugated and those over whom Assyria wielded influence. That economic subjugation would often occur in advance of armed conflict; as a result the merchants in Nahum may represent economic and bureaucratic oppression. The scribes and officials also represent layers of bureaucracy, which could be considered the infrastructure of Assyria's economic domination.

## TRANSLATION MATTERS

Among Nineveh's endless bureaucrats are merchants, scribes, and some sort of official, מנזר (putative, derived from the inflected form מנזריך). According to the *DCH* the translation options are "conjuror," "consecrated one," "courtier," "exorcist," "guard," "official," and "prince." *HALOT* prefers "courtier"; BDB, "consecrated ones." Though many scholars regard מנזר as a loan word from Akkadian *manzaru*, the *TDOT* treats it as a form of נדר, "vow." A brief survey of *manzaru* in *CAD* affirms a generic reading of "official."

Both the fourth prophecy and the book conclude in verses 18-19, where the address changes to the second-person masculine singular to address the unnamed king of Assyria. All of his support has been stripped from him, and he is alone. His officials, "shepherds" and "nobles," are dead.[40] The Targum is more explicit: "Your warriors have been defeated." The king's surviving people flee to the mountains with no one to gather them, אין מקבץ (v. 18). The king is mortally injured, literally "broken," with no treatment available to aid his healing (v. 19). Assyria will not recover from the fall of Nineveh. Everyone who hears the report of Nineveh's fall—and thus Assyria's fall—will celebrate and clap their hands. Nahum asks a final question that ties the book together and makes clear the rationale for the destruction: "For upon whom has your evil not passed perpetually?"

For Nahum Nineveh/Assyria gets what she deserves because of what she has done, just like Thebes before her. The judgment rendered upon Nineveh and Assyria is more than the vengeance of God for the attacks on Israel and Judah. It is a measure of justice for Assyria's offenses against the whole world.

40. I read ישכנו . . . נמו, "slumber . . . dwelling [in sleep]" as "residing in the sleep of death."

# Conclusion: Contextual Hermeneutics

# *A Womanist Reading of Nahum: Nahum's God Is Not My God*

The rhetoric of Nahum is vicious and violent. The proclamations are engineered to elicit a set of responses from Israelite/Judean hearers that would encompass approval and even celebration of the physical and sexual violence marshaled against Nineveh, including her sexual violation by Israel's God. Renita Weems reminds us that the powerful, dominating God-figure would have been comforting to the tiny and much abused principality that was Israel at virtually any phase of its existence.[1] The canonization of Nahum's proclamations in their current form testifies to the reception of the collection as Scripture, perhaps even as "good news" (Nah 1:15 [2:1 MT]) to Israelites and Judeans who knew Assyrian domination[2] and for their descendants after them who knew Babylonian, Greek, and Roman subjugation. Nahum's near total absence from Jewish and Christian liturgy, however, is another kind of testimony. For Francisco García-Treto, the book of Nahum is "a book that

1. Renita J. Weems, *Battered Love: Marriage, Sex, and Violence in the Hebrew Prophets* (Minneapolis: Fortress, 1995), 20.
2. Valerie Bridgeman, "Nahum," in *Africana Bible*, ed. Hugh Page Jr., et al. (Minneapolis: Fortress, 2010), 195–96.

makes the church uncomfortable, and one that the church seldom, if ever, opens."[3] The lack of engagement with the text in the classical midrash, Talmud, and Zohar suggests a similar discomfort.

Generations of white, male, mainstream or "malestream" scholarship has been untroubled by the book of Nahum or has minimized it by distancing metaphorical and rhetorical violence from actual violence. Feminists have rightly identified the dilemma this book and texts like it present for readers for whom Nahum is Scripture:

> Within these verses, God, characterized as male, is regularly threatening, in judgment, to rape, or otherwise sexually abuse, the cities of Israel, Judah and their neighbors, all characterized as female. Metaphorically then, God is seemingly quite willing to perpetrate repeated sexual assaults and abuse on women. Such texts are the ultimate in biblical texts of terror. Not only is God a passive participant in the sexual assaults on and abuse of women in the narrative portions of the Hebrew Bible by his lack of intervention on behalf of the raped and abused, God is an active perpetrator of such sexual violence against women in the prophetic corpus of the Bible.[4]

The sanction and sanctification of sexual violence is misogynist whether in secular or sacred texts or contexts. In sacred spaces that sanction can be presented as incontrovertible. Not unexpectedly, misogyny in the text of Nahum occurs in a highly patriarchal framework in which the male figures dominate the female figures. God and the king are male; each is a patriarch and a warrior. Nineveh and Judah are females in the care of their respective patriarchs. The actual women, slaves, and the lion-queen are subject to the Assyrian king. All of the king's actual and metaphorical women are subjugated by Israel's male God as an affront to the king. The despoliation of Nineveh's womenfolk restores the honor of Jacob, a masculine construction of Israel (contra the feminine presentation of Judah) in 2:2.[5] The violence of Nahum transcends the brutal

3. Francisco O. García-Treto, "Nahum," in *The New Interpreter's Bible: General Articles and Introduction, Commentary, and Reflections for Each Book of the Bible, Including the Apocryphal/Deuterocanonical Books* (Nashville: Abingdon, 1994), 596.

4. F. Rachel Magdalene, "Ancient Near Eastern Treaty-Curses and the Ultimate Texts of Terror: A Study of the Language of Divine Sexual Abuse in the Prophetic Corpus," in *A Feminist Companion to the Latter Prophets*, ed. Athalya Brenner, FCB 8 (Sheffield: Sheffield Academic, 1995), 327.

5. Julia O'Brien, *Nahum*, Readings: A New Biblical Commentary (London: Black, 2002), 65.

spectacle rape of the city-woman. The patriarchal framework in which it occurs is itself violent.

The proclamations of Nahum make it easy to reduce the world to "us" and "them." This is especially true for those for whom the proclamations of Nahum are God's word. In readings without nuance the prophecies are good news for those whom God loves and defends and protects—or at least avenges—and they are bad news for those on whom God takes revenge. The desire for an omnipotent, responsive avenger, if not protector, in this crucified and crucifying world is entirely understandable.[6] As a black woman raised in the black church on stories of deliverance, I want God to defend and protect me against racism and sexual violence in every space in which I find myself. And in some cases, after the fact, I too want vengeance on an epic scale.

When I read Nahum I see rhetoric based on the presumption that it doesn't matter what happens to some bodies, and the bodies of women— non-Israelites and gentile women in particular—can be brutalized in fact or in rhetoric to make a point. I also find a corollary for the assault on Nineveh in American history; it is akin to a spectacle lynching whose victim survived. Neither the horrors borne of the poet-prophet's pen nor those of the lynching tree are relegated to the biblical or more recent past.

Nahum's Iron Age value system is alive and well in the Digital Age. I am writing after the emergence of the Black Lives Matters movement and find parallels between the disregard for the lives of the people of Nineveh (and others in the canon) and the disregard for the lives of whole populations in the present age. The disparate rate of police shootings of black men when compared to other demographics, murder rates of black and brown trans women, rates of crime against non–gender conforming people, and rampant Islamophobia all point to disposable populations in the eyes of some.

While Nahum's rhetoric is extraordinarily vicious, it is not without parallel in the biblical text; Nahum's god is not entirely unrelated to the God of the Hebrew Scriptures. I distinguish between them nonetheless. I find myself in the company of Gerlinde Baumann: "As a woman who is always potentially threatened with sexual violence on the basis of my gender, I cannot count on the solidarity of this God who himself

---

6. The recent success of Marvel's *Avenger* franchise demonstrates a popular receptivity to the theme.

commits sexual violence."[7] So, Nahum is not good news for me. As a religious reader, priest, and preacher, I cannot own Nahum's God as my own. I need to distinguish between the God of the (in the) text and God beyond the text.

Nahum's God is immutably male; his virulent maleness resists the inclusive language that many womanists and feminists use to translate and interpret the Scriptures. Nahum, book and prophesying person, depends not only on the gender binary fundamental to biblical Hebrew but also on rigid gender roles. Even with the dizzying array of subject and object pronouns, the text inscribes and reinscribes a binary gender paradigm. Nineveh and the nearly invisible Ishtar are the most transgressive characters, and they are sexually brutalized in order to put them in their gendered place. The God who rapes is no God to me.

For García-Treto, Nahum's God is a cautionary tale against nationalistic gods and associated theologies in which enemy peoples become demonized and the deity, forswearing love for all humankind, becomes more demon than God.[8] Nahum's God has no difficulty using the violence of the oppressors against them and either does not distinguish between the guilty and the innocent or finds every infant, child, woman, and man in Nineveh equally guilty and deserving of brutal vengeance.[9] One way of understanding Nahum's God is that the God who batters Israel will batter on behalf of Israel. This theology is not unique to Nahum; it can be found throughout Torah and Prophets. Nahum's portrait of God is not the only troubling one in the Hebrew Bible. The legacies of those portraits shaped modern nations and their conflicts and the history of peoples on virtually every continent. The systematic pillaging of my people, physically and sexually, to build this country and generate its wealth was justified by a God in the text very much like Nahum's.

While I can find no redemption in or for Nahum's God, I find I can relate to Nahum, poet and proclaimer, as a "tortured man who lives amidst the violence of war."[10] Reading texts like Nahum, Ezekiel, and Obadiah through the lens of trauma theology helps me to make sense

7. Gerlinde Baumann, "Nahum: The Just God as Sexual Predator," in *Feminist Biblical Interpretation: A Compendium of Critical Commentary on the Books of the Bible and Related Literature,* ed. Luise Schottroff and Marie-Theres Wacker (Grand Rapids: Eerdmans, 2012), 439.

8. García-Treto, "Nahum," 603.

9. Ibid., 597.

10. Baumann, "Nahum: The Just God as Sexual Predator," 439.

of them. The horror of war is generative, begetting horror after horror in text and theology.

Finally, Nahum leaves me with unanswerable questions:

For whom is Nahum good news today?

Who would choose a battering God?

Would anyone on the margins of racial, ethnic, gender, or identity hierarchies willingly embrace the God of Nineveh?

Can Nahum be anything more than revenge fantasy pornography?

# *Habakkuk*

# Author's Introduction

# *The Prophet Who Talks Back*

On its surface, the proclamations of Habakkuk might seem to have little to commend them for womanist or feminist study. The book contains no obvious gendered rhetoric, no female characters or actors, and no women. Yet, Habakkuk is a text about a prophet crying out on behalf of his community, which is a fundamental understanding of prophetic ministry in womanist and other Africana interpretive communities. The cry of Habakkuk, "How long, O Lord"[1] has been a staple in black preaching and a heart-cry of many womanists. It has also been a common hermeneutical response to the extra-judicial killings of black women, men, and children by police and in police custody, especially in recent times.[2] Habakkuk's interaction with the divine prefigures some womanist ways of relating to the world, the divine word, and the God in and of both.

1. In most places for simplicity I use "God" to render YHWH rather than "Lᴏʀᴅ," as does the NRSV, to resist explicitly gendering the deity, and I use "Gᴏᴅ" when quoting biblical text with יהוה, in keeping with conventions for rendering the Tetragrammaton. Here I use the familiar form of the quotation to introduce the discussion.

2. I began preparing this manuscript in the summer of 2015, during the burgeoning of the Black Lives Matter movement.

The book of Habakkuk has been shaped in such a way as to give the sense of dialogue, or, in the vernacular of the black church, call and response. The dialogue between Habakkuk and God has some parallels in the book of Job. The prophet[3] Habakkuk's primary question is one of theodicy, as is Job's primary motivation to seek God. Each book is heavily redacted into its current form. The books do have, however, significant points of departure. The discourse in Job is more serial monologue than dialogue. Another major difference between Habakkuk and Job is that Habakkuk entreats God on behalf of his people, not himself. Perhaps the most significant departure between the two corpora is the response of God to the complainant. God overwhelms Job with power and majesty, interrogating him, questioning Job's temerity to question God, casting his human frailty and comprehension in sharp relief to the God of storm, wind, all creation, its mysteries, and even its monsters. Conversely, in Habakkuk, God is a willing conversation partner, taking the prophet's complaints and questions seriously, answering them (to some degree),[4] and even responding to follow-up questions.

The books of Job and Habakkuk each offer a model of prayer that is honest, demanding, and confrontational in the same space as traditional, liturgical, reverently pious prayer. Habakkuk boldly calls on God to account for God's conduct. Habakkuk is not entirely satisfied with what he has heard and presses God for more answers, more clarity. In womanist parlance, Habakkuk talks back to God. Habakkuk is not easily soothed, swayed, or convinced; he takes a wait-and-see approach to God's declared intent. He is audacious in questioning God; in womanist terms, his audacity is womanish.[5] Further, God tells Habakkuk to "make it [his prophetic vision] plain" (2:2). Such language becomes not only

---

3. As is common for prophetic books "the prophet" is a literary character in the text, a poet crafting the dialogue in the book, and an ancestral prophetic figure whose proclamations have been preserved and/or revised or to whom these prophetic utterances have been ascribed in some combination.

4. Though God responds to Habakkuk, God does not answer the specific charges Habakkuk raises. The reader/hearer cannot discern whether God understands God's self to be directly answering Habakkuk's questions.

5. I am using the term "womanish" from Alice Walker's definition: "Usually referring to outrageous, audacious, courageous or willful behavior. Wanting to know more and in greater depth than is considered 'good' for one. Interested in grown-up doings. Acting grown up. Being grown up. Interchangeable with another black folk expression: 'You trying to be grown'" (Alice Walker, *In Search of Our Mothers' Gardens: Womanist Prose* [San Diego: Harcourt Brace Jovanovich, 1983], xi).

synonymous with the task of preaching in the black church but also a core commitment of womanists.[6]

The book of Habakkuk also presents the prophet as crafting a beautiful psalm that praises the power and fidelity of God in the same work in which the prophet questions what God is doing, a pattern echoed by the deep faith and piety of womanists who demand their own answers from God and know questioning and praising are not antithetical. Habakkuk's contested positionality, a prophet with apparent ties[7] to the dominant religious institution, vexes interpreters who understand authentic prophets to be found outside of institutions so they can legitimately critique them. If Habakkuk is indeed affiliated with the Jerusalem temple—which cannot be determined with any degree of certainty—that does not undercut his ability to function as a prophet.[8] The insider/outsider polemic is as problematic as are all rigid binaries. Womanists and feminists who maintain religious affiliations while critiquing those institutions and who accept biblical texts as Scripture while critiquing them and their depictions of God may find some solidarity with Habakkuk when read as an insider prophet. The wrestling of Habakkuk, text and prophet, with the core issues of theodicy—the justness of God, the power of God, and the actions/inactions of God in the face of undisputed evil—further commends the text to a womanist reading.

The book is composed of three chapters that roughly correspond with its three parts following the superscription: (1) 1:2–2:8 is an artfully crafted dialogue between Habakkuk and a wider unseen audience and God that transitions abruptly to (2) a brief collection of five "woe" prophecies in 2:6-20 (which overlap with the previous unit as 2:6-8 is both the end of the dialogue and the beginning of the woe prophecies) and (3) a psalm in 3:1-19. The subunits of the dialogue and the individual woes are delineated in their respective sections. The dialogue shifts from one speaker to another, Habakkuk to God and back again. In a number of exchanges, the speaker is not clearly identified, though in

---

6. Katie Geneva Cannon, "Womanist Interpretation and Preaching in the Black Church," in *I Found God in Me: A Womanist Reader*, ed. Mitzi Smith (Eugene, OR: Cascade, 2014), 56–67, at 63. See also the account of the founding of the Black Religious Scholars Group (BRSG) and their guiding vision to "make it plain" by Stacey M. Floyd-Thomas in *Black Church Studies: An Introduction* (Nashville: Abingdon, 2007), xv.

7. The precise liturgical instructions in chapter 3 have led some to speculate that Habakkuk was a priest or otherwise connected to the liturgical corps in Jerusalem.

8. Julia M. O'Brien, *Nahum, Habakkuk, Zephaniah, Haggai, Zechariah, Malachi*, AOTC (Nashville: Abingdon, 2004), 62–63.

most cases the speaker can be determined by the content of the address. The book contains some textual plurality and a few passages that defy honest translation, particularly in chapter 3. As a rule I will follow the reconstructions in the NRSV unless otherwise specified.

For all its vibrant language, the book is surprisingly vague. When does Habakkuk prophesy? In what historical context? What is the violence Habakkuk sees in 1:2? Is the threat external or internal to Israel/Judah? Who are the righteous and the wicked who appear repeatedly? How are they related to the Chaldeans? Are the Chaldeans going to punish the wicked or are they the wicked? How will the Chaldeans bring about an end to the violence Habakkuk laments? How is the violence Habakkuk decries related to the "violence of Lebanon"? What is the content of the vision on which the prophecy hinges in 2:2? How long will Habakkuk and his people see and endure violence? In spite of his questions and in spite of God's responses, neither Habakkuk nor the reader gets clear answers, if any, to these questions.

The character Habakkuk lives beyond this brief book. He appears in Bel (and the Dragon) in verses 1, 33–39 as the son of Jesus of the tribe of Levi, sent by God to comfort and strengthen Daniel with his own supper in the lions' den. He appears in the pseudepigrapha in *Lives of the Prophets* as a contemporary of Daniel but as a Simeonite. In Zohar A 7b, the rabbis date him to the time of Manasseh and as the Shunammite woman's son from 2 Kings 4.[9] Church Fathers associate Habakkuk with Daniel and Jonah and Jeremiah and Ezekiel.[10] His name in Hebrew, *Havaquq*, and Greek, *Hambakoum*, reflect a likely Akkadian origin for his name, *Habbaququ/Hambaququ*, a type of flora, possibly a type of basil (*HALOT*) or a fruit tree (*CAD*). The Akkadian provenance of Habakkuk's name provides little help with the dating of the book.

The text of Habakkuk received significant attention from the Qumran community, which produced the Habakkuk *Pesher* (1QpHab), a specialized biblical commentary genre, on Habakkuk 1:1–2:20. In the *pesher*, the vagueness of the biblical text is remedied and redressed with contemporary issues and concerns of the community from the first century BCE. Its adoption by the community presages its subsequent popularity as one of the better known prophets in the Book of the Twelve. Conversely, Habakkuk has a modest footprint in rabbinic literature, single mentions

---

9. That identification is made based on the similarity between Habakkuk, חבקוק, and the verb חבק, "to embrace." Elisha's promise is that she will "embrace," חבקת, a son.

10. Marvin A. Sweeney. "Habakkuk, Book of," *ABD*, 3:1.

in *Bavli Sotah* 49a and *Shir HaShirim Rabbah* 8:15, and more extensive conversations in the Zohar.[11] Habakkuk became more legendary in *Seder Olam Rabbah* and the *Lives of the Prophets*, and, in recent years, the book inspired authors outside of biblical studies, including Harriet Beecher Stowe.[12] Liturgically, Habakkuk 3 is read as the *haftarah* on the second day of Shavuoth (Pentecost), and Habakkuk 1:1-4 and 2:1-4 are read together twice in Ordinary Time during Year C of the Revised Common Lectionary with a rich history in the early and medieval church.[13]

11. See Zohar A 7b, B 44a, and C 195a.
12. Richard Coggins and Jin H. Han, *Six Minor Prophets through the Centuries: Nahum, Habakkuk, Zephaniah, Haggai, Zechariah, and Malachi* (New York: Wiley & Sons, 2011), 37–39.
13. Ibid., 48–49.

# Habakkuk 1:1–2:6

# *The Prophet Who Talks Back and the God Who Hears*

## Superscription (Hab 1:1)

Habakkuk is a "burden"-bearing prophet; his prophetic work is categorized as a מַשָּׂא, like the prophecies of Isaiah, Ezekiel, Nahum, Zechariah, Malachi, and the words of King Lemmuel's mother preserved as Proverbs 31. He "envisions,"[1] חזה, his proclamations like Isaiah, Amos, Obadiah, Micah, and Nahum. The framing of the superscription infers the entire book could be regarded as the fruit of Habakkuk's envisioning, while 2:2-3 makes reference to a specific "vision," חזון, whose content is not clear. The JPS often translates חזון simply as "prophecy."[2] The most common prophetic formulae, "Thus/So says God" and "an utterance of God," do not occur in the text. The third

---

1. This vision-based prophecy is distinct from sight-based prophecy articulated with the verb ראה, "to see"; i.e., Isaiah sees God in 6:1 but envisions his prophecies (Isa 1:1; 2:1; 13:1). The cognates of משא refer to both bearing burdens and oracular prophetic utterances.

2. Use of "prophecy" versus "vision" is inconsistent in the JPS. See 1 Sam 3:1; Jer 14:14; 23:16; Obad 1:1; Mic 3:6; Nah 1:1; Hab 2:2-3. Compare Isa 1:1 with 29:7 and see Ezek 7:13, 26; 12:22-24, 27; 13:16; and Hos 12:11.

*Habakkuk 1:1*

1:1The oracle that the prophet
Habakkuk saw.

chapter has its own superscription, which allows one to understand 1:1
as pertaining solely to chapters 1–2.

Since his prophecy has been presented as חזון . . . חזה, "envisioning
. . . a vision," and he does not say he has "seen" or "gazed" upon God
as Moses (ראה and נבט) and Isaiah did (ראה), the encounter would seem
to have happened in a vision-state; yet, no discussion of methodology or
technology to induce the state is evident. Either Habakkuk is able to enter
the vision-state at will or God responds to his call by granting access.
No mention is made of the divine council or any supernatural beings ac-
companying God. The contents of the prophetic vision accessed through
חזה, envisioning, are distinguished from the things Habakkuk "sees" in
the natural world, ראה, and those which he "gazes [upon]," נבט, in 1:3.

Habakkuk is actually called a prophet in the book's superscription (like
Haggai and Zechariah), which is rare among the prophetic texts. Unlike
Isaiah, Jeremiah, Haggai, and Zechariah, he is not called a prophet in
the body of the text that bears his name. The text reveals nothing of his
origins; the one personal characteristic of the prophet that emerges is his
apparent literacy. God directs him to write his prophetic vision in 2:2,
and Habakkuk provides performance notes for his psalm. Those notes,
one of which opens the psalm in 3:1 and the other of which closes it in
3:19, also include technical language common in psalms. The inclusion
of guild-related performance notes raises the possibility Habakkuk was
affiliated in some way with the liturgical work of the Jerusalem temple,
whose psalms include similar performance guidelines.

Whether or not affiliation with the Jerusalem temple is even a possibility cannot be determined because there are no explicit dating indices in
the superscription or body of the work. The mention of the "Chaldeans"
in 1:6 is hardly determinative but suggests interpreting the rise of the
Babylonians, i.e., Chaldeans, at the behest of God to punish Assyria for
its oppression of Israel and Judah. Even if the mention of the Chaldeans
is only a literary device, the text assumes a posture of surprise that the
Chaldeans are coming. Broadly, the text seems to interpret the rise of the
Neo-Babylonian Empire in the seventh century BCE. J. J. M. Roberts convincingly argues that by the time the Babylonians defeat the Egyptians at

Carchemish in 605 BCE their advance would no longer have had shock value.[3] At the same time, the book of Habakkuk seems to articulate a shift in how the Babylonians were perceived before and after the fall of Jerusalem. In one reading the brief text seems to fold time, moving from a powerful Assyria to a powerful Babylon to a declining Babylon within a few chapters, without explicitly naming (all of) the players or key events. If the text dates from Babylon's ascendancy, then the dismantled Assyria can hardly be the threatening "wicked." Egypt before their defeat at Carchemish is a possibility if the wicked are external to Judah.[4] Habakkuk does not even address his audience by name; neither "Israel" nor "Judah" appear in the text to help identify the political context. At best, historical context in Habakkuk is suggestive.

## Dialogue (Hab 1:2–2:6)

The book of Habakkuk begins with a dialogue between Habakkuk (and silent observers) and God. With the superscription the text is a performance ready three-part drama:

| | |
|---|---|
| Narrator: | 1:1 |
| Habakkuk: | 1:2-4 |
| God: | 1:5-11 |
| Habakkuk: | 1:12–2:1[5] |
| God: | 2:2-5[6] |
| Habakkuk: | 2:6-8[7] |

3. J. J. M. Roberts, *Nahum, Habakkuk and Zephaniah: A Commentary* (Louisville: Westminster John Knox, 1991), 83.

4. Francis I. Anderson, *Habakkuk: A New Translation with Introduction and Commentary*, AB 25 (New Haven: Yale University Press, 1974), 168.

5. The breaks around 1:15-17 in the NRSV unnecessarily separate it from the rest of Habakkuk's speech here.

6. I have chosen not to break the unit at v. 9 following the Masoretic major break פ in order give Habakkuk all of the "woe" prophecies. Most scholars agree the "woe" prophecies belong to Habakkuk even though the transition from God's speech to Habakkuk's is not clearly marked. (The MT has two forms that indicate the end of a passage: a soft break marked with a ס and a hard break indicated by a פ. The relevant marker, ס or פ, most often comes at the end of the line.)

7. Habakkuk 2:6-8 simultaneously concludes the opening dialogue and transitions to the woe prophecies without a clear demarcation.

²O Lord, how long shall I cry for
    help,
    and you will not listen?
Or cry to you "Violence!"
    and you will not save?
³Why do you make me see
    wrongdoing
    and look at trouble?
Destruction and violence are
    before me;
    strife and contention arise.
⁴So the law becomes slack
    and justice never prevails.
The wicked surround the
    righteous—
    therefore judgment comes
        forth perverted.

⁵Look at the nations, and see!
    Be astonished! Be astounded!
For a work is being done in your
    days

that you would not believe if
    you were told.
⁶For I am rousing the Chaldeans,
    that fierce and impetuous
        nation,
who march through the breadth of
    the earth
    to seize dwellings not their own.
⁷Dread and fearsome are they;
    their justice and dignity proceed
        from themselves.
⁸Their horses are swifter than
    leopards,
    more menacing than wolves at
        dusk;
    their horses charge.
Their horsemen come from far
    away;
    they fly like an eagle swift to
        devour.
⁹They all come for violence,

How long Holy One . . . ?

Habakkuk has some questions for God, and his questions are prophecy
every bit as much as are God's responses. Habakkuk's prophecy begins
with his interrogation of God in 1:2-4; more specifically, Habakkuk begins with prayer. Arguably the entire book is prayer. Prayer is one of the
bulwarks of Christian womanist practice, often characterized by the same
kind of blunt speech Habakkuk employs. Habakkuk lends itself easily to
womanist interpretation with the character of Habakkuk himself providing a, perhaps, unlikely proto-womanist protagonist. Womanists place
a premium on the well-being of the community in addition to concern
for the individual. Though he uses the first person in his protest-prayer,
Habakkuk calls God out on behalf of his people; his well-being is tied to
the well-being of his community (1:14). Yet, Habakkuk does not lose sight
of all humanity as God's creation. It is well within the role of prophets
to advocate on behalf of their people, especially the most marginalized,
but those prophets who emphasize social and economic justice tend to

with faces pressing forward;
  they gather captives like sand.
¹⁰At kings they scoff,
  and of rulers they make sport.
They laugh at every fortress,
  and heap up earth to take it.
¹¹Then they sweep by like the wind;
  they transgress and become
    guilty;
  their own might is their god!

¹²Are you not from of old,
  O Lord my God, my Holy One?
  You shall not die.
O Lord, you have marked them
    for judgment;
  and you, O Rock, have
    established them for
    punishment.
¹³Your eyes are too pure to behold
    evil,
  and you cannot look on
    wrongdoing;

why do you look on the treacherous,
  and are silent when the wicked
    swallow
  those more righteous than they?
¹⁴You have made people like the
    fish of the sea,
  like crawling things that have
    no ruler.

¹⁵The enemy brings all of them up
    with a hook;
  he drags them out with his net,
  he gathers them in his seine;
  so he rejoices and exults.
¹⁶Therefore he sacrifices to his net
  and makes offerings to his
    seine;
for by them his portion is lavish,
  and his food is rich.
¹⁷Is he then to keep on emptying
    his net,
  and destroying nations without
    mercy?

address their proclamations to their fellow human beings for redress and not to God as does Habakkuk.

Unlike his fellow prophets, Habakkuk does not begin his prophetic discourse with a declaration from God. Prophets mediate between divinity and humanity at the instigation of either and can and do initiate those conversations.[8] As presented, Habakkuk instigates this conversation. Only Habakkuk's anguished cry serves as a summons or invitation to his God. The prophet chooses a cry voiced by others in his tradition. "How long" as a cry to God to explain God's self is a recurring feature in the psalms,[9] particularly relevant because the psalm with which Habakkuk closes shares some technical language with the psalm corpus. In

8. Wilda Gafney, *Daughters of Miriam: Women Prophets in Ancient Israel* (Minneapolis: Fortress, 2007), 23.
9. See Pss 13:1-2; 35:17; 74:10; 79:5; 80:4; 89:46; 90:13; 94:3; 119:84; Isa 6:11; note that Ps 31:1 shares the same text, עד־אנה יהוה, for the cry, "How long, Holy One."

*Habakkuk 1:2–2:6 (cont.)*

²:¹I will stand at my watchpost,
and station myself on the rampart;
I will keep watch to see what he will say to me,
and what he will answer
concerning my complaint.
²Then the LORD answered me and said:
Write the vision;
make it plain on tablets,
so that a runner may read it.
³For there is still a vision for the appointed time;
it speaks of the end, and does not lie.
If it seems to tarry, wait for it;
it will surely come, it will not delay.
⁴Look at the proud!
Their spirit is not right in them,

but the righteous live by their faith.
⁵Moreover, wealth is treacherous;
the arrogant do not endure.
They open their throats wide as Sheol;
like Death they never have enough.
They gather all nations for themselves,
and collect all peoples as their own.

⁶Shall not everyone taunt such people and, with mocking riddles, say about them,
"Alas for you who heap up what is not your own!"
How long will you load yourselves with goods taken in pledge?

the Torah and Former Prophets, God is the one who asks "how long."[10] Among the prophets, Isaiah (6:11) and Zechariah (1:12) each address the question to God a single time, while Jeremiah makes it a rhetorical question repeatedly without invoking the divine Name.[11] Habakkuk's use of the cultural liturgical lament—"How long?"—may point toward his knowledge of and participation in worship at the temple. Use of the element does not clarify in what capacity he may have functioned; the psalms and their characteristic parts are not relegated to the period in which the temple stood. Habakkuk's cry originated from his context, the plight of his people.

Habakkuk's proclamation is a complaint (in the legal sense) on his own behalf and the people for whom he speaks. Contra Ehud Ben Zvi who

10. Exod 10:3; 16:28; Num 14:11, 27; 1 Sam 16:1. The prophets Eli and Elijah use the question dramatically, as do Job's interlocutors; see 1 Sam 1:14; 1 Kgs 18:21; Job 8:2; 18:2; 19:2.
11. Isa 6:11; Jer 4:14, 21; 12:4; 13:27; 23:26; 31:22; 47:5-6.

asserts Habakkuk's questions are rhetorical, I contend Habakkuk, like Job, seeks answers from the divine.[12] Like Job, Habakkuk is a timeless theological wrestling with theodicy in the context of a relationship with God in which expectations are not being met. Habakkuk is not afraid to say so; he does not couch his words with honorifics of reverential address. He demands the Divine account for God's self. He holds God responsible for what he and his people are experiencing: "Why do you make[13] me see . . . ?" His proclamation is also protest speech. Habakkuk more than objects to what he sees. He is moved to engage and confront what he sees strategically. Habakkuk is dissatisfied with God's lack of response to his entreaties and demands to know how long God will give him the silent treatment. The passion of his address bespeaks a sense of intimacy between God and prophet. He expects God to hear and respond to him.

Habakkuk's opening question includes an accusation: "How long, Holy One, shall I cry out and you do not hear while I cry to you 'Violence!' and you do not save?"[14] God is not listening and has not been listening for some time. Habakkuk's need is urgent. He expects his cries of "violence," חמס, would prompt divine intervention and deliverance, but he has been disappointed. His language is descriptive but not specific. Verse 3 features a litany of dysfunction: "iniquity," עון; "trouble," עמל; "destruction," שד; more "violence," חמס; "disputation," ריב; and "contention," מדון. The charges reflect the experiences of a subjugated, oppressed people. While the book of Habakkuk cannot be clearly dated to Assyrian or Babylonian imperial dominion, the text is clearly postcolonial and almost certainly pre-Persian and would continue to be meaningful during successive periods of Israelite and Judean subjugation and occupation. Some of Habakkuk's rhetoric addresses unjust economic practices, which makes the text easy to read in solidarity with other prophets as a critique of one segment of Israelite society that economically oppresses another. J. J. M. Roberts translates שד in 1:3 as "plunder," emphasizing economic despoliation, which he understands to be the result of internal conflict.[15] Elements of both readings against external and internal oppressors pervade the work. The language of disputation and contention in verse 3

12. Ehud Ben Zvi, "Habakkuk," in *The Jewish Study Bible*, ed. Adele Berlin and Mark Zvi Brettler (Oxford: Oxford University Press, 2004), note on 1:2-4, 1227.

13. חדאני, Hiphil.

14. I use my translations throughout unless otherwise indicated.

15. Roberts, *Nahum, Habakkuk and Zephaniah*, 87–89.

mitigates toward internal conflict, specifically, abusive litigation. Litigation in response to abusive economic practices or unjust adjudication of disputes would account for Habakkuk's characterization of the *torah* and justice as dysfunctional in verse 4. Francis Anderson proposes the possibility that Habakkuk is the litigant who brings a case to or against God on behalf of his people. This portrait of the prophet as well as his actions has a further similarity with the book of Job.[16]

Habakkuk's original cry is "Violence!" Unlike some of the other vocabulary for oppression that can take many forms of violence, including social, political, and economic, חמס refers explicitly to physical force causing injury or harm. The threat from unchecked violence is immediate, disabling, and potentially lethal. Habakkuk and his community are in crisis, crying out to God, and God is silent. Habakkuk's cry and the context from which it emerged are resonant with generations of the faithful across millennia: from enslaved Israelites to enslaved Africans in the Americas, and from Jews being hunted and slaughtered by Nazis to Muslims, Christians, and Yazidis being slaughtered today, not to mention the institutionalized religiously constructed rapes of Yazidi girls and women by Daesh.[17] The text does not reveal what kind of violence—interpersonal or state violence—occurs or who inflicts this violence, or on whom in the community the violence is inflicted. Whether or not Habakkuk himself is a victim is also uncertain. The violence about which Habakkuk laments is not gendered in his articulation, yet structural and interpersonal violence affect women and children as much as, if not more than, men.

Habakkuk's final allegation (v. 4) in his first speech is quite serious. The law, Torah (תורה), has become פוג, powerless, ineffective. Torah functions here in its broadest sense as revelation from God that includes individual laws, statutes, customs, and the larger system of jurisprudence, including accounts of their issuance that would be codified in/as the Torah. Torah could also refer to religious, particularly priestly, teaching and interpretation of written Torah in addition to the text itself. Subsequently, a body of oral Torah was collected, codified, and canonized. Contempo-

---

16. Anderson, *Habakkuk*, 131.

17. An acronym for *al-Dawla al-Islamiya fi al-Iraq wa al-Sham*, the Arabic name of the terror group initially called the "Islamic State" in Iraq, Syria, and other parts of the Levant. Daesh is the preferable nomenclature to many who reject the religious characterization of the group as the word *daesh* in Arabic has derogatory interpretations that enrage the group.

rarily, interpretations of Torah are also Torah, specifically those framed as religious teaching. The charge that Torah has failed is a strong one and points back to the One who gives Torah, God. Habakkuk's challenge is akin to womanist and feminist challenges of Scripture, which is also Torah in the fullest sense of the word. As a result of the incapacitated Torah, מִשְׁפָּט, justice, has been aborted, לֹא יֵצֵא לָנֶצַח, literally, "never goes forth," and, when it does emerge against all the odds, it is deformed, מְעֻקָּל, "crooked." Evidence of that perversion is an inversion in the power dynamics between the righteous and the wicked. The language is powerful, heartfelt, and easy to identify with even though the reader has no idea what exactly has happened to Habakkuk and his people.

In spite of its powerful, poignant language, the proclamation is quite vague, perhaps intentionally so. It functions as a biblical boilerplate. Who are the righteous and the wicked? The former are somewhat easy to identify: they are primarily an element of Judean/Israelite society whose Scriptures these are. Habakkuk is an Israelite prophet speaking to his own people. If the passage has broader implications, then they are secondary. Torah is an Israelite identity marker, and the twisting or perversion of Torah is an internal concern. The expression "the righteous," הַצַּדִּיק, virtually always refers to those who qualify among Israel and is rarely further explicated.[18] Use of the preposition עַל־כֵּן, "therefore," makes clear justice (or judgment) goes out perverted, deformed, because the wicked surround the righteous (v. 4).

The wicked can be understood as an internal Israelite element like the righteous but can also be read as an external enemy. Possibly the Israelites are making unjust judgments and perverting Torah, or an enemy power is impinging on Israel's or Judah's ability to follow Torah, particularly in matters of governance or dispute resolution. The mention of neither the nations in verse 5 nor the Chaldeans in verse 6 resolves this question though it widens the scope of the text to the international level.

The text does not document an arrival for God who responds in 1:5-11. The shift in speakers becomes apparent in part when Habakkuk stops addressing God as God. In addition, the imperatives of 1:5-11 bear the weight of divine authority. The use of the first person to deploy the Chaldean nation as a tool is clearly divine prerogative. Other passages

---

18. The expression occurs frequently in Job, Psalms, Proverbs, and Ecclesiastes and, among the prophets, in Isaiah, Jeremiah, Ezekiel, Amos, and Malachi. In the Torah, "the righteous" and "the wicked" appear only in Gen 18:23-25, in the account of the destruction of Sodom.

are not so clear. Determination of the speaker in 1:15-17 and 2:6-8 is more difficult. God's response indicates God has heard all Habakkuk has said and would seem to have been present or at least attentive from the beginning of Habakkuk's cry. Unlike the situation with Job, God does not rebuke Habakkuk for his questions or his tone. God's response takes Habakkuk's question seriously and enters into conversation with the distraught prophet. God directs Habakkuk's sight to the nations where God is already at work. The work, God concedes, would be impossible to apprehend without prior instruction. God's reply assures Habakkuk God is indeed active in response to the terrible things Habakkuk has seen and experienced. Throughout the discourse, God and Habakkuk repeatedly use the language of seeing to frame their conversation: Habakkuk 1:3, 5, 13; 2:1-4, 19; 3:6-7, 10.

God's response is not just to or for Habakkuk. God speaks to an unidentified audience in the second-person plural, arguably Habakkuk's community on behalf of whom he has been crying out. What is not clear is whether this audience includes the wicked along with the righteous of 1:4. If the wicked are external oppressors, then they would be absent. God commands the unidentified people with a series of imperatives to look, ראו, at the nations and see הביטו (Hiphil, "gaze"), to astonish themselves (by looking) and to (be) astounded by what they see (התמהו תמהו, the Hitpael followed by the Qal of תמה). Because, however, they cannot or will not see, God assures the community the work God is doing is happening now, "in your [pl.] days," but they wouldn't believe it even if they were told. Then God proceeds to tell them something of the divine plan. The "work that is being worked"[19] in their days (v. 5) along with God's active rousing of the Chaldeans, כי־הנני מקים (v. 6), is already underway when Habakkuk cries out. The language of rousing is strong and includes the first-person singular suffix on the interjection[20] and a Hiphil participle. God is (already) doing this work by God's self: *Look-it-is-I who-makes-rise!* God has not been inattentive. Habakkuk cannot see what God is presently doing.

God's plan already in motion is to rouse a sleeping giant, the Chaldeans. While technically a distinct people from the Babylonians, in the biblical text the Chaldeans and the Babylonians are generally conflated.[21]

---

19. In the expression פעל פעל, *phoal poel*, "a work is being done," the Qal participle follows the noun.

20. Following Beth LaRocca-Pitts I teach that "Behold!" and "Look!" are too weak for the force of the particle הנה. Her suggested translation is, "Oh shit!"

21. See, for example, 2 Kgs 25:24; Ezra 5:12; Isa 13:19; Jer 40:9; among many others.

Whether, or even if, the Chaldeans are the remedy to Habakkuk's complaint is unclear. God's response is inscrutable, which is another parallel with Job. The Qumran Pesher commentary on Habakkuk reads *"Kittim"* here, referring to the Romans in their context. Some biblical scholars made the same emendation in advance of the discovery of the Dead Sea Scrolls, albeit identifying the *Kittim* as the Greeks.[22]

God's response begins with a wider scope, the (Gentile) nations, and has several implications. Habakkuk should be able to interpret what he sees in other nations as the hand of God at work. Now that it has been explained, Habakkuk should be satisfied. Without more specificity, God's response reads as a status update, "I've been busy." Then God provides a detailed and highly allegorical description of the Chaldeans that does not translate easily without specifying their purpose. They are sharp ("bitter"), מר, and speedy, נמהר (v. 6), dreadful and frightful, אים ונורה (v. 7).[23]

Unlike the Israelites, the Chaldeans are the source of their own justice; they have no Torah. Their horses are faster than leopards or wolves and their riders have the stamina of eagles (v. 8). They are coming, and coming quickly, for more of that same violence, חמס (v. 9), and will take captives like sand, the very matter Habakkuk bemoans. Who, however, will they take captive? Will they pursue Israel or an enemy oppressing Israel? That the Chaldeans mock kings and other rulers and their defenses (v. 10) would not seem to bode well for Israel's oft-embattled monarchy; it is an equally poor tiding for those who would hold Israel or Judah in thrall. Are the Chaldeans coming to help defend the righteous against the wicked, a foreign enemy, or are they coming to punish the wicked in Israel? Whether or not the military might of the Chaldeans is supposed to comfort or terrify the Israelites is unclear. Such is God's response to Habakkuk. Yet, this response is bewildering. God responds to Habakkuk very much as God does to Job and leaves the reader puzzled with no small number of questions.

The passage ends with verse 11, which is difficult to translate; I address the issues more fully in the Translation Matters section on page 87. I suggest the following: "Then a wind/spirit swept on and they [the Chaldean nation] passed through and became guilty, whose strength was their own god." Alternately, Roberts proposes reading the Chaldean king

22. Richard Coggins and Jin H. Han, *Six Minor Prophets through the Centuries: Nahum, Habakkuk, Zephaniah, Haggai, Zechariah, and Malachi* (New York: Wiley & Sons, 2011), 53.

23. The description of the Chaldeans in vv. 6-11 is in the singular because of the antecedent הגוי, "the nation," in v. 6. Anderson avoids this difficulty by preserving the singular subject "he" in his translation (*Habakkuk*, 3–4).

as the subject of the entire passage.[24] God is stirring up the Chaldeans for divine purposes but does not want Habakkuk or his community to be too taken with them.[25] The verse seems to frame the arrival of the Chaldeans with some ambiguity in keeping with their description as powerful but deadly. The sense is: as quickly as the wind blows or changes direction, what may have looked like a liberating force becomes or reveals itself to be something else entirely, אשם, guilty.

## TRANSLATION MATTERS

Habakkuk 1:11 includes a somewhat rare word for God/god, אלוה, *eloah*, occurring some fifty-seven times, compared to אל, which appears 236 times (as generic "god" in addition to seventy-nine times as the proper name El), and אלהים, which appears over 2,600 times. אלוה is most likely to be the singular form within the plural אלהים, accounting for the ה; the root cannot be אל; its plural is אלים. The final ה in אלוה is pointed with a *mappiq* giving אלוה the appearance of a feminine form; however, like יה, *Yah*, אלוה takes masculine verbs in the Hebrew Bible. While the former, יה, is used as a feminine form of the divine name in some contemporary egalitarian Jewish contexts, replacing יהוה and taking feminine verbs in prayers and liturgy, the same does not appear to be the case for אלוה.

Habakkuk's response begins in verse 12 and indicates awe for God, if not for the plans of God: "Are you not from time-before-time, GOD my God, my Holy One? You cannot die."[26] Alternately, Julia O'Brien proposes another reading, specifically, Habakkuk is pointing out that the eternal deity is not affected by mortal concerns.[27] If this reading is accurate, then it would indicate a pushback against God's response to Habakkuk's complaint and a reminder of how urgent Habakkuk's concern is to those for whom death is a reality. Habakkuk affirms that an unidentified "they,"[28] perhaps the wicked from verse 4, have been destined for adjudication. The legal terms "judgment," משפט, and "reproof," להוכיח, parallel each other. According to this reading, "they" might be an internal Judean

---

24. See Roberts, *Nahum, Habakkuk and Zephaniah*, 97.

25. Ibid., 91.

26. See the Translation Matters section on p. 88 for a discussion of the *tiqqune sopherim*, scribal emendation, and options for translation here.

27. Julia M. O'Brien, *Nahum, Habakkuk, Zephaniah: A Commentary* (Louisville: Westminster John Knox, 2004), 69.

28. A masculine singular subject, often translated "they" or "you" for purposes of gender inclusivity whose identity cannot be ascertained conclusively, can be traced throughout the first two chapters of Habakkuk.

element, with the Chaldeans becoming the instrument of judgment. Another possibility is that "they" refers to the Chaldeans, and Habakkuk is objecting to God's use of them. In this reading, Habakkuk is strongly critiquing God's plan, finding it seriously wanting and counter to his own understanding of God's nature. What is clear is that Habakkuk's questions have not been answered to Habakkuk's satisfaction, and so he takes up his complaint again.

## TRANSLATION MATTERS

Habakkuk 1:11 is difficult because the number and gender of its subjects and verbs do not correspond and the referent of the verse is not easily identified. If this verse is a continuation of the previous description of the Chaldeans, then the masculine singular subject of חלף, "to sweep," would be הגוי, "the nation," from verse 6, as is the case for all of the descriptive language in verses 6-10. The verb is followed by the normally feminine רוח.[29] The Hebrew word רוח, however, does not make sense as the subject of "he swept," nor is there a feminine verb. NRSV and JPS understand the subject to be the Chaldeans who "sweep on" or "pass by." Both translations add a preposition and a definite article to complete the phrase with "like the wind." The verb ויעבר, "and he/it passed over," follows רוח, which adds to the confusion of being able to identify the subject. The Hebrew word עבר, "pass over," is a synonym for חלף, "sweep," though nearly all translations render it as "transgress," which makes it parallel to the next verb, ואשם, "and he/it became guilty."[30] Roberts takes רוח for the subject, adding the definite article, "Then the spirit passed on." This translation leaves the identity of "the spirit" unclear.[31] Was the spirit God's, i.e., the means of Habakkuk's communication with God? If so, it would be odd for it to pass on in the middle of their conversation; each has further remarks to make. Furthermore, the Masoretic *nikkudim* group ויעבר with אף חלף רוח. Curiously, in the only other text in which חלף and רוח coincide, Job 4:15, רוח is also paired with a masculine verb. The final phrase is the most lucid, זו כחו לאלהו: "their[32] strength becomes their god."

29. There are a handful of times that רוח takes masculine verbs, slightly less than 3 percent, eleven out of 378. See Gen 6:3; Num 11:31; 1 Kgs 22:24; Isa 57:13; Hos 4:19; Mic 2:7; Hab 1:11; Pss 51:10; 78:39; 147:18; 2 Chr 18:23. Anderson provides a more detailed analysis in his commentary (*Habakkuk*, 160–65), though his count differs significantly from mine.

30. Roberts takes אשם as a first-person imperfect, "I was astonished" (*Nahum, Habakkuk and Zephaniah*, 91).

31. See ibid.

32. Habakkuk uses a rather rare relative pronoun here in 1:11, זו, meaning "that/ which/who/whom," which appears only fifteen times in the canon, including twice in the *Shirah*, Exod 15:13, 16.

## TRANSLATION MATTERS

The *BHS* apparatus documents a *tiqqune sopherim*, correction by the Masoretic scribes for Habakkuk 1:12; however, Ehud Ben Zvi raises doubt he does not clarify on the tradition in his commentary on the verse in the Jewish Study Bible even though Rashi affirms it.[33] Ginsburg classifies it as one of eighteen emendations to the MT by the Masoretes for theological reasons.[34] The putative original תמות יהוה, "you shall not die," presents the concept of a mortal God even as Habakkuk rejects it. The shift to נמות יהוה, "we shall not die," eliminates the theoretical or rhetorical possibility of God's death, but the phrase makes no sense. Habakkuk and his people shall die (eventually), perhaps sooner rather than later, given the violence that has provoked his outcry. "You shall not die" makes sense in the context—God is eternal. This phrase is either an exclamation in awe or a reminder the mortal Habakkuk and his people experience the current threat in a way the immortal God cannot.

In verse 13 Habakkuk points out God's behavior is inconsistent. God cannot look upon "trouble," עמל, in verse 3, yet God is beholding the treacherous, בוגדים, a distinction made without a difference. Habakkuk wants to know why God watches while the wicked gobble up the righteous. God's mysterious plan and recitation of the impressive attributes of the Chaldeans have not satisfied him. In 1:14-16 Habakkuk counters God's characterization of the Chaldeans with his own bleak estimation of the nature of humanity as God has created them. His assessment is somewhat at odds with the creation account in Genesis. Eschewing mammals, Habakkuk compares humanity with (cold-blooded) fish and aimless vermin who lack the hierarchy and organization imposed by a leader. That is how he sees the Chaldeans and apparently his own people. Habakkuk contends humanity is now little more than a disorganized swarm of insects or larvae, רמש, from Genesis 1:24, and fish and fish food to be harvested at will by unknown persons or forces. (NRSV supplies "[t]he enemy" in v. 15, which is not present in the MT.) God is the One who has done this to humankind.

Throughout the passage the masculine singular subject is likely the same and can be traced back to the Chaldean nation in 1:6. The end of verse 17 would seem to confirm this point: "Is he [the Chaldean nation] therefore to continually empty his net and slay [other] nations without pity?" Habakkuk is critical of God's plan to turn the Chaldeans—a blunt

33. Ben Zvi, "Habakkuk," 1228.

34. Christian D. Ginsburg, *Introduction to the Massoretico-Critical Edition of the Hebrew Bible* (New York: Ktav, 1966), 358.

instrument at best—loose on the world. How will this plan defend the righteous from the wicked? Habakkuk is not certain how God's Chaldean experiment will help, and so he resolves to wait, watch, and see. His resistance to God's proposal does not find a ready comparison in the canon outside of the book of Job. In Genesis 18:23-32 when Abraham haggles with God over the lives of the people of Sodom, Abraham is very circumspect. He repeatedly entreats God not to be angry. Habakkuk's language is much stronger. Habakkuk's discourse continues through 2:1.

In 2:1 Habakkuk makes clear that God has not really addressed his complaint to his satisfaction, if at all. His language indicates he sees his own words as more than a complaint or a lament: they are a "rebuke," תוכחת, or reproof to God. Not surprisingly Targum Jonathan softens Habakkuk's rebuke of God and makes it a "request." Habakkuk waits and expects an answer: "I shall keep watch to see what [GOD] shall say in/ to me." Habakkuk's expectation that God will respond "within" him, בי, may reflect the vision state in which this discourse occurs. The last phrase of 2:1 presents some difficulty: "and what I may return regarding my rebuke." The NRSV joins the JPS in departing from the MT with "what he will answer," which makes sense in the broader context but disregards the first-person verb אשיב, "I will return." The NRSV is following the Syriac *wmn mtyb ly*, "what he returned to me." The JPS does not explain the choice. The LXX and DSS correspond to the MT.

### Watchwomen on the Ramparts of Life

"I will stand my watch and station myself on the ramparts." The image evoked for me is that of women waiting on the parapets of their homes for their loved one to return from sea. They wait and wonder if, when, how. The patience that must have taken and the strength required to survive those days of waiting! These women waited out their days not knowing what to expect. Would their husbands return home in one piece? Would they be dangerously wounded or ill? Would they even be alive?

The women would have to be full of resolve, willing themselves to be patient, to have the strength to deal with both the best- and the worst-case scenarios.

Women are trained to wait. We wait to grow up when we are young, to fall in love, to find out or decide if children are in our future, to be pregnant or to miscarry—and to deal with both. As mothers we wait for our children to return when they go out; as lovers we wait for our loved ones.

As a Jewish woman this reminds me of the mothers who send their children off to school

or their lovers/partners off
for the day and stare after
them wondering if they will
return home at day's end or be
caught up in an act of terror
and violence. As a member of
the worldwide sisterhood of
women this reminds me of all
other Israelis and Palestinians
and women of so many other
countries who send their loved
ones off in the morning and

worry about their return at day's
end.

So we all stand our watch over
those we love, with patience and
strength, wondering if they will
be safe or if they will be victims
of violence. And we all wait for
God's answer to Habakkuk's
question, *Ad Ana Adonai?* "How
long God?" (1:2).

*Rabbah Arlene Goldstein Berger*

The place of the brief, and perhaps only theoretical, sojourn Habakkuk
takes while waiting for a divine response to his "watch [place/post]" is
not necessarily a physical place. The notion of the prophet as "watcher"
occurs regularly in prophetic literature and mirrors a regular description
of God who, without slumber or sleep, watches over both Israel and the
divine word.[35] Habakkuk seems dug in; he will wait for God to respond
to him no matter how long that response will take. The response appears to be immediate, and Habakkuk reports it in the next verse. Very
little connects God's follow-up comments in 2:2-5 with God's previous
response in 1:5-11 or Habakkuk's repeated question in 1:2-4 and 2:13 in
particular. Yet God does respond. The response would seem to indicate
God's care and concern for Habakkuk even if the response does not sat-
isfactorily address his concerns or answer his questions. The paradigm is
familiar from Job. God has an intimate conversational relationship with a
few characters, though persons with whom God converses repeatedly in
an ongoing conversation are quite rare.[36] The more common pattern is a
single address from God to a human conversation partner regardless of
who initiates the conversation. God is clearly aware of and responsive
to Habakkuk's urgency in his limited mortal timeframe. Even Habakkuk
does not seem to expect God to respond so quickly.

When Habakkuk expresses reservation about God's reply and plan,
God counters with some directions and some assurance. Habakkuk

35. See Jer 1:2; 7:11; 31:28; 44:27; Ezek 3:17; 33:7; Hos 9:8; Ps 1:6; 33:14; 121:4; 145:20;
146:9.

36. The obvious exemplars are Abraham, Moses, and Job.

is to write out his חָזוֹן, his prophetic vision. Whether that vision is the conversation he has been having with God or something else is unclear. Habakkuk joins only Moses, Isaiah, Jeremiah, and Ezekiel in receiving instruction to write a divine word or vision, which underscores how little literacy figured in the early dissemination of Israelite prophecy.[37] Furthermore, God calls Habakkuk to make the vision plain, to write it so a runner may read it. The medium, הַלֻּחוֹת, "the tablets" with the definite article, indicates a specific set of tablets of which the reader is unaware. Just how many tablets are intended is not specified. Tablets, לֻחוֹת, are normally wood; hence the modifier "of stone" comes into play for those tablets that are not made of wood. The instruction is obscure. Are the letters to be large and plain so someone running by can read it like a billboard? That makes little sense, given the fact that people read aloud (just as they prayed). Running and reading aloud do not seem like a good mix. The instruction suggests a brief account of the vision, short enough to fit on the tablets, something less than any of the proclamations in Habakkuk, and points to an expectation of some literacy among the general public. Just what this truncated vision is has not been revealed or made clear. The instructions also point to a time in the near or distant future for the vision's fulfillment.

Without clarifying what exactly should be inscribed in the tablets, God continues offering words of assurance in verses 3-5 that do not address the violence for which Habakkuk demands an account. Rather, God assures Habakkuk there is still a prophetic vision for the appointed time that will not be delayed but neither does it seem immediate.[38] This reality does not exactly address Habakkuk's concerns; he is not looking for God to intervene by whatever means on some appointed day. He and his people need help now. They are suffering from violence and predation now. As with the text following the introduction of the Chaldeans, a question surfaces as to what is the antecedent for the masculine singular

---

37. See Exod 17:14; 34:27; Deut 31:19; Isa 8:1; 30:8; Jer 22:30; 30:2; 36:28; Ezek 24:2; 37:16; 43:11; Hab 2:2. Nahum also writes his oracles but does not acknowledge having been directed to do so. Furthermore, Baruch writes Jeremiah's narratives and prophecies, which leads many scholars to conclude that Jeremiah is not sufficiently literate or is otherwise incapable of producing his own corpus.

38. The time frame is significantly altered in the Epistle to the Hebrews (10:37-38). The "appointed time" becomes a "little while" but encompasses millennia, apparently leaving Habakkuk and his people on their own. Furthermore, even though the time frame is only a "little while" in Hebrews, the time (of Christ's return) has presumably not yet occurred.

pronouns and verbs in 2:3: "There is still a vision . . . he/it speaks . . . he/it does not lie . . . if he/it tarries . . . wait for it/him . . . it/he will surely come . . . it/he will not delay." The ambiguity has led some scholars to read the antecedent as God. In later Jewish and Christian exegesis the subject is the Messiah.[39] In the LXX, a mix of genders, as well as feminine vision (ὅρασις) and masculine (appointed) time (καιρὸν), does little to sort out the antecedent.[40]

The vision will speak of the end and will not lie, but the end of what? Is the end to be the end of violence against Habakkuk's people? Will this prophecy answer these questions: How long will he and his people have to endure violence? Why did God not respond to his cry before now? What exactly is God going to do about Habakkuk's cry? One of the difficulties in interpreting the book of Habakkuk is that the contents of the vision are never clearly identified. It may be the contents of some or all of the subsequent units comprise the vision. Or, the contents of the vision are not disclosed in Habakkuk.

God calls Habakkuk's attention to the "puffed up," עפלה, "proud" (NRSV), whose spirits are not "right" or "upright," ישרה (v. 3). While not called wicked, the puffed up are clearly contrasted with the righteous in verse 4. They are not like the righteous who live by their own faithfulness; in the LXX the righteous live by the faithfulness of God.[41] Drawing on the familiar myth of Mot (Death) swallowing up Baal, verse 5 describes the proud recipients of treacherous wealth as ultimately transient, though greedy as the grave (Sheol), and lethal as Death. The description of the opposition expands to an international scale in the final lines of God's speech in the dialogue. "They," the puffed up, arrogant and proud, collect and accumulate peoples and nations to devour. Yet, they are not specified as a nation themselves. This ambiguity pervades the conflict at the heart of Habakkuk portrayed at times as one who is between Israel and an invading, oppressing, or occupying force, and al-

---

39. Rambam's (Maimonides') twelfth principle of faith (in the Messiah) is articulated liturgically in the *Ani Maamim* with this passage referring to the still-anticipated messiah: "I believe with a full heart in the coming of the Messiah, and even though he may tarry I will still wait for him." In Heb 10:37-38 the antecedent becomes "the one who is coming," the Messiah, where Habakkuk is understood to prophecy the return, not advent, of the Messiah, Jesus.

40. The NETS uses the pronoun "it" and identifies the subject of each verb following the vision as the appointed time.

41. I will address אמונה and its translation and interpretation in the Translation Matters section that follows.

ternately as one between different economic classes within Israel, which makes the rhetoric suitable for redeployment and reinterpretation. The description of the puffed up becomes a launching pad for Habakkuk's woe prophecies in the next section.

## TRANSLATION MATTERS

Habakkuk 2:4c: "The righteous person shall live by their faithfulness." Hebrew אמונה means "faithfulness," "trustworthiness," "reliability" (*DCH*), "steadfastness" (*HALOT*), or "fidelity" (*BDB*). As a verb אמן means "to be trustworthy" throughout its *binyan*;[42] in the Hiphil it has the specific meaning "to trust in" as in Habakkuk 1:5. The NRSV translation, "the righteous live by their faith," is influenced by Christian exegesis. In the LXX and citations of Habakkuk 2:4 in the New Testament, πίστεως (genitive of πίστις) renders אמונה, even though πίστις has the same sense of "faithfulness," "reliability," "fidelity," and "commitment" (BDAG). In the Christian Scriptures πίστις also means "faith" or "belief," principally in Jesus. As a result Christian Bibles like the NRSV nearly exclusively translate אמונה here—and only here—as "faith"; the CEB is a notable exception.[43] The line is well known in Christian contexts in large part because of its multiple reiterations in the subsequent Christian canon, in Romans 1:17; Galatians 3:11; and Hebrews 10:38.

אמונה occurs forty-nine times in the Hebrew Bible; the NRSV translates it as "faithfulness" twenty-four times and "faithful/faithfully" six more times. "Truth/truthfully," "honestly," "enduring," "steady," and "stability" make up the bulk of other uses, making the choice of "faith" in Habakkuk 2:5 an obvious anomaly. The distinction between faith and faithfulness is significant. Faithfulness is how a person lives, what she does; faith is what she believes. The description of the proud and puffed up that contrasts with the righteous in Habakkuk 2:5 centers on what they do, not on what they believe. In the LXX the righteous person lives by God's faithfulness articulated in the first person, πίστεώς μου, "my faithfulness." If πίστεώς μου were "my faith," then we should have to wonder in what or whom does God have this faith and how does the righteous person live by that. Whether the attribute pertains to divinity or humanity, faithfulness is the appropriate translation here. Appearing regularly as an attribute of God, אמונה is God's faithfulness, not God's faith. Finally, because of the ubiquitous masculine grammar it cannot be determined whether the righteous person will live by human fidelity or God's faithfulness.

---

42. *Binyan* refers to a word root with three consonants.
43. The NETS translates "faith" but notes "faithfulness" as an alternative in the footnote.

**TRANSLATION MATTERS**

Sheol is the underworld in Israelite cosmology. Transliterated and not translated, Sheol evokes darkness, dampness, and dankness (Job 17:13, 16; 21:13). It
is the place of the dead, always hungry for more (Isa 5:14; Prov 27:20; 30:16). In
Habakkuk 2:5 the wealthy are as greedy as Sheol. The image of a mouth is often
associated with Sheol (Num 16:30; Prov 1:12). It is configured as a place of judgment and punishment and a place devoid of distinctions (Ps 9:17). Occasionally
Sheol is described as a place of torment (Ps 116:3). Rarely, the living go down to
Sheol when the earth swallows them alive in a divinely orchestrated geological
catastrophe (Num 16:33). It is full of traps and snares (1 Sam 22:6). In theory, no
one can return from Sheol (Job 7:9), however, the female ghost-lord,[44] בעלת־איב,
of Endor brought Samuel up from Sheol (1 Sam 28:7-14) on request with relative
ease. (She has been misrepresented as a medium who is possessed; however, she
exerts mastery over the ghost, not it over her.)

44. While "mistress" or "lady" generally translate בעלת, neither term carries the same
force or authority of their masculine counterparts, "lord," "master," or, occasionally,
"husband." Neither "ghost-mistress" nor "ghost-lady" connotes mastery. Each lacks
the gravitas of "ghost-lord."

# Habakkuk 2:6-20

# *Proclamations of Woe: The Bad News Blues*

## Woe Prophecies (Hab 2:6-20)

The dialogue between Habakkuk and God ends with a series of five "woe" prophecies, so named because they begin with the interjection "Woe!" הוֹי, translated "alas" in Habakkuk in the NRSV. The onomatopoetic interjection is more of a cry than a word; *hoy*, like its more familiar form "oy," is not a word but an articulation of distress.[1] In prophetic discourse it is attention-getting rhetoric that commands the attention of the hearer for what follows. The prophetic forms "woe to X" and "woe to you who Y" are among the most common, employed by Isaiah, Jeremiah, Ezekiel, Amos, Micah, Nahum, Habakkuk, and Zephaniah. Here the woes are retributive, with the transgressor receiving a punishment that parallels the infraction. The shift from God's speech in 2:2-5 to Habakkuk's proclamations in 2:6-20 is not marked with an indication from the narrator or editor that the speaker has changed.

While not always marked, previous changes in the speaker have been relatively easy to follow: After the superscription, Habakkuk addresses

---

1. In other passages it is "ah," "woe," or "oh."

*Habakkuk 2:6-20*

⁶Shall not everyone taunt such people and, with mocking riddles, say about them,
"Alas for you who heap up what is not your own!"
How long will you load yourselves with goods taken in pledge?
⁷Will not your own creditors suddenly rise,
and those who make you tremble wake you up?
Then you will be booty for them.
⁸Because you have plundered many nations,
all that survive of the people shall plunder you—
because of human bloodshed, and violence to the earth,
to cities and all who live in them.

⁹"Alas for you who get evil gain for your house,
setting your nest on high
to be safe from the reach of harm!"
¹⁰You have devised shame for your house
by cutting off many peoples;
you have forfeited your life.
¹¹The very stones will cry out from the wall,
and the plaster will respond from the woodwork.

¹²"Alas for you who build a town by bloodshed,
and found a city on iniquity!"
¹³Is it not from the LORD of hosts
that peoples labor only to feed the flames,
and nations weary themselves for nothing?
¹⁴But the earth will be filled
with the knowledge of the glory of the LORD,
as the waters cover the sea.

God in 1:2. The shift in 1:5 is not marked, but the language "I am raising the Chaldeans" is the language of divinity, not humanity. Chapter 2 begins after a soft break marked by a ס in the MT, indicating the reading can be ended at that point. Further, the one who will watch speaks in the first person, "I will." The commitment to watch and see what happens in response to the previous dialogue makes sense for Habakkuk, not God. There is not another Masoretic break[2] in the text until the end of 2:8. If verses 6-8 are reckoned as the end of the divine speech, then God is credited with the first "woe" prophecy that begins in verse 6 and either

2. The Masoretic Text (MT) has two forms that indicate the end of a passage: a soft break marked with a ס, and a hard break indicated by a פ. The relevant marker, ס or פ, most often comes at the end of the line. There are other markers that indicate the midpoint and end of individual verses.

15"Alas for you who make your
neighbors drink,
pouring out your wrath until
they are drunk,
in order to gaze on their
nakedness!"
16You will be sated with contempt
instead of glory.
Drink, you yourself, and stagger!
The cup in the LORD's right hand
will come around to you,
and shame will come upon
your glory!
17For the violence done to Lebanon
will overwhelm you;
the destruction of the animals
will terrify you—
because of human bloodshed and
violence to the earth,
to cities and all who live in
them.

18What use is an idol
once its maker has shaped it—
a cast image, a teacher of
lies?
For its maker trusts in what has
been made,
though the product is only an
idol that cannot speak!
19Alas for you who say to the
wood, "Wake up!"
to silent stone, "Rouse
yourself!"
Can it teach?
See, it is gold and silver plated,
and there is no breath in it at
all.

20But the LORD is in his holy
temple;
let all the earth keep silence
before him!

speaks all of them or the speaker changes without notice and Habakkuk takes over the form at some point.

The first "woe" comes in the second phrase of Habakkuk 2:6 and contributes to the difficulty of knowing to whom to credit the verse, as does the lack of any break in the text other than the *sof pasuq*[3] at the end of verse 5. Breaking the text between verses 5 and 6 means Habakkuk responds to God's description of the puffed up, proud, and wealthy with the woe prophecies. Upon hearing that description, Habakkuk asks: "Shall not everyone make a proverb against these [people], raising poetic-satire, riddles and saying, 'Woe to the one who accumulates what is not theirs!'" Dividing the text between verses 5 and 6 assigns Habakkuk the remainder of the proclamations since the text offers no indication of a change in speaker.

The individual woe prophecies are marked by the introduction of each successive "woe," followed by a masculine singular participle, "Woe to

3. The *sof pasuq* marks the end of an individual verse very much like a period.

the one who [does the action of the relevant verb]" translated in the second person in the NRSV and here for gender inclusivity. Each concludes with a soft (ס) or hard (פ) Masoretic break as indicated:

1. Habakkuk 2:6-8 פ
2. Habakkuk 2:9-11 פ
3. Habakkuk 2:12-14 ס
4. Habakkuk 2:15-17 ס
5. Habakkuk 2:18-20 פ[4]

These proclamations, like the larger book, are vague enough to be multipurpose. They seem to apply to Babylon more than any other external threat, retaining their utility to critique unjust practices within Israel/ Judah as well as future threats. Primarily the proclamations seem to prophesy the fall of Babylon to Persia in retribution for its excess against Judah, particularly in and around the fall of Jerusalem and the pillaging of the temple, which appears at the close. The characteristics that convict Babylon also convict any individual who uses their wealth to impoverish and subjugate a sister or brother Judean.

Prophecy 1: "Woe to you who multiplies [things] to yourself!" The first woe prophecy in Habakkuk 2:6-8 is part of Habakkuk's response to God's critique of those puffed up by wealth and pride in the previous verses, verses 4-5. The "woe" line that gives this genre its name comes as the second clause of the verse. The first clause is Habakkuk's speculation that everyone, כלם, would taunt and ridicule such people. The prophecy is written as Habakkuk's musings. Habakkuk supplies the words "everyone" has for those puffed up people; those words are the woe prophecy in verses 6-8. "Woe!" to people such as these. The proclamation includes a warning and prediction that those who have survived them in the many nations they have plundered will turn the tables on them and take them as spoils. The punishment is suitable for the puffed up and wealthy of 2:4-5 as a class and a wealthy and proud nation subjugating Israel/Judah, making clear the economic costs of occupation and colonization.[5]

---

4. There is also a ס after v. 18 but none after v. 19.

5. The MT actually has "wine," היין, rather than "wealth," הון, in v. 5; both intoxicants, vv. 15-16, and wealth, vv. 6-8, appear in the oracles, making either reading possible given their similarity.

In keeping with the previous international focus on the Chaldeans who sneer at monarchs and fortifications in 1:6-11, these malefactors, who plunder many nations, are external to Judean society (v. 8). The target is an imperial power, which ravages and despoils nations using economic oppression. Imperial economic exploitation is enabled and enforced with physical violence through military might. Imperial violence targeted individuals and communities indiscriminately, leaving behind bloodshed in their wake. They are accused of enriching themselves with pledges as surety for debt, an action that evokes a predatory merchant class from within or without Israel: "How long will you load on yourselves pledges?" To the degree the proclamation is read against Babylonian imperialization, the pledges are the persons of Judah whom Babylon holds hostage in deportation and in thrall for those who were left behind.

Typically, throughout the book of Habakkuk, the scope of this proclamation is broader than the affairs of Judah or Babylon. The plunder of many nations, the spilled blood of human beings without regard to national or ethnic identity, the violence perpetrated against communities (cities), and the violence against the earth are outrages that will be answered with commensurate reciprocal retribution.

Prophecy 2: "Woe to you who gains unjust gain for your house!"[6] In the second woe prophecy, 2:9-11, the castigated nation is charged with cutting off so many peoples, so many other nations, that its own life is now forfeit. The inclusion of the non-Israelite nations and the judgment resulting from their dispossession indicates a God whose concern is broader than the well-being of Judah. Justice knows no borders and is reciprocal. Instead of accruing riches for the national house or dynasty, the persons puffed up with pride and wealth have accrued only shame. The language also functions for individual creditors who enrich themselves and their houses through unjust gain. Their guilt will be uncovered no matter how many they exterminate because the stones and rafters of the plundered houses will cry out, testifying to the dispossession of their former occupants. The outcry of inanimate objects adds a cosmic dimension to this proclamation encompassing Judah, Gentile nations, and, now, building materials taken from the earth which, though shaped by human hands, nevertheless remain in "earshot" of their creator. The conjunction, כִּי, "for," connects verses 10 and 11 and provides the rationale for the death sentence: the wicked have forfeited their life for, כִּי, the outcry of stones and plaster testifies to what they have seen.

---

6. "House" can also mean "dynasty," which may be more appropriate here.

Prophecy 3: "Woe to you who builds a city through bloodshed!" The third prophecy, 2:12-14, is a testimony to the sovereignty of God. God's sovereignty is cosmogonic as indicated by the divine title, יהוה צבאות, "God of celestial-warriors."[7] The nation that builds cities and towns, i.e., constructs an empire, should know the labor of its people, but instead it yields only kindling; all its efforts are for naught (2:12). Instead of a corrupt empire covering the earth, the earth will be filled with knowledge of Israel's God, who is an alternate colonizing force and no mere tribal deity. More specifically, the earth will be filled with knowledge of the glory of God, כבוד יהוה, as the sea is filled with water.[8] Since the כבוד is an extension of God, it is also the presence of God that makes the statement shocking—all nations, including the Gentile nations, will have intimate knowledge of and access to God. Previously, only Moses had that kind of access on an ongoing basis.[9] Jewish exegesis has wanted more distance between God and the nations. Thus, the JPS offers an alternative translation: the earth will be full of the "awe" of God. This translation is likely influenced by the Targum: "the earth will be full of the fear [דחלתא] of God."

Prophecy 4: "Woe to you who makes your neighbor drink!" The fourth prophecy, 2:15-17, builds on the language in the second prophecy and ties it to the third prophecy with another verse on "glory." Using language that would not be out of place in a contemporary conversation about date rape, Habakkuk warns his target against forcing (משקה, Hiphil) a neighbor to drink in order to gain sexual access to the neighbor, using the biblical idiom "gaze upon their nakedness" in 2:15. In Habakkuk's analogy, however, fury or wrath, חמה, is the intoxicant. The prophecy applies whether the target is an empire or an individual. Both empires and individuals were guilty of using their power to have their way with the persons or peoples who are subject to them; both left behind a rising gorge of anger in those they oppressed. Nakedness, מעור, encompasses everything from stripping captives to robbing and/or humiliating them to every degree of nonconsensual and coercive sexual contact in the

7. The expression evokes countless celestial bodies in military formation; the traditional gloss, "hosts," no longer adequately conveys this meaning. The masculine singular noun צבא is used of human armies; the feminine plural form צבאות is used exclusively for the divine armies.

8. The concept conveyed by the final phrase in Hab 2:14 is similar to the one in Isa 11:9, but the language varies significantly. Hab 2:14: לדעת את כבוד יהוה כמים יכסו על ים. Isa 11:9: כי מלאה את הארץ דעה את יהוה כמים לים מכסים. כי תמלא הארץ.

9. Ezekiel's dramatic interactions with the כבוד occupied a relatively brief period of his life, and Isaiah's vision of the Divine was a singular occurrence.

context of invasion and occupation. Switching to the second person to address his target directly, Habakkuk declares that they will not benefit from the ubiquity of divine glory; rather, they will be sated with shame. So, they should get themselves drunk—whether with wine or wrath is unclear. They should be so drunk that they stagger like a freshly circumcised man or, perhaps, stagger around displaying their circumcision or lack thereof.[10] In retribution, they who have forced others to drink will in turn, literally and/or figuratively, be forced to drink from the cup in God's right hand (v. 16).

## TRANSLATION MATTERS

Primarily an adjective (thirty-five out of its thirty-seven occurrences), ערל means "uncircumcised." The word functions as a slur (Judg 14:3; 1 Sam 17:26, 36; 31:14; 2 Sam 1:20) and, when used for non-Israelite peoples, becomes a distinguishing characteristic governing the peoples' relationship to Israel and its Torah, marking them as outsiders (Exod 12:48; Ezek 44:7, 9). When not functioning diagnostically, ערל is used metaphorically with reference to lips (Exod 6:12, 30), hearts (Lev 26:41; Jer 9:26; Ezek 44:7, 9), and ears (Jer 6:10) and means "thick" or "encumbered," which signifies speech impediments and lack of appropriate response to the divine, whether deliberately or not. The root, ערל, functions as a verb only outside of Habakkuk, specifically in Leviticus 19:23, with reference to fruit that is to be treated as "uncircumcised," i.e., "forbidden." The grammar in this particular verse is torturous: "You all shall circumcise its fruit's uncircumcision, three years it must be uncircumcised to you all. Do not eat it." Interpretation of ערל in that passage has included understanding the produce to have been trimmed, burned, or simply declared forbidden. None of the interpretations of ערל with regard to fruit help with the Habakkuk passage.[11]

The translation "stagger" for the Niphal imperative הערל in Habakkuk 2:16 is circuitous if not euphemistic. Because the preceding verse includes drinking, drunkenness, and nakedness, and verse 16 also includes an imperative command to drink, שתה, linked with והערל, the resulting state is clearly a consequence of the drinking and is understood to be to the point of drunkenness, as in the previous verse. What might the passive command mean in that context? "Be [seen as] uncircumcised!" In other words, conduct yourself in such a way (in your drunkenness) so there is no doubt you are uncircumcised, either because you have exposed yourself or because your behavior is consistent with the stereotyped expectations for the uncircumcised.

10. See discussion of הערל in the following Translation Matters section.

11. Baruch Levine, *Leviticus: The Traditional Hebrew Text with the New JPS Translation*, JPS Torah Commentary, ed. Chaim Potok, Nahum M. Sarna, Jacob Milgrom, and Jeffrey H. Tigay (Philadelphia: Jewish Publication Society, 1989), 132–33.

The focus of the proclamations may seem to have shifted from national and international to interpersonal. Since, however, conquest is sexualized in rhetoric and tactic, the analogy holds on both scales. In verse 17 the mention of the destruction of animals and violence done to the earth call to mind modified *cherem* annihilations in which men, boys, and sexually experienced women are slaughtered; marriageable and prepubescent girls are seized as captive brides; towns, fields, and livestock are burned; and, in some cases, the ground is salted to prevent resettlement.[12] This proclamation can and should be read in an imperializing context with the others. Getting the neighbors drunk to expose them can refer not only to the actual practice of using intoxicants to facilitate sexual assault but also to getting colonized peoples addicted to the spoils of empire, which can lead to their own destruction. Ambiguity in Habakkuk extends the reach of the rhetoric and makes it perpetually available for reinterpretation.

The appearance of Lebanon in verse 17, heretofore unmentioned, brings with it an entirely new rationale for retribution, "for violence of Lebanon." The NRSV and JPS understand the violence to be against Lebanon; however, there is no preposition. Given that the text was, at one level, read against Babylon, the reference to Lebanon would be a reference to Nebuchadnezzar's substantial cedar harvest used to supply his many building projects.[13] Destruction of the forests, which provided timber for the Jerusalem temple and other Israelite projects, leads to catastrophic consequences for animals in its ecosystem. Verse 17 continues the grand scope of the proclamation addressing humankind and animals. The human and natural worlds are both subject to violence and bloodshed, but it is humans who are the perpetrators in the prophecy's rhetoric. Woe to the one who inflicts violence on the earth itself. This last phrase is duplicated from verse 8. While the phrase may be an unintended duplication, it fits well here (better than in the first proclamation, where it lacks any other reference to the earth or natural domain).

---

12. In Deuteronomy and Joshua these annihilations were complete and included women, men, children, and livestock; see Deut 2:34; 3:6; 13:15; Josh 6:21; 10:1, 28, 35, 37, 39-40. See Judg 9:45 for the salting of the land.

13. Francis I. Anderson, *Habakkuk: A New Translation with Introduction and Commentary*, AB 25 (New Haven: Yale University Press, 1974), 251.

## TRANSLATION MATTERS

Habakkuk 2:18 uses a variety of terms for "idol," פסל, carved stone; מסכה, metal, cast or forged image; and the assonant and alliterative אלילים אלמים, *elelim illemim*, valueless (אליל) voiceless (אלם) things. The first two terms are used slightly more throughout the canon, namely, thirty-one and twenty-nine times, compared with twenty-one.

The fifth prophecy, 2:18-20, begins with a verse seemingly unrelated to the previous four proclamations, absent a "woe" prophecy. Habakkuk 2:18 is a polemic against idols[14] that begins with a rhetorical question as to the idols' worth, יעל, "use," "benefit," or "profit." Habakkuk derides idols as human-made and "teaching lies" in spite of the fact they cannot speak. As in the first prophecy, the "woe" in the fifth prophecy does not begin the proclamation. Here the "woe" is not even in the first verse. The "woe" of the fifth prophecy occurs in verse 19.

Prophecy 5: "Woe to you who says to the wood [of an idol], Wake up!" The second phrase similarly ridicules the one who would try to rouse a stone carving. Unimpressed with the silver and gold ornamentation on the idols, Habakkuk points out that, however ornate, the images are inanimate, void of רוח, spirit/breath. It may be that the connection between this prophecy and the previous one is that the idols are a feature of the religion of the people, nation, or empire being castigated, but the text does not quite make that link.

The woe prophecy ends with the idols being juxtaposed to God (2:19), a declaration of the abiding presence of God in the Jerusalem temple, and a call to reverential silence (v. 20). The conclusion maintains the cosmic scale of verse 17 and previous lines: "GOD, the Holy One, is in God's holy temple. Silence in God's presence all the earth!" This concluding verse transitions into the psalm that is Habakkuk 3:1-19, which is like a call to worship that prepares a congregation for the liturgy. Verse 20 functions as the final verse of the final proclamation, though it is a dramatic shift in tone from the prophecy proper.[15]

As a collection, the woe prophecies offer a powerful critique of imperializing practices interspersed with a few laugh lines crafted for a public

14. I address the vocabulary for idols in the Translation Matters section immediately above.

15. Ending the final prophecy with v. 19 would seem to be contraindicated by the major break, פ at the end of v. 20.

delivery. The target of the proclamations is vague, and even the mention of Lebanon in 2:17 is confusing. One wonders at a prophet who is bold enough to demand answers of God and then questions the response he gets but shrinks from naming the nation about whom he is prophesying.

# Habakkuk 3:1-19

# *Habakkuk's Hymn,*
# *"Holy One, I Have Heard . . ."*

## Psalm (Hab 3:1-19)

The psalm-prayer that comprises the third chapter of Habakkuk has its own superscription, which allows it to stand alone. Arguments have been made that the psalm is not original to the book; however, those arguments rely on the unconvincing claim that a biblical book would not legitimately include such diverse genres. There are also a number of thematic links between the psalm and the first two chapters of Habakkuk. Additionally, the fact the Qumran *pesher* does not comment on Habakkuk 3 may indicate that the text functioned liturgically and not that it did not exist at the time, especially since it was found at Murabba'at. On the contrary, a credible argument is that the poetic form of the prayer marks it as older than Habakkuk 1–2.[1] Stephen Cook argues convincingly that the prayer's victory chant form points to its original composition by a woman as an oral or literary work.[2] In his analysis Cook

---

1. Francis I. Anderson, *Habakkuk: A New Translation with Introduction and Commentary*, AB 25 (New Haven: Yale University Press, 1974), 260–61.
2. Stephen Cook, "Habakkuk 3, Gender, and War," *lectio difficilior*, no. 1 (2009): 6, http://www.lectio.unibe.ch/09_1/steve_cook_habakkuk_3.html.

3:1A prayer of the prophet
Habakkuk according to
Shigionoth.
2O LORD, I have heard of your
renown,
and I stand in awe, O LORD, of
your work.
In our own time revive it;
in our own time make it known;
in wrath may you remember
mercy.
3God came from Teman,
the Holy One from Mount
Paran.

*Selah*

His glory covered the heavens,
and the earth was full of his
praise.
4The brightness was like the sun;
rays came forth from his hand,
where his power lay hidden.

5Before him went pestilence,
and plague followed close
behind.
6He stopped and shook the earth;
he looked and made the
nations tremble.
The eternal mountains were
shattered;
along his ancient pathways
the everlasting hills sank low.
7I saw the tents of Cushan under
affliction;
the tent-curtains of the land of
Midian trembled.
8Was your wrath against the
rivers, O LORD?
Or your anger against the
rivers,
or your rage against the sea,
when you drove your horses,
your chariots to victory?

asks, "What does it suggest about the poem/speaker's gender that she/ he regards her/his feet like those of does and not male deer?" His work raises the question of how to identify male, female, and androgynous voices, all of which he finds in Habakkuk 3:1-19.

The psalm that constitutes Habakkuk 3 has traditional language found in and beyond the book of Psalms. It names itself as prayer, תפלה, formally a subgenre of psalms, found in the superscriptions of Psalms 72, 102, and 142, and, informally, prayer in general. It has liturgical elements found only in the book of Psalms, such as the particle *selah* used as a refrain in verses 3, 9, and 13 for dramatic effect. In each placement *selah* marks a climactic moment, whether through maintaining a moment of silence or some cacophonous sound. God appears, *selah!* God fires God's bow, *selah!* God crushes the enemy, *selah!* The psalm in Habakkuk also has allusions to and/or quotations of material from Psalms 18 and 77: making the psalmist's feet like those of a deer (Ps 18) and remembering and recalling the works of the divine warrior, particularly against primeval

⁹You brandished your naked bow,
  sated were the arrows at your
    command.    *Selah*
You split the earth with rivers.
¹⁰The mountains saw you, and
  writhed;
  a torrent of water swept by;
the deep gave forth its voice.
  The sun raised high its hands;
¹¹the moon stood still in its exalted
  place,
  at the light of your arrows
    speeding by,
  at the gleam of your flashing
    spear.
¹²In fury you trod the earth,
  in anger you trampled nations.
¹³You came forth to save your
  people,
to save your anointed.

You crushed the head of the
  wicked house,
  laying it bare from foundation
    to roof.    *Selah*
¹⁴You pierced with their own arrows
  the head of his warriors,
  who came like a whirlwind to
    scatter us,
  gloating as if ready to devour
    the poor who were in
    hiding.
¹⁵You trampled the sea with your
  horses,
  churning the mighty waters.

¹⁶I hear, and I tremble within;
  my lips quiver at the sound.
Rottenness enters into my bones,
  and my steps tremble beneath
  me.

waters (Ps 77). The psalm-prayer also contains opening and closing technical performance notes that otherwise occur only in Psalms. The work concludes with common elements from psalms of praise: "I will rejoice" and "I will exult."

The vision of Habakkuk 2:2 may be articulated in Habakkuk 3, in particular verses 3-7. The psalm is composed of these elements:

1. Superscription: 3:1

2. Personal Prayer: 3:2

3. The Divine Warrior: 3:3-15[3]

4. Personal Response: 3:16-19

3. The Divine Warrior unit is in two pieces: a march to battle describing God in the third person in vv. 3-7 and a section addressing the divine directly in the second person in vv. 8-15.

I wait quietly for the day of calamity
to come upon the people who
attack us.

[17]Though the fig tree does not
blossom,
and no fruit is on the vines;
though the produce of the olive
fails,
and the fields yield no food;
though the flock is cut off from the
fold,

and there is no herd in the stalls,
[18]yet I will rejoice in the LORD;
I will exult in the God of my
salvation.
[19]GOD, the Lord, is my strength;
he makes my feet like the feet
of a deer,
and makes me tread upon the
heights.

To the leader: with stringed
instruments.

## Superscription (Hab 3:1)

The beginning of the psalm's superscription parallels the superscription that opens the book of Habakkuk. The genre is identified first. In Habakkuk 3 the genre is identified as תפלה, "prayer"; in Habakkuk 1 the genre is המשא, "the utterance." Next, each superscription identifies its presumptive author, Habakkuk. The prayer-psalm is identified as לחבקוק, which can mean either "to Habakkuk" or "for Habakkuk." In the Psalm corpus ל indicates liturgical directions for worship leaders,[4] authorship, and, perhaps, dedication.[5] Similarly, the book identifies its contents as "the utterance which Habakkuk envisioned." Whether the prayer dates from the still-undetermined time of Habakkuk cannot be determined any more than the context of the book as a whole. Quite possibly Habakkuk either appropriated an older well-known composition or the psalm and book are composed in his name with or without material from him. Both the psalm superscription and the book's opening superscription in chapter 1 identify Habakkuk as a prophet. Neither superscription provides any further identifying information. Finally, the psalm superscription includes a technical instruction for the performance of the psalm, the gen-

4. See Pss 4; 6; 22; et al.
5. Some doubt exists as to whether the psalms traditionally credited to David were written by him or for him, even if he composed and dictated some of them. His shepherding background would not necessarily have prepared him with sufficient literacy to write the psalms. See Pss 39 and 62, which are both *l'David* and *l'Jeduthun*. Which is the author and which is the dedicatee?

erally untranslated עַל שִׁגְיֹנוֹת, transliterated as "according to Shigionoth." The term occurs in the singular form in the superscription of Psalm 7, which is a "Shiggaion to/for David." The term is plural in Habakkuk, and its meaning is inferred by context. According to *DCH* a *shiggayon* is a song of ecstasy unless it is a song of lament or excitation—in other words, some sort of song. These two uses of *shiggayon* are the only occurrences of the term and consequently they provide insufficient evidence to determine a root with any certainty.

## Personal Prayer (Hab 3:2)

In a canonical reading of Habakkuk, chapter 3 is a continuation of the dialogue in chapters 1–2. The prophetic interlocutor is gone and has been replaced by a contemplative Habakkuk. He reflects on what he has heard and seen: God at work in the wider world and in his people's past. God's "renown" is rooted in God's primary identity, literally God's "name." God's "work," here פָּעֳלֶךָ, points back to פֹּעַל פֹּעֵל, *phoal poel*, the "work" God promises to "work" in 1:5. Habakkuk's request that God "revive" the divine work is actually a plea to God to bring it back to life, חַיֵּיהוּ. That language suggests for Habakkuk that no sign of God's work in the world exists at the present moment; God's previous work is dead and buried. In his supplication, Habakkuk entreats God to balance righteous wrath with unmerited mercy. The request evinces a pastoral dimension of Habakkuk's ministry that may be unexpected to those who see prophetic identity as constructed around righteous indignation and external institutional critique. In Africana contexts, prophetic and pastoral are interrelated, not diametrically opposed.

Habakkuk acknowledges what he has heard about God, very much like Job in 42:5: "I had heard of you by the hearing of the ear." Still pushing God to respond to his cry of *How long*, Habakkuk asks God to do in his time what God had done in his people's past. Habakkuk's efforts to reconcile what he has been taught about God and what he is experiencing has parallels in virtually every community that interprets Scripture.

## The Divine Warrior (Hab 3:3-15)

At some point—the timeframe is not clear—Habakkuk sees Israel's divine warrior with his own eyes (Hab 3:3-15). The divine warrior motif is one of the oldest in the Hebrew Bible, with notable exemplars in Exodus 15:1-27; Deuteronomy 33:1-29; Judges 5:1-31; Nahum 1:1-15; and Psalm

68:1-35. The motif is deeply rooted in Canaanite mythology and pervades the ANE.[6] In these biblical exemplars of the divine warrior God appears as storm god with similarities to the Canaanite Baal Haddu.[7] Like Baal, God's weapons are the forces of nature: thunder, lightning, storm, whirlwind, earthquake and ground collapse, rain, flood, plague, pestilence, and chaos restrained and released at will. God also holds "rays," קרנים, which evokes the image of the lightning bolts borne by Baal. The same root can mean either "horn" or "ray," famously leading to a tradition Moses descended Sinai with horns sprouting from his head. Common in the regional stories is the divine warrior armed with bow and arrows (Hab 3:9, 11, 14) and mounted on horse and/or chariot (vv. 8, 15). The plurality of horses and chariots in verse 8 gestures toward the celestial armies, the troops or "hosts" whom God commands at will in Habakkuk 2:13.

The rivers and sea of Habakkuk 3:8 and the deep in verse 10 are allusions to the Babylonian creation and flood myths.[8] Evoking the Numbers tradition of the exodus (Num 10:12; 12:16; 13:3, 26), Habakkuk tells the story of God's triumph in the wilderness of Sinai, referred to as Paran. Paran (along with Seir) is also used as a synonym for Sinai in Deuteronomy 33:2, which is the only other passage that refers to Paran as "Mount." Distinct from the Deuteronomic tradition, God also comes from Teman in Habakkuk 3:3. The Hebrew Bible associates Teman with Edom, and in every interaction with God except in Habakkuk, Teman is subject to harsh and lethal judgment.[9] The one tradition in which God emerges from Teman is the extrabiblical Kuntillet Ajrud inscriptions.[10]

The psalm also echoes a number of post-exodus traditions: Habakkuk describes seeing the moon stand still (3:11), which recalls the story

---

6. See Frank Moore Cross's classic study: *Canaanite Myth and Hebrew Epic: Essays in the History of the Religion of Israel* (Cambridge: Harvard University Press, 1976).

7. Haddu is the personal name of the deity more commonly known by the title *baal*, meaning "lord," "master," or, occasionally, "husband."

8. Anderson, *Habakkuk*, 350–51.

9. See Jer 49:7, 20; Ezek 25:13; Amos 1:12; Obad 1:9.

10. Kuntillet Ajrud is an eighth-century BCE installation in the Sinai Desert where inscriptions that mention YHWH have been found along with images on pottery fragments, some of which may have been intended to represent YHWH and Asherah. One relevant text is liturgical blessing "by YHWH of Teman and his Asherah," which many read as an indication that YHWH and Asherah were worshiped as a (conjugal?) couple. YHWH emerges from ("of the") Teman in a second text. A third text includes a battle theophany. William W. Hallo and K. Lawson Younger Jr., *The Contexts of Scripture*, vol. 2: *Monumental Inscriptions* (Leiden: Brill, 2003), 171–72.

in Joshua 10:12-14 where the sun does indeed stand still. Further, the descriptions in Habakkuk 3:7-10 bear a strong resemblance to Psalm 77:17-18. Habakkuk 3:7-10 and Psalm 77:17-18 share vocabulary and imagery: in each the divine warrior targets waters wielding arrows, and in each the response is trembling articulated with the root רגז. In the psalm, the deep responds with trembling (v. 16) to the assault; in Habakkuk 3:7 the tent-curtains tremble. In each case, God fights water with water: the clouds pour out water in Psalm 77:17, and in Habakkuk 3:10 God brings forth a torrent of water.

Although the NRSV begins the composition in the past tense, "God came," in 3:2, the passage uses the imperfect, so it can be read/heard in the future or even present tense. The NRSV rendering contributes to the sense that Habakkuk is seeing these events in a vision, perhaps the one prophesied in 2:2. A mix of perfect and imperfect verbs in 3:2-5 makes locating this visionary experience in any one timeframe difficult. In Habakkuk's theophany, God's appearance is not veiled in storm and cloud and, departing from the Torah traditions, neither cloud nor pillar is present. Rather than obscuring God,[11] the divine glory covers the heavens, providing a backdrop against which God can be, unexpectedly, seen. Subsequent interpretive traditions limit visions of God to Moses, but Isaiah (chap 6), Ezekiel (1:1–3:15), and Micaiah ben Imlah (2 Kgs 22:19-23) clearly see God, and it is implied that Jeremiah (1:4-10) does so as well. God is visible to Habakkuk; God's splendor, הוד, covers the heavens. God's strength, God's "power" in the NRSV, however, is hidden; the amount of divinity mortal eyes can behold is limited. The effects of God's power are visible in God's wake. God changes the contours of the earth in verses 5-6 by appearing, looking, walking and stopping, and bringing plague and pestilence.

From his perspective, perhaps his prophetic perch on the rampart in 2:1, Habakkuk describes God's victorious actions in 3:10-15, where he addresses God in the second person repeatedly, which emphasizes their relationship and continues the dialogical form of chapters 1–2. Habakkuk refers to God as "Holy One" in 3:3, thus repeating the divine address from 1:12. In 1:12 Habakkuk refers to God as his own God in very personal terms, "YHWH my God, my Holy One."[12] Habakkuk testifies in

---

11. See Exod 24:16-17; 40:34-35; Lev 9:6; Num 14:10; YHWH appears as glory, a nimbus which can be seen shrouding the essence of the deity.

12. That address is not used in the Torah. It predominates in Isaiah (thirty times) and occurs once or twice in a small number of other prophetic books.

the first person that he personally saw the fate of Cushan and Midian (v. 7). Israel's bitter conflict[13] with Midian overlapped Moses' marriage to the Midianite Zipporah (Exod 2:16-22) and his acceptance of the counsel of her father the priest of Midian (Exod 18:13-23). The conflation of Midian with Cush(an) occurs only here in Habakkuk.[14]

Habakkuk of chapter 3 is still the prophet who questions God in chapters 1–2. In Habakkuk 3:8 he interrupts his narration of the theophany to ask what would be a rhetorical question had anyone else asked it, but given his previous conversation with God, he just may expect a response: Was God angry with the waters of rivers and sea that seemed to receive the brunt of God's wrath? Broadly, those waters represent the forces of chaos on which God founded the world and the waters of the Sea of Reeds that would have thwarted the escape of the Israelites from Egypt. For Habakkuk, that chaos also signifies, most likely, the enemy forces oppressing his people against whom he has been crying out to God. Answering his own question, Habakkuk proclaims God's fury at the (non-Israelite) nations (v. 12), the "wicked house" or dynasty (v. 13), and their military leader. The warrior has come to a bad end: his skull is cracked open, and he has been bludgeoned with his own staff (v. 14).[15] The final act of the divine warrior in verse 15 is to trample the enemy. The fact that the enemy is insubstantial water and treacherous seas is irrelevant. God tramples them anyway, churning them to froth.

In his past/present vision, Habakkuk sees God save his people, God's people, described as God's anointed, מְשִׁיחֶךָ, in Habakkuk 3:13 (though the term does not refer to the collective people in other passages). God's anointed is God's special servant, usually an individual, a messiah-king identified as or with David or a legitimate Davidic heir (see 2 Chr 6:42;

---

13. The rationale for this conflict is contrived with Moses and YHWH calling for the extermination of the Midianites for offenses that the Torah plainly states were committed by another group, the inhabitants of Baal Peor, even killing a couple on their wedding day whose Midianite-Israelite union mirrored that of Zipporah and Moses. See Num 25 and 31.

14. The term Cushan occurs only as a place name in Hab 3:7 and as a personal name, King Cushan-Rishathaim of Aram, in Judg 3:8, 10. There is much doubt about the referent in the Judges passage given that Aram is more than 280 miles northeast of Midian, the former in Mesopotamia, the latter on the coast of the Red Sea. Cush proper corresponds with portions of central Africa, including portions of Egypt, Sudan, and Ethiopia, and in this passage, it is rendered Αἰθιόπων in the LXX.

15. The instrument of the warrior's death is a tribal staff (מַטֶּה), not an arrow (חֵץ) as in the NRSV.

Pss 84:9; 89:38, 51; 132:10). The text may refer to a specific fallen or deposed Judean king or the hope for a continued monarchy.

## Personal Response (Hab 3:16-19)

With two separate reflections, Habakkuk responds to what he has seen
and experienced. The first reflection describes his physical response (v.
16). He is shaken, trembling like the tent-curtains of Midian he saw in 3:7.
He stills himself to wait for the affliction of the ones who have afflicted
him and his people. While resting in that space Habakkuk produces a
psalm within his psalm.

In verse 17, Habakkuk begins his second response by describing ca-
lamitous economic scarcity. He uses agricultural and ecological terms;
the language is hyperbolic. Two of the traditional seven species[16] of
indigenous comestible crops have failed—figs and olives. The lack of
blossoms on the fig tree means no future pollination and a precipitous
decline in the production of figs, which, if unchecked, could result in
a total loss: no fresh or dried figs, no fig cakes or wine, no fig-based
medicines.[17] Lack of olives and their oil used medicinally, as fuel, and
ritually would have been devastating on its own. The seven-year period
required to nurture an olive tree before it bore fruit would mean the
after effects of this blight could not easily be turned around. The lack of
grapes would mean a lack of dried and fresh fruit, wine, and vinegar
as foodstuffs and for medicinal use, and vinegar and tannin for use in
curing leather and other manufacturing processes. The next loss is a
sweeping generalization: all field crops. This loss would include wheat,
barley, spelt, millet, lentils, and more. The loss of flora is devastating
but not all encompassing. The loss of fauna is catastrophic. The loss of
flocks and herds, sheep, goats, cattle, and oxen represents a loss in material wealth, meat, and dairy and also a loss in investment and income in
terms of breeding stock.

These catastrophes, however, may not have actually befallen Habakkuk and his people. Habakkuk introduces the list with "if." *If* these things

---

16. Deuteronomy 8:8 extols the goodness of the land of Canaan in part by listing
the food already available there: "a land of wheat and barley, of vines and fig trees
and pomegranates, a land of olive trees and honey."

17. Figs are a known laxative, used in antiquity and modernity, and Hezekiah's
fig poultice in 2 Kgs 20:7 has an equine counterpart in the literature from Ugarit (see
Ziony Zevit's commentary in the *Jewish Study Bible*, 768).

happen, or better, *even if* these things happen, Habakkuk will rejoice in God. The paired celebratory verbs include the common גיל and עלז, which occurs only here and in Zephaniah 3:14. The "why" of this mini-psalm is a thread that ties it to the preceding verses about the divine warrior. God is the God of Habakkuk's salvation and, by extension, the God of Habakkuk's people. The economic and ecological disaster is a poetic foil for Habakkuk's confession of trust. Like Job, Habakkuk has questioned God. Like Job, Habakkuk has had a response from God. Like Job, Habakkuk has received a divine encounter rather than a direct answer to his question. Throughout his conversation with and interrogation of God, Habakkuk has questioned God's methods and remained skeptical. Now acknowledging whether the current situation changes or not, whether God intervenes in a way that makes sense to him or not, he will praise God. That praise includes a line largely duplicated from Psalm 18:33 (itself duplicated in 2 Sam 22:34): "[God] sets my feet like the feet of a deer." In Habakkuk 3:19 there is a verb, וישם; in Psalm 18 and 2 Samuel there is no verb and translators supply "makes."

---

### TRANSLATION MATTERS

YHWH *adonai*: YHWH is the most frequent and perhaps best-known example of the scribal emendation category *qetiv/qere*, "what is written"/"what is read." The sacred four letters of the Tetragrammaton are pointed with the vowels of אדני in most cases (but occasionally אלהים), which results in the circumlocution "the LORD" that represents the unpronounceable Divine name with large and small capital letters indicating YHWH rather than אדן. On occasion the inflected form of אדן, "my lord," אדני, appears in tandem with YHWH. The most common arrangement by several orders of magnitude is *adonai* YHWH, which occurs nearly three hundred times as compared to fewer than ten when excluding unrelated proximal placement. Habakkuk uses the rarer configuration, YHWH *adonai*, in 3:19. Most translations render "YHWH my lord" as "God, the Lord"; the KJV uses the more common "the Lord God" while the JPS uses "God my Lord."

---

One might wonder why Habakkuk seemingly invents an epic ecological and economic catastrophe that evokes the specter of famine rather than return to the violence about which he has been crying out in the first two chapters of the larger work. J. J. M. Roberts suggests that Habakkuk and his people are routinely subjected to Babylonian violence and already enduring the dehumanizing violence of oppression and subjugation.[18] The agricultural metaphor may also reflect one dimension of violence to which Habakkuk's people have been subjected, the economic violence of the woe prophecies, notably 2:5-11. Reading the agricultural loss in terms of plunder and excessive taxation may make more sense. This reading would make the internal psalm and its larger enveloping psalm not just anti-oppression rhetoric but specifically anti-Babylonian rhetoric. The prophet's confession is that even if things get worse—and he conjures an epic scenario—even then he will praise the God whose saving acts he has seen.

The final verse of the psalm may well be Habakkuk's response to his own question in light of the lack of an answer from God: *How long?* However long it takes, God is my strength. That knowledge gives him strength and endurance, represented as the sure-footedness of a deer in verse 19. The sentiment is a fitting conclusion to the work as a whole. The final words of the verse are a second set of liturgical instructions, to play it on נגינות, stringed instruments, which occur repeatedly in identical instructions in the psalms.[19]

18. J. J. M. Roberts, *Nahum, Habakkuk and Zephaniah: A Commentary* (Louisville: Westminster John Knox, 1991), 157.

19. Pss 4; 6; 45:8; 54; 55; 61; 67; 76. An apparent suffix on נגינותי represents a small textual oddity; here and in Isa 38:20 the word is treated as the feminine plural in spite of resembling the first common singular pronominal suffix.

# Conclusion: Contextual Hermeneutics

## *How Long, Holy One?*

*How long, Holy One?* Habakkuk's unanswered question rings throughout the ages, echoed by those who have asked this question from his time to ours and those who continue to ask it in an array of anguished contexts. The details of Habakkuk's situation, intentionally vague, are lost to us. The text does preserve the impetus for his cry: the violence that afflicts Habakkuk and his people. "How long?" is the cry of those subject to violence in its many forms: physical, structural, economic, sexual, international, and interpersonal violence. The world Habakkuk describes corresponds to the world I know and the world my ancestors knew. This congruence is one reason why the book of Habakkuk figures prominently in Jewish and Christian exegesis and is particularly beloved in Africana Christian contexts.

The cry "How long, Holy One?" echoes from those shackled in and by slavery's chains, through those systematically oppressed by law and tradition enforced by night riders with flaming crosses, to those shot and strangled, beaten and wrestled down by those trusted to protect and serve. It is the cry of black women whose families and bodies have been systematically ravaged by the benefactors, adherents, and evangelists of white supremacy. "How long?" is the cry of the oppressed. It is the cry of those on the bottom of power curves and hierarchies. It is the cry of women, people of color, non-gender-conforming people, people with

particular ranges of mobility and abilities, the poor, undocumented im-
migrants, and minority communities who do not see themselves reflected
in those with power over them or the cultural norms they produce. "How
long?" is the cry of a faithful prophet and likewise the cry of faithful
people. For those who need it, Habakkuk grants permission to question
God, not just about the state of the world, but what God is doing in it and
about it. Habakkuk offers a womanish model of faithfulness through his
questioning God, demanding a response, and determining for oneself if
God's response is valid.

Habakkuk's cry demonstrates the other direction of prophetic discourse, from the prophet to God on behalf of the people. He says his
piece, and God listens. Habakkuk's plain speech and direct approach
have corollaries in the prayers of black women through the ages, who
have told and tell God what we want, think, and need. Habakkuk's cry
reveals the expectations he has about God shared by many for whom
he is canonical: He expects God to respond to his cries. He expects God
to do something about the state of the world. He cannot fathom what
is taking God so long to act. Habakkuk's expectations of God form the
contours of their relationship from his perspective. He expects God to
accept his questioning and provide him with answers that make sense.
God conforms to Habakkuk's expectations to some degree. In Habakkuk
God is responsive and accessible, sovereign and active in the world. This
portrait of God is familiar and comforting.

Habakkuk is sure that what he sees all around him is inconsistent
with what he knows about the world that is subject to God's sovereignty.
Torah, an extension of that sovereignty, has been perverted, twisted,
weakened, paralyzed, and rendered unjust. To the degree that Torah also
represents jurisprudence and legal structures, a womanist reading of
Habakkuk finds the Torah that is the justice system in the United States
similarly perverted and deformed, demonstrated by the over-policing of
black and brown bodies and communities, disparate judicial outcomes,
black, Hispanic, and poor defendants, and over-representation of African
Americans in prison and on death row.[1] Like Habakkuk, black women
have seen too much horror to be satisfied with glib responses and clichés,
even from God. Like Habakkuk, we may trust God is turning the world
around, but we will stand on our perches to be sure, and if we do not
like what we see, we will call God out again and again. Like Habakkuk,

---

1. Michelle Alexander, *The New Jim Crow: Mass Incarceration in the Age of Colorblindness* (New York: New Press, 2012), 98–99.

we know God doesn't flinch or shrink in the face of scrutiny and can handle our questions, cries, and reservations.

Habakkuk is one of many who "dare to indict God for his [sic] failure to manage this world in a way a good, just, and competent Creator should."[2] I've noted Habakkuk's many similarities with Job—that world-renowned God-questioner. An important difference is the conclusion of their respective volumes. Job gets a fairytale ending: more of everything than he had before, including new children to replace those who had been killed, and God validated his theology, leaving the fate of his interlocutors in his hands to some degree. Habakkuk is left waiting for his change to come.[3]

The juxtaposition of the prayer-psalm and divine interrogation bring to mind the proliferation of African American spirituals that "cry out for justice and call for accountability" at the same time Africans in the Atlantic basin were subjected to the depredation of chattel slavery and arguably every form of violence chronicled by Habakkuk.[4] In her reading of Habakkuk, Job, and African American history and the spirituals, Cheryl Kirk-Duggan finds coherence that explains Habakkuk's appeal to African Americans broadly and womanists in particular:

> Habakkuk protests that God neither hears nor acts and thus negates Law and justice, even as he recalls God's saving acts. Neither Habakkuk nor Job question God's power under God-permitted injustice and suffering. A believer can endure pain without losing faith through divine self-disclosure. Habakkuk's struggle with redemption and righteousness in the midst of evil is the victim's struggle. The books of Job and Habakkuk show that life is a daily series of deaths to human desires and deeds, as faith leads toward perfection within God.[5]

The combination of Habakkuk's interrogation and rebuke of God with his prayer to and praise of God is not all that different from the tension

---

2. Francis I. Anderson, *Habakkuk: A New Translation with Introduction and Commentary*, AB 25 (New Haven: Yale University Press, 1974), 132.

3. The phrase "my change is gonna come" is a paraphrase of Job 14:14 from the King James Version of the Bible. The KJV is a common referent in African American preaching and broader religious and cultural discourse. Sam Cooke's iconic "A Change Is Gonna Come," released in 1964 by RCA Victor, has subsequently become canonical in many African American contexts, including the Black Lives Matter movement.

4. Cheryl A. Kirk-Duggan, "African-American Spirituals: Confronting and Exorcising Evil through Song," in *A Troubling in My Soul: Womanist Perspectives on Evil and Suffering*, ed. Emilie Townes, Bishop Henry McNeal Turner studies in North American Black Religion, vol. 8 (Maryknoll, NY: Orbis Books, 1993), 150–71.

5. Ibid., 165.

with which many womanists and feminists engage the biblical text. Like Habakkuk, many womanists for whom this text is canonical look at God's saving acts in and beyond the canons of Scripture and continue to trust in God in spite of present circumstances. Womanists and feminists who are religious readers can and do simultaneously question and challenge the text and its God and participate in religious communities.

*How long, Holy One?* For Habakkuk or those who echo his cry, no answer comes. Indeed, "The answer to the question 'How Long, Oh Lord?' may be 'Never.' But with righteous indignation we must continue to offer the complaint of Habakkuk with the courage of Esther."[6]

6. Ibid., 171.

# Zephaniah

## Author's Introduction

# *A Cataclysm Is Coming: Where You Gonna Run?*

Zephaniah's[1] brief three chapters begin with what looks like the end of the world, and then they move to the salvation of a faithful remnant at the book's conclusion. The language and imagery of the book of Zephaniah is strong, cataclysmic, apocalyptic, and eschatological. Divine judgment is one of the major themes presented under the rubric of *the day of YHWH,*[2] a motif that pervades the prophetic corpus and extends beyond it.[3] Articulation of the day varies, and multiple formulae of this

---

1. As is the case with most prophetic books, the same name refers to the book and the prophet in whose name the book is offered, even when the final form of the book is the result of a later author or redactor.

2. The traditional rendering of יהוה יום is "the day of the LORD." In most places for simplicity I use "God" to render YHWH rather than "LORD," as does the NRSV, to resist explicitly gendering the deity, and I use "GOD" when quoting biblical texts with יהוה in keeping with conventions for rendering the Tetragrammaton. I will, however, use the expression "day of YHWH" to avoid the gender implications of NRSV's "day of the LORD" and because the day is particular to Israel's God addressed as YHWH and not associated with other divine names or titles in the Hebrew Bible.

3. The expression also occurs in Mal 4:5 as well as in the New Testament: 1 Cor 5:5; 2 Cor 1:14; 1 Thess 5:2; 2 Thess 2:2; 2 Pet 3:10.

"day" appear throughout the Hebrew canon, inclusive of the book of Zephaniah. Sometimes the motif is just "the day"; other times it is "that day." In Zephaniah the day of YHWH is a day of retribution. The book is characterized by extremes. On the one hand, it proclaims that all the earth will be destroyed; on the other hand, it announces that a remnant shall survive. God is highly anthropomorphized in the text: "I will stretch out my hand" (1:4); "I will search Jerusalem with lamps" (1:12); "God will stretch out God's hand" (2:13); and "I will rise as a witness" (3:8). For those who survive, Zephaniah offers words of restoration and comfort. The book is, in a word, dramatic.

Zephaniah is one of the few prophetic books that introduces its author/speaker, its geographical setting, and its temporal context. These three elements in particular differentiate Zephaniah from the books of Nahum and Habakkuk, with which Zephaniah is often bundled. The book is set in the days of Josiah the reformer, making the prophet Zephaniah a contemporary of Huldah, Josiah's court prophet. Unlike Huldah, Zephaniah does not serve or address the king. Whether or not Zephaniah was even acquainted with the monarch, whose rule frames his prophecies as presented, cannot be ascertained. The content of Zephaniah, however, particularly the polemic against foreign and syncretistic worship, is broadly supportive of Josiah's reform.

Zephaniah's proclamations address Jerusalem and Judah, Israel and Zion (Zeph 1:4; 3:14), with Zephaniah naming specific neighborhoods in Jerusalem (Zeph 1:10-11). Zephaniah also addresses the four Philistine cities: Gaza, Ashkelon, Ashdod, and Ekron (Zeph 2:4), along with a number of other nations with whom Israel/Judah has been in conflict: the Cherethites or Cretans and Canaan, which is characterized as a Philistine holding in Zephaniah 2:5; Moab and Ammon in Zephaniah 2:8-9; Nubia (biblical Cush) in Zephaniah 2:12; and Nineveh and Assyria in Zephaniah 2:13.

Contact between Zephaniah and a number of Hebrew Bible texts, far beyond the day of YHWH motif, is considerable. Adele Berlin has identified an impressive list of shared language and imagery with repeated elements between Zephaniah and Genesis, Deuteronomy, Kings, Isaiah, Jeremiah, Ezekiel, Hosea, Joel, Amos, Micah, and Habakkuk that is exclusive of day of YHWH material.[4] The most significant contact between Zephaniah and other biblical literature is with other prophetic books, most notably Isaiah, Jeremiah, and, to a lesser degree, Micah. It

---

4. Adele Berlin, *Zephaniah*, AB 25A (New Haven: Yale University Press, 1974), 15–16.

cannot be determined whether the shared material between Isaiah and Zephaniah originates with one or the other prophet, due in part to the multistage formation of the book of Isaiah. Significant overlap also occurs between Zephaniah and Genesis. That intertextuality ranges from quotes, e.g., Isaiah 47:8 and Zephaniah 2:15,[5] and allusions such as Isaiah 1:15/Zephaniah 1:1 and Isaiah 34:12-16/Zephaniah 2:13-15, to thematic sampling such as creation elements being swept away in Zephaniah 1, an event that represents an undoing of Genesis 1–2.

Feminist interest in Zephaniah has often focused on the expression בת ציון, which can be translated as either "Daughter Zion" or "[the] Daughter of Zion." (I explore this point in the Translation Matters section on pp. 188–89 and in the Contextual Hermeneutics section.) Zephaniah offers many more areas for womanist and feminist exploration. As is the case for many biblical texts, under the skin of the narrative are women and girls who are rendered invisible in the text. Making visible the women and girls submerged in the text prompts more questions. For example, how might royal women and their daughters have participated in the activities for which the "king's children," traditionally translated as the "king's sons," are condemned in 1:8?[6] Did women participate in the censured worship of Baal and Milcom referred to in 1:4-5? Since the superscription roots Zephaniah in a historical context that is shared with other biblical literature, the fate of women who are present for or affected by the events described are another area of exploration. The issue of female characters from texts set in the same period and location also invites questions. For example, did the prophets Huldah and Zephaniah have any contact with each other? The intersection of race (or ethnicity in the biblical text) and gender is a particular place of feminist inquiry, but intersectionality is the lived reality of womanist biblical scholars, making Zephaniah's genealogy a fruitful field for womanist inquiry.

The text of Zephaniah varies significantly across the MT, LXX, Targum, Peshitta, and Vulgate. The pronouncements of Zephaniah are full of wordplay, puns, alliteration, assonance, double entendre, and a fair number of obscure expressions rendered in quite diverse ways across

5. Examples of intertextuality include "I am, and there is no one besides me" in both Isa 47:8 and Zeph 2:15: אני ואפסי עוד. Further, in Isa 45:22, אני־אל ואין עוד, "I am God and there is none other," and Isa 46:9, אנכי אל ואין עוד אלהים ואפס, "I am God and there is none other, I am God and there is no one like me."

6. The same expression, בני המלך, can mean "king's sons" or "king's children." I chose to read it as inclusive since no textual reason exists to limit the reference to one gender.

the ancient versions, though versification is largely consistent across the versions. The singular exception is LXX 3:1 which is 2:15 in the MT, DSS, Targum, Peshitta, and Vulgate. Zephaniah is well represented among the Dead Sea finds.[7] In addition, Zephaniah spawned at least two now fragmentary commentaries or *pesharim* on Zephaniah from caves 1 and 4: 1QpZephaniah 1:18–2:2 and 4QpZephaniah 1:12-13 at Qumran. Also in existence is a fragmentary fourth-century Coptic *Apocalypse of Zephaniah*, some or all of which was known to Clement.[8]

I have divided Zephaniah's proclamations into six prophecies.[9] I rely largely on the ס breaks[10] in the Masoretic Text:

  I.  Superscription 1:1

 II.  Prophecy 1: Zephaniah 1:2-9

III.  Prophecy 2: Zephaniah 1:10-18

 IV.  Prophecy 3: Zephaniah 2:1-3[11]

  V.  Prophecy 4: Zephaniah 2:4-15

 VI.  Prophecy 5: Zephaniah 3:1-13

VII.  Prophecy 6: Zephaniah 3:14-20

---

7. A number of scrolls and fragments of the Twelve come from cave 4: 4QXII[b] (Zeph 1:2; 2:13-15; 3:19), 4QXII[c] (Zeph 2:15), 4QXII[e] (Zeph 1:4-6, 9-10, 13-14; 2:10-14; 3:4–4:4; 5:8; 8:3-4, 6-7; 12:7-12), and 4QXII[g] (Zeph 3:3-5). Additionally, a scroll of the Twelve exists from Muraba'at, MurXII. This scroll contains Zeph 1:1; 1:11–3:6; 3:8-20. These Hebrew traditions are largely congruent with the Masoretic Text (MT). In existence is also a Greek manuscript that includes Zephaniah from Nahal Hever, 8HevXIIgr with Zeph 1:1-6, 13-18; 2:9-10; 3:6-7.

8. See *Stromateis* 5.11.77.

9. I am using "proclamations" to describe the content of Zephaniah and "prophecies" to describe discrete prophetic units within the book.

10. In the MT individual passages are delineated with a soft break marked with a ס and a hard break indicated by a פ, most often at the end of a verse.

11. Though the ס break follows Zeph 2:4, I am breaking the text at v. 3 because the proclamation against the Philistine cities fits better with the proclamations against foreign nations in 2:5-15.

# Zephaniah 1:1-9

## *Zephaniah and the Day of YHWH: Sea, Won't You Hide Me?*

### Superscription (Zeph 1:1)

The elements of Zephaniah's superscription require significant discussion. The name Zephaniah likely means "hidden," "secreted," or "treasured" by YHWH as in the hiding of Moses, which uses the same verb, צָפַן, in Exodus 2:2. The name is well represented in seals and seal impressions (*bullae*) primarily from the sixth to eighth centuries BCE; the *Dictionary of Classical Hebrew* (*DCH*) identifies fifteen of these seals.[1] The prophet Zephaniah is not attested in other biblical literature; however, in the Hebrew Scriptures, the name Zephaniah is shared by three or four persons, all of whom are associated with Jerusalem:

1) Zephaniah ben Tahath was a Kohathite psalmist (1 Chr 6:36 [1 Chr 6:21 MT]).[2]

---

1. David J. A. Clines, ed., *The Dictionary of Classical Hebrew*, vol. צ-ר (Sheffield: Sheffield Phoenix, 2011), 152.
2. Someone else is identified as ben Tahath in 1 Chr 6:24 (1 Chr 6:9 MT).

*Zephaniah 1:1*

¹:¹The word of the Lᴏʀᴅ that came to Zephaniah son of Cushi son of Gedaliah son of Amariah son of Hezekiah, in the days of King Josiah son of Amon of Judah.

2) Zephaniah ben Maaseiah was the second-ranked priest in the temple hierarchy at the time of the Babylonian exile (Jer 52:24-27 and 2 Kgs 25:18-21).

3) Josiah ben Zephaniah functions as a makeshift treasurer in Zechariah 6:10-14. His father, Zephaniah, is not further identified.[3]

4) Zephaniah ben Cushi ben Gedaliah ben Amariah ben Hezekiah is the prophet to whom the book that bears his name is attributed.

The form of the superscription in Zephaniah is a common formula, duplicated in the respective first verses of Hosea and Micah: "The word of Gᴏᴅ that came[4] to [PN][5] in the days of [monarch's PN] of [monarchy]." Amos's superscription deviates slightly from the pattern; it incorporates his shepherding context in Tekoa. Joel and Jonah have abbreviated forms that omit the personal names of the relevant monarchs. Jeremiah has multiple superscriptions that vary the end of the form to add a specific context: "concerning the drought" (14:1), "concerning the nations" (46:1), "concerning the Philistines before Pharaoh struck Gaza" (47:1), and "concerning Elam, at the beginning of the reign of King Zedekiah of Judah" (49:34).

The vast bulk of Zephaniah's superscription is the disclosure of the prophet Zephaniah's identity. Zephaniah's genealogy is fifteen out of the superscription's twenty words in Hebrew. Zephaniah's five-generation pedigree is by far the longest of the prophetic genealogies.[6] According

---

3. John Berridge considers the Zephaniah in Zech 6 to be the father of Josiah and offers the possibility that he may be the same person as Zephaniah ben Maaseiah in Jer 52:24-27 and 2 Kgs 25:18-21; see "Zephaniah," *ABD*, 6:1075.

4. The phrase דבר־יהוה אשר היה אל is literally "the word of YHWH that happened to X," suggesting a multisensory encounter with the word rather than the traditional "the word of the YHWH came to X."

5. Hosea's PN (personal name) includes genealogy; Micah's does not. Micah's genealogy includes a geographic reference; Hosea's genealogy does not.

6. Of the fifteen prophets with books attributed to them in the Hebrew Bible, seven are presented as "Name *ben* X." The rest have no genealogy but only occasional references to homeland or other descriptive information. The fifteen Latter Prophets are

to the text, Zephaniah's ancestors are: his father Cushi, his grandfather Gedaliah, his great-grandfather Amariah, and his great-great-grandfather Hezekiah, *if* the genealogy contains no gaps. The second and fifth names, Cushi and Hezekiah, have provoked the most scholarly investigation. The length and composition of the genealogy is the subject of much scholarly speculation. A common but not universally accepted understanding is that the genealogy stretches back to King Hezekiah of Judah, reading the otherwise uncharacterized "Hezekiah" as the venerated monarch and the lengthy genealogy as a disclosure of Zephaniah's noble heritage. Alternative interpretations consider the length of the genealogy an attempt to legitimize Zephaniah because of his father's name and what they imagine it reveals. In those arguments (see below) Hezekiah is either the monarch or non-royal Israelite or Judean with the same culturally significant name. As is common in the prophetic books, Zephaniah is not called a prophet in the work credited to him.[7]

## *Zephaniah ben Cushi*

Zephaniah is the son or descendant[8] of a person identified as Cushi, a name that evokes the ancient African nation of Nubia called Kush/Cush in the Hebrew Bible. This area corresponds with parts of contemporary Egypt, Sudan, and Ethiopia. Likewise, according to the legendary genealogy in Genesis 10:6-20, Cush, כוש, is the ancestor of peoples in North, East, and Central Africa, Mesopotamia, and Canaan. Cush will come to be identified with ancient Ethiopia via its translation as Αἰθιοπία, *Aithiopia*, in the Greek-speaking world. The LXX simply transliterates Cush as Χους more frequently[9] than it translates it as Αἰθιοπία, Ethiopia.[10] The etymology of the Greek term Αἰθιοπία, Ethiopia, "burnt face,"[11] seems

---

Isaiah, Jeremiah, Ezekiel, and the Twelve (Minor Prophets). Daniel, though grouped with the prophets in the LXX and Christian Bibles that are based on the LXX, is placed with the Writings in the Hebrew Bible.

7. Only Habakkuk, Haggai, and Zechariah are called prophets in the superscriptions to their books.

8. Whether or not names in a genealogy represent only the space of a single generation is uncertain. Some genealogical formulae intentionally skip generations as in the case of "son of David."

9. Gen 10:6-8; 2 Sam 18:21-23, 31-32; 1 Chr 1:8-10.

10. Gen 2:13; Num 12:1; Hab 3:7.

11. Αἰθίοψ stems from αἴθω, "burned," and ὄψ, "face," therefore "swarthy face" (*Thayer's Greek-English Lexicon of the New Testament*), "blackamoor" (*Strong's Greek Lexicon*), and "burnt-face" and "negro" (Liddell and Scott, *An Intermediate Greek-English*

to communicate a phenotypic component to the identities of Cush and Cushites that most interpreters have understood to mean that Nubians had darker skin than their Afro-Asiatic neighbors.[12] The only physical description of the Nubians in the Hebrew Scriptures is גוי ממשך ומורט, "a nation tall and smooth," in Isaiah 18:2 and 7.[13] Cush also functions as an element in several names. Cush is the proper name for at least one other Israelite, namely, Cush of Benjamin[14] in the superscription to Psalm 7, and Cush appears as an onomastic element in the name of a Mesopotamian[15] monarch, Cushan-rishathaim in Judges 3:8, 10.

Cushi, כושי, Zephaniah's father's name, is a gentilic in form, i.e., "Cushite," which would normally mean a person with a Cushite ethnic identity. The apparent gentilic form raises the question for some scholars as to whether Cushi is indeed a personal name (either given at birth or a moniker based on his appearance), an ethnic identity indicator, or a combination of the two. The question ignores the fact that Cushi does not occur with the definite article in the superscription, which would indisputably identify it as a gentilic, i.e., "the Cushite." Therefore, I argue that what is being signaled is a personal name, Cushi, not a person being

---

*Lexicon*). According to Herodotus, "The men of the country are black because of the heat"; see *Histories* 2.22.3. He is discussing the lands through which the Nile flows. Sections 1 and 2 make reference to Egypt, Libya, and Ethiopia.

12. In Western interpretation the base skin tone against which that "darker" has been constructed has been imagined to be white skin, ignoring the fact that biblical Israel is an Afro-Asiatic and not a European people. Some rabbinic speculation on Israelite phenotypes, however, presumed a brown base tone or a range of colors from black to white. In B. Bek. 45b: *A-white-man should not marry a white-woman lest they produce* בוהק, *a-too-white-child, and a-black-man should not marry a-black-woman lest they produce* טפוח, *a-too-black-child*; in m. Neg. 2:1: *R. Ishmael stated: the children of Israel—may I be an atonement for them!—are like eshcara-wood neither black nor white but of an intermediate shade*. For further exploration of blackness in rabbinic texts, see Wil Gafney, "It Does Matter If You're Black or White, Too Black or Too White, but Mestizo Is Just Right," in *Re-Presenting Texts: Jewish and Black Biblical Interpretation*, ed. W. David Nelson and Rivka Ulmer, Society of Biblical Literature Consultation on Midrash (Piscataway, NJ: Gorgias, 2013), 43–51.

13. The RSV and NRSV translate the description as "tall and smooth"; Joseph Blenkinsopp renders the phrase as "hairless and anomalously elongated" in *Isaiah 1–39*, AB 19 (New Haven: Yale University Press, 1974), 308. Some significant disagreement exists, however, among ancient and contemporary texts as to whether the expression is even a physical description, let alone positive or negative.

14. The reading is contested: LXX has Χουσι, Cushi, in the form of a personal name, while the Targum makes the Benjaminite Saul ben Kish of Benjamin.

15. *Aram-naharaim* is "Aram of the-two-rivers," a euphemism for Mesopotamia, known for its two rivers: the Tigris and Euphrates.

described as a Cushite; this reading, however, does not mitigate against Cushite heritage for Zephaniah and his father (see below). In support of this reading, the name Cushi recurs for a different person in a genealogy almost as long as Zephaniah's genealogy, specifically, Jehudi ben Nethaniah ben Shelemiah ben Cushi in Jeremiah 36:14. Furthermore, the LXX, Targum, Peshitta, and Vulgate omit the definite article in the Hebrew text of 2 Samuel 18:21-31 and record Cushi/Χουσι as a personal name there as well, signaling an ancient understanding that Cushi was indeed a personal name. In Zephaniah the name Cushi is connected with the land of Cush/Kush, Nubia, which appears repeatedly in the text (see Zeph 2:10; 3:12).

Speculation about the name, origin, race, and ethnicity of (either) Cushi reveals much about the assumptions and understanding of race that shape biblical scholars and our scholarship.[16] Questioning whether Cushi is a gentilic and whether it indicates African identity is extremely freighted in a Western interpreting context, particularly in the Americas. Constructions of race and ethnicity read into and out of the Bible justified the colonization of Africa, Asia, and the Americas, the institutionalization of race-based slavery, and the dispossession and attempted genocide of indigenous peoples. Persons of African descent have looked for persons of African descent in the Scriptures to affirm their worth and dignity virtually from the introduction of the Scriptures. Seeking such affirmation in the Scriptures was tantamount to using the Scriptures against themselves—or, better, their use against subjugated communities as an implement of domination, occupation, and colonization.[17] Scholarly efforts to understand what is being signified by the name Cushi occur within these contexts. Interpretations that presume the name Cushi and its association with African lands and people were perceived negatively in biblical texts derive from postbiblical constructions of race, valorization of whiteness,[18] and demonization and othering of blackness. These elements were and are

---

16. For example, see the baseless claim that Cushi was a slave because he was black as pointed out by Judith E. Sanderson, "Zephaniah," in *The Women's Bible Commentary*, ed. Carol A. Newsom and Sharon H. Ringe (Louisville: Westminster John Knox, 1998), 240.

17. Such "Blacks in the Bible" projects often seemed to accept the Eurocentric premise that biblical characters were white with a few exceptions. Focus on the introduction of the Scriptures to persons of African descent and attempts to identify African characters in the text can discount the significance of the geographical contexts of the Scriptures and their peoples and neglect the implications of that Afro-Asiatic context.

18. The valorization of whiteness is one aspect of the white supremacist cultural and aesthetic values that underlie what is otherwise called "Western civilization."

pervasive in the context in which biblical scholarship occurred and occurs in the West, particularly from the seventeenth century forward.[19] Similarly, readings that presume a binary in which the name Cushi signals Cushite, Nubian, heritage over against Israelite identity are equally products of a world in which identity is racialized, in which whiteness is postulated as normative and the ideal against which others are identified. I accept the *plene* reading of Cushi as a proper name, which is not disconnected from the nation and people of Nubia, and I contend the name was likely part of Zephaniah's family onomasticon because of Cushite ancestry in his family. Still, some voices argue against an ethnically contextual reading of Cushi, to wit, Adele Berlin: "It is more likely, however, that Cushi is simply a personal name (cf. 'Cush the Benjaminite' in Ps 7:1). I see no reason to link it with Ethiopia or with a dark-skinned person. Nor do I perceive a connection with 'Cushites' in 2:12 or 'rivers of Cush' in 3:10."[20]

In truth, Israelite identity was complex and composite, incorporating multiethnic heritages normatively. The paternal reckoning of Israelite identity meant that the children of Israelite men with Israelite and non-Israelite women were legitimate. The practice was regular and recurrent. Hence the tradition of rape and abduction-marriage as acts of war comes into play.[21] Forced marriage and impregnation of captive women contributed to an Israel with diverse ethnic heritages. Notable examples of Israelites with plural heritages include Moses' own children with a Midianite wife (Exod 2:16-21)[22] and the offspring of a number of the patriarchs and their offspring, all of whom gave rise to a multiethnic Israel.[23] Intermarriage was a regular practice in ancient Israel in spite of its

19. See Rodney Steven Sadler's excellent survey of the relevant scholarship, *Can a Cushite Change His Skin? An Examination of Race, Ethnicity, and Othering in the Hebrew Bible* (New York: T & T Clark, 2005), 64–70.

20. Adele Berlin, *Zephaniah*, AB 25A (New Haven: Yale University Press, 1994), 67.

21. Rape-marriage is the forcible marriage of women and girls, regularly subsequent to military conquest and abduction on individual or corporate scales. Numbers 31:9-12, 17-18, 32-35 details Israelite rape-marriages with Midianite women; Judg 21:8-24 describes the Israelites abducting women from among their own people in the tribe of Gad at Jabesh-Gilead and from the sacred site of Shiloh. Rape-marriage coexists with virulent anti-exogamous language in the Torah (Deut 7:1-4) and Former Prophets (Josh 23:12-13) along with broad prohibitions against intermarriage for the priests (Lev 21:14-15).

22. If Moses had other unrecorded offspring with his second wife (Num 12:1), then they would have Nubian heritage.

23. Among the patriarchs who intermarried are Judah and Simeon, who married Canaanite women, and Joseph, who married the African (Egyptian) Asenath. These

selective but occasionally vociferous censure.[24] Nubians were present in the Levant, and in Judah in particular, from the fourteenth to the seventh centuries BCE.[25] They were prominent and well integrated into Judean society in the eighth and seventh centuries and therefore were available for intermarriage.[26] The offspring of Israelite or Judean men with Nubian women would be recognized as Judeans. They, in turn, would become appropriate Judean marriage partners, generating generations of legitimate Judean children with Nubian heritage.

The choice of the name Cushi most likely reflects Cushite identity of Zephaniah's grandmother, the wife of Gedaliah, and/or her family, or possibly a more distant relative. Such intermarriage likely also accounts for Jehudi ben Nethaniah ben Shelemiah ben Cushi in Jeremiah 36:14.[27] The marriage of high-ranking Judean men in the military or royal bureaucracy to Nubian women and their offspring would account for the presence of persons with Nubian ancestry with access to the highest levels of the Israelite military and monarchy. The presence of Nubians in biblical narratives is not treated as an uncommon phenomenon. Examples include the Nubian messenger[28] serving David and Joab in 2 Samuel 18:21-31 and the Cushite who prompted the writing of Psalm 7 (framed as an enemy of David but not because of his identity/ethnicity). That an Israelite would have Nubian ancestry just as some Israelites had Egyptian heritage is not only possible but also unremarkable based on biblical narratives.[29]

---

intermarriages meant that the twelve Israelite tribes came from diverse ethnic stock, and, in the case of the half-tribes of Ephraim and Manasseh, they were fully half Egyptian or African.

24. Abduction and rape-marriage of enemy girls and women was sanctioned (and occasionally sanctified by prophetic or even divine commandment), but voluntary intermarriage was regularly opposed—sometimes lethally. Compare the command to save enemy girls and women in Num 31:18 with the execution of Cozbi bat Zur and Zimri ben Salu in Num 25:6-9. Additionally repeated injunctions not to marry foreign women are given (Deut 7:3; Ezra 9:12; Neh 10:30; 13:25).

25. See Sadler, *Can a Cushite*, 40–45, 63–69, 78–80, 108–11.

26. Gene Rice, "The African Roots of the Prophet Zephaniah," *JRT* 36 (1979): 24.

27. Ibid., 28.

28. The messenger is called "the Cushite" repeatedly (הכושי, לכושי) but on one occasion in 2 Sam 18:21 appears without the definite article, an apparent haplography.

29. P. Kyle McCarter Jr., *II Samuel*, AB 9 (New Haven: Yale University Press, 1974), 408. See also Marvin A. Sweeney, *Zephaniah: A Commentary on the Book of Zephaniah*, ed. Paul D. Hanson, Hermeneia 36 (Minneapolis: Fortress, 2003), 49.

*Amariah ben Hezekiah, Gedaliah ben Amariah*

The third and fourth names in Zephaniah's genealogy, Gedaliah and Amariah, occur repeatedly in the Hebrew Scriptures, five and ten times, respectively, though none of these persons can be identified with the persons of the same name in Zephaniah's lineage.[30] The identification of Amariah and Gedaliah in Zephaniah's genealogy is largely dependent on the identity of Hezekiah—Gedaliah is ben Amariah and Amariah is ben Hezekiah. I presume Hezekiah to be King Hezekiah of Judah (discussed below), though no other reference to Amariah ben Hezekiah who appears in Zephaniah's genealogy is extant. The options for understanding the inclusion of Amariah (and his son Gedaliah) in Zephaniah's genealogy but not in the genealogies of Hezekiah in Kings and Chronicles are that Amariah ben Hezekiah was either unknown to the compiler(s) of the genealogies in Kings and Chronicles or known but deemed insignificant to them. I contend that Amariah was indeed the son of King Hezekiah of Judah, but as neither his heir nor a combatant attempting to seize the throne, he, like the bulk of other offspring, daughters or sons, was excluded from the royal genealogies.

Royal genealogies in Kings and Chronicles trace the lineage of Judean monarchs and regularly limit[31] the mention of offspring to successors,[32] those competing for succession,[33] and, in some cases, those who experience horrific fates[34] deemed germane to the narrative. The fact that these royal succession genealogies accurately represent the progeny of the monarchs is unfeasible for a number of reasons. The polygyny of Israelite and Judean monarchs, like that of monarchs throughout the ancient world—and parts of the modern world—is well documented. The number of royal offspring recorded in the Hebrew Bible does not

---

30. See the corresponding entries in the *ABD*: Roger Utti, "Amariah," 1:173, and Robert Althan, "Gedaliah," 2:923–24.

31. David is a notable exception; his progeny are named in some detail in the Hebrew Bible. See 2 Sam 5:13-16; 1 Chr 3:1-9.

32. That is the case for the Judean monarchs listed in 1 Chr 3:10-17 and the introduction of each successive monarch in Kings, i.e., 1 Kgs 15:1-2, 9-10, etc.

33. The detailed listing of David's potential heirs forms the background of the struggle for succession even before his death. A similar case can be made for the mention of Josiah's four sons in 1 Chr 3:15, several of whom served as or were designated as his successor during the decline of the Judean state. See also 2 Kgs 23:30, 34; Jer 37:1.

34. Amnon's rape of Tamar and Absalom's assassination of Amnon in 2 Sam 13 and Ahab's seventy sons executed by Jehu in 2 Kgs 10:1-7 are examples of such horrific fates that advance the narratives in which they are embedded.

correspond to reasonable expectations of fertility, given the number of sex partners listed (and those that can be reasonably inferred). Neither do reported offspring correspond meaningfully to the lifespans of monarchs as recorded.

For example, in spite of reckoning seven hundred royal women among Solomon's primary wives and crediting him with three hundred secondary wives (1 Kgs 11:3), the Hebrew Bible acknowledges only a single son fathered by Solomon, namely, his successor Rehoboam. In a narrative about his administrative prowess, Solomon is credited with two daughters, Taphath and Basemath, who are married to some of his bureaucrats in 1 Kings 4:11, 15. Rehoboam's dual genealogies prove the case in point. His royal genealogy lists a single son, his successor Abijah, in 1 Chronicles 3:10 while the narrative in 2 Chronicles 11:21-23 credits him with sixty daughters and twenty-eight sons from his eighteen primary and sixty secondary wives. The rare acknowledgment of Rehoboam's fertility buttresses the David mythos since the woman Rehoboam loves above all others is Maacah bat Absalom ben David (2 Chr 11:21).

The relative lack of royal daughters mentioned in the Hebrew Bible is not simply an artifact of the ratio of female to male characters in the canon. One effect of limiting the record of a monarch's offspring to his— or in Athaliah's case, her—successor is the near elimination of royal daughters from the Hebrew Bible except when they are deemed to serve a narrative purpose.[35] Surprisingly, a significant number of royal wives,[36] particularly queen mothers, exist,[37] most of whose names are preserved, which further highlights the paucity of royal daughters in the Hebrew Bible. Most likely, Hezekiah has daughters as well as sons who are not

35. See the stories of Merab and Michal, Saul's daughters (1 Sam 14:49; 18-19; 2 Sam 3:13-14; 6:16-23; 21:8-9), and the abducted princesses in Jer 41:16 and 43:6.

36. Some twenty primary or major royal wives are named in the Hebrew Bible; factoring in all of the women with whom David produced children adds at least another eight to fourteen, depending in part on whether the offspring listed in 1 Chr 3:5 has one or more mothers. I discuss all of these royal women at some length in Wilda Gafney, *Womanist Midrash: A Reintroduction to the Women of the Torah and of the Throne* (Louisville: Westminster John Knox, 2017).

37. The senior royal woman in Judah was the mother, not wife, of the ruling monarch. Some were graced with the title גבירה, Great Lady, which indicates that a Queen Mother could be suspended from some official duties. See 1 Kgs 15:13 // 2 Chr 15:16; see also 2 Kgs 10:13; Jer 13:18; 29:2. The title is also used for royal women in other contexts (1 Kgs 11:19) and for slaveholding women (Gen 16:4, 8; 2 Kgs 5:3; Isa 24:3, etc.).

recorded in his official genealogy, thus making the genealogical claims in Zephaniah's superscription reasonable and feasible.

Zephaniah is not the only text claiming offspring for Hezekiah omitted by his royal genealogies. Sennacherib's account of his assault on Jerusalem attributes an unknown number of daughters to Hezekiah.[38] In Sennacherib's chronicle, Hezekiah sends his daughters and other "palace women," likely as royal hostages, with a heavy tribute to Sennacherib. The account is noteworthy for its intersection with the biblical narrative in 2 Kings 18:13-18, particularly its specification of the exact amount of gold given in tribute in the biblical narrative. According to verse 14, this tribute amounted to thirty talents. Variances between the accounts can be explained by reluctance on the part of biblical tradents to reveal the full extent of Hezekiah's submission and/or some exaggeration on the part of Sennacherib. Mordechai Cogan and Hayim Tadmor make the intriguing suggestion that the Assyrian reckoning of the silver tribute (eight hundred talents) exceeds the biblical tally (three hundred talents) because the Assyrian reckoning includes the value of silver stripped from the temple doors (see 2 Kgs 18:16), though the biblical account mentions only gold taken from the doors.[39]

That Amariah ben Hezekiah as well as the unnamed daughters attributed to Hezekiah by Sennacherib would be excluded from the royal genealogies focusing on succession is feasible. Also reasonable is that Zephaniah would know his own lineage, particularly if it connected him to one of Judah's great monarchs. The otherwise unknown Amariah and Gedaliah in Zephaniah's genealogy are best understood if King Hezekiah of Judah is their father and grandfather. Thus, their identities hang on the identity of Hezekiah in Zephaniah's genealogy.

I suggest that Amariah was a child of Hezekiah's latter years, born after Manasseh. It is unlikely Amariah was Manasseh's older brother. It is hard to imagine the text remaining silent on the passing over of a firstborn son to succeed his father as monarch. It is possible to calculate that Hezekiah fathered the son who would succeed him, Manasseh, at forty-two based on: (1) his age at ascension, twenty-five, (2) length of rule, twenty-nine years, and (3) the age of Manasseh at his ascension,

---

38. William W. Hallo and K. Lawson Younger Jr., "Sennacherib's Siege of Jerusalem," in *The Contexts of Scripture*, vol. 2: *Monumental Inscriptions* (Leiden: Brill, 2003), 302–3.

39. Mordechai Cogan and Hayim Tadmor, *II Kings*, AB 11 (Garden City, NY: Doubleday, 1974), 229.

twelve.[40] In the ancient world, for a man in his forties to father his first son would be remarkable if not impossible, given that most men married and began producing children in their teens. The length of Hezekiah's rule would have given him an additional twelve years after the birth of Manasseh to father another son—indeed, many children of both genders.

## Hezekiah

The fifth and last name in Zephaniah's genealogy would seem to be the most significant since the genealogy is deliberately extended beyond the customary range to include this particular Hezekiah. The Hebrew Bible features either two or three persons named Hezekiah, depending on whether the Hezekiah in Zephaniah's genealogy is indeed King Hezekiah of Judah. In addition to Hezekiah the king of Judah who reigned from 715 to 687 BCE, another Hezekiah—also called Ater in Ezra 2:16 and Nehemiah 7:21 and 10:17—comes to the fore.[41] If the Hezekiah in Zephaniah's genealogy is not the monarch of Judah, then he is a third distinct Hezekiah since Zephaniah's ancestor Hezekiah would have lived at least four generations before the seventh-century setting of the book of Zephaniah. The Hezekiah that appears in Ezra–Nehemiah is set two centuries later, specifically in the fifth century BCE. I understand Zephaniah's forebear Hezekiah to be the sovereign of Judah since no other Hezekiah who dates from the appropriate period appears in the canon and/or is significant enough to justify a four-generation genealogy. This conclusion has sparked disagreement among scholars with some proffering the notion of a distinguished but nonroyal Hezekiah as a character reference to compensate for the imagined stain of Cushite ancestry.[42] That argument is rooted in postbiblical racism and constructions of race, not the biblical canon. The argument also fails on efficacy since an alternative Hezekiah and his bona fides cannot be identified. As is often the case with biblical genealogies, the length of a generation is difficult to ascertain, and the time frame represented does not easily

40. Michael Ufok Udoekpo, *Re-Thinking the Day of YHWH and Restoration of Fortunes in the Prophet Zephaniah: An Exegetical and Theological Study of 1:14-18; 3:14-20* (Bern: Lang, 2010), 84.

41. Gary Herion, "Hezekiah" and Jonathan Rosenbaum, "Hezekiah King of Judah," in *ABD*, 3:189.

42. See Joseph Blenkinsopp, *A History of Prophecy in Israel* (Louisville: Westminster John Knox, 1996), 150.

correlate with other dating indications in the text.[43] Finally, a family connection to the monarch Hezekiah and his prophet Isaiah and their generally favorable relationship may account for the amount of inter-textuality between the two works.[44]

Few legitimate difficulties exist for reading the Hezekiah in Zepha-niah's lineage as the Judean monarch. The conflict between Zephaniah's account of Hezekiah's genealogy and the extant royal genealogies of He-zekiah that attribute only one son, Manasseh, to Hezekiah in 2 Kings 20:21 and 1 Chronicles 3:13 is easily resolved by the fact that royal genealogies regularly limit offspring to the successor of the monarch. The Peshitta's identification of the distal ancestor as "Hilkiah" against all of the other textual witnesses is a minority report; yet, it merits consideration.[45]

At least ten men in the Hebrew Scriptures are named Hilkiah, ex-cluding the one who appears in Judith's genealogy.[46] Since the lengthy genealogy would seem to connect Zephaniah to an exceptionally sig-nificant ancestor, Hilkiah would have to be prominent. The most likely candidates would be Hilkiah who managed Hezekiah's household (2 Kgs 18:37) and Ezra's great-grandfather (Ezra 7:1). Whether they are the same person remains unclear.[47] Hilkiah, the high priest who served under Josiah (2 Kgs 22:3-4), and Jeremiah's father (Jer 1:1), also named Hilkiah, are not feasible for chronological reasons. That the Peshitta does not identify Hilkiah further to make him clearly known mitigates against this reading if the purpose is to present an ancestor of some standing. Reading with the MT, LXX, Qumran texts, Targum, and the Vulgate against the Peshitta, the lengthy genealogy links Zephaniah with Hezekiah the Judean monarch. Hezekiah was arguably the most significant Judean monarch after the division of the monarchies. Given the lack of direct contact between Zephaniah and Josiah, the ancestral link to King Hezekiah of Judah—their shared great-grandfather—may be an alternative set of bona fides for Zephaniah.

---

43. Udoekpo, *Re-Thinking the Day of YHWH*, 85.

44. Carol J. Dempsey, *Amos, Hosea, Micah, Nahum, Zephaniah, Habakkuk*, New Collegeville Bible Commentary 15 (Collegeville, MN: Liturgical Press, 2013), 120.

45. Marvin A. Sweeney notes that in some Old Aramaic scripts *zayin* and *lammed* are easily confused so חלקיה/חלקיהו, "Hilkiah," might be a misreading of חזקיה/חזקיהו, "Hezekiah" (*Zephaniah*, 48).

46. Roger Utti, "Hilkiah," in *ABD*, 3:200.

47. Utti (ibid.) understands that Ezra's father is Josiah's high priest, while others reckon Ezra's father is Hezekiah's chamberlain (see Berlin, *Zephaniah*, 66).

*Setting of Zephaniah*

According to the superscription, Zephaniah prophesies in the days of King Josiah ben Amon of Judah who reigned from 640 to 601 BCE. The text does not acknowledge any contact between Zephaniah and Josiah, though Zephaniah's first proclamation rhetorically addresses the monarch's offspring in Zephaniah 1:8. Nothing indicates that Zephaniah delivered any of his prophecies in person to the monarch, to any member of the royal family, or to any officials.

The setting of Zephaniah is roughly contemporaneous with the books of Nahum (663–612 BCE)[48] and Jeremiah (626–586 BCE). Arguably dating from the early seventh century in which the text is set, Zephaniah's preaching follows the preaching of Amos and Hosea in the North (both mid-eighth century BCE) and Micah and Isaiah in the South (who follow shortly thereafter). Zephaniah likely overlaps with the prophets Micah and Isaiah; certainly some contact exists between the corpora. Zephaniah 2:12 may anticipate or refer to the fall of Kush[49] between 666 and 664 BCE. Similarly, the following verses in Zephaniah 2:13-15 interpret or predict the fall of Nineveh and Assyria in 612 BCE. At the very least, in Zephaniah Assyria is in decline but still a force with which to be reckoned. The lack of a prophecy against Egypt in Zephaniah suggests a time when Egypt was in such decline it was not imagined to be able to recover. Egypt's decline would place the collection before Egypt reconstituted its coastal holdings between 633 and 618 BCE.[50] No mention of Babylonia is made.

Locating Zephaniah's individual prophecies with respect to Josiah's reign and reform is difficult. The critiques of idolatry could have been given in support of the reform or afterward to stamp out any remaining residue. References to the king's children or sons could refer to either Josiah and his siblings or to his own children. Given that Josiah was so young (eight years old) when he ascended the throne, Zephaniah's preaching could have functioned to set the tone for the new regime. This tone would have been one of fidelity to God, which was in stark opposition to the tone of Josiah's father and grandfather, the notorious idolaters Manasseh and Amon, respectively.

48. See the dating of Nahum in my introduction earlier in this volume.
49. "Kush" denotes the ancient African nation also known as Nubia. "Cush" is the traditional rendering of כוש the biblical nation (and an element in some personal names) that is identified with Kush and associated with the Garden of Eden and Mesopotamia in Genesis traditions.
50. Berlin, *Zephaniah*, 119.

## Prophecy 1 (Zeph 1:2-9)

The prophecies of Zephaniah are shocking. His first words announce the end[51] of everything on the surface ("face," פְּנֵי) of the earth.[52] This prophecy, like the bulk of those that follow, presents God as speaking in the first person. In other proclamations the prophet will interrupt God as if to elucidate the divine declamation.[53] This initial prophecy has two portions: verses 2-6 announce God's judgment and punishment, and verses 7-9 are the first[54] of two reflections on the day of YHWH.

Verse 2 is a six-word stand-alone prophecy (in Hebrew) declaring the end of everything, buttressed by the formula "an utterance of GOD." Translation and interpretation of the first two words are entirely dependent on their vowels because these words are consonantally identical, אסף אסף. The Masoretes vocalize the phrase as *asef asof*, reading it as two different verbs, the infinitive absolute אסף, "gather," followed by the first-person jussive of סוף, "destroy," in the Hiphil, meaning "I will utterly destroy." Alternatively, it is common for the conjugated form to follow the infinitive absolute of the same lexeme to indicate certainty, i.e., "truly, truly"[55] as the LXX (Ἐκλείψει ἐκλιπέτω) and Targum (שיצי אישיצי) render the phrase. The Peshitta supplies an external pronoun (*m'brw m'br*) and reads both verbs as "gather," i.e., "I will remove." The Vulgate defaults to "gather" but in the sense of "assemble" (*congregans congregabo*). These words seem to have been chosen for their phonemes and their verbal articulation. Whether the verbs are "sweep," "end/destroy," or one of each, the sense is that God definitively acts and nothing can endure that force. The verb is repeated in verse 3, "I [God] will sweep away—or destroy—human and animal. I will sweep/destroy fish of the sea."[56] What is occurring here is the undoing of creation, a reversal of its generation in Genesis 1. When read in this way the opening phrase of Zephaniah's prophecies becomes one of a series of six first-person verbs through which God brings about the day of YHWH.

---

51. אסף אסף, *asof asef*, "I will surely bring to an end."

52. Zephaniah addresses Judah and Jerusalem and foreign nations; in the corpus ארץ refers to both the land of Judah and the whole earth, sometimes slightly more one than the other.

53. Sweeney, *Zephaniah*, 102.

54. The second discourse on the day of YHWH is in the second prophecy, Zeph 1:10-18.

55. E.g., "in the day that you eat of [the tree of life], מות תמות, you shall surely die" (Gen 2:17).

56. In Zeph 3:8, 18, אסף appears as "gather."

*Zephaniah 1:2-9*

²I will utterly sweep away
everything
from the face of the earth, says
the LORD.
³I will sweep away humans and
animals;
I will sweep away the birds of
the air
and the fish of the sea.
I will make the wicked stumble.
I will cut off humanity
from the face of the earth, says
the LORD.
⁴I will stretch out my hand against
Judah,
and against all the inhabitants
of Jerusalem;
and I will cut off from this place
every remnant of Baal
and the name of the idolatrous
priests;
⁵those who bow down on the roofs
to the host of the heavens;

those who bow down and swear
to the LORD,
but also swear by Milcom;
⁶those who have turned back from
following the LORD,
who have not sought the LORD
or inquired of him.

⁷Be silent before the Lord GOD!
For the day of the LORD is at
hand;
the Lord has prepared a sacrifice,
he has consecrated his guests.
⁸And on the day of the LORD's
sacrifice
I will punish the officials and the
king's sons
and all who dress themselves
in foreign attire.
⁹On that day I will punish
all who leap over the threshold,
who fill their master's house
with violence and fraud.

In the following verses, Zephaniah details the layers of annihilation. This annihilation will encompass all[57] life on the surface of the earth, as represented by humankind and animals, including the extinction of the birds above and the fish below the surface of the earth. The language is evocative of the deluge (Gen 6:7; 7:4; 8:8) but should not be identified with it.[58] Curiously, flora is not mentioned. The wicked receive special attention; they are sentenced to "stumbling"[59] before they and the rest of humanity are cut off from the surface of the earth.

57. Zephaniah uses the word "all" repeatedly—"all the inhabitants of Jerusalem" (1:4), "all the inhabitants of the earth" (1:18), and "all the earth" (3:8). His repeated pronouncements of total destruction, however, are followed by accounts of survivors and remnants.
58. See Sweeney, *Zephaniah*, 63.
59. "Stumbling blocks," or perhaps "ruin" (see Isa 3:6, the only other occurrence), is an object of the sweeping. The Hebrew is not clear here.

In verse 4 the prophecy turns toward Judah and Jerusalem and reveals the reason for the harsh judgment—the worship of Baal Haddu[60] (who receives a feminine article in the LXX and is identified as a goddess in the NETS).[61] In the Hebrew Bible Baal refers to the Canaanite storm god often presented as God's chief rival for Israel's devotion. Extirpation of Baal worship was a key element of Josiah's purge in 2 Kings 23:3-20; however, Josiah's purge extended far beyond the elements named in Zephaniah. Josiah's reform also targeted the worship of Asherah and Molech (2 Kgs 23:4, 6-7, 10), the vestments or houses of foreign male religious officiants (2 Kgs 23:7),[62] idolatrous priests and the worship of astrological phenomenon (2 Kgs 23:5), legitimate priests who presided in places other than the Jerusalem temple (2 Kgs 23:8-9), foreign elements in the temple (2 Kgs 23:11), the personal altars of Amon and Manasseh (2 Kgs 23:12), altars Solomon built for Astarte, Chemosh, and Milcom (2 Kgs 23:13), sacred pillars (2 Kgs 23:14), and the shrines at Bethel and Samaria (2 Kgs 23:15, 18-20). Zephaniah's focus on Baal (1:4), Milcom (1:5), and the idolatrous priests (1:4) may indicate that Josiah's purge was largely successful insofar as only a remnant of the former practices endured. God's declaration in Zephaniah 1:4, "I [will] stretch out [נטה] my hand [against]," anticipates a catastrophic recompense for idolatry. The expression occurs about ten times, primarily in the prophetic litera-ture.[63] Its object is more often than not a foreign land or people. Only here in Zephaniah 1:4 and Ezekiel 16:27 is the quarry Judah/Jerusalem.

---

60. Haddu is the personal name of the deity more commonly known by the title *baal* which means "lord," "master," or, occasionally, "husband."

61. Baal regularly receives the feminine article in the LXX and often is translated as a goddess or "She-Baal"; see, e.g., Judg 2:13; 4 Rgs 1:2–3, 6, 16; 21:3; 2 Sup 23:17; Hos 2:8; 13:1; Soph 1:4; Jer 2:8, 23, 28; 7:9; 11:13, 17; 12:16; 19:5; 23:13, 27; 39:29, 35. (In the LXX Rgs, Reigns = Kings; Sup, Supplements = Chronicles; and Soph, Sophonias = Zephaniah.) The feminine Baal is a heifer in Tobit 1:5. See Albert Pietersma and Benjamin G. Wright, *A New English Translation of the Septuagint: And the Other Greek Translations Traditionally Included Under That Title* (New York: Oxford University Press, 2007).

62. For the difficulty in translating בתי, see Cogan and Tadmor, *II Kings*, 286. The NRSV translation of הקדשם as male "temple prostitutes" cannot be sustained. Simply no evidence exists that these religious workers (or their female counterparts not present in this text) used sex as part of their professional religious practice. They are holy persons, sacred to another deity, and therefore taboo.

63. Exod 7:5; Jer 6:12; 51:25; Ezek 6:14; 14:9, 13; 16:27; 25:13, 16; 35:3; Zeph 1:4. A synonymous expression with a different verb occurs in Exod 3:20, ושלחתי את ידי.

The rhetoric of Zephaniah indicts Israel's priests, הכהנים, along with idolatrous priests, הכמרים. The NRSV neglects the sanctioned priests; it collapses the two groups into one, while the Targum erases the scandalous priests. In the MT the idolatrous priests are עם, "among," "within," or "part of" the larger established community of Israel's priests.[64] The הכמרים priests are heterodox. They may be irregularly ordained or outside of the proper lineage, or they may worship deities other than Israel's God along with (not instead of) God.[65] Israel's syncretistic priests—those who worship Israel's God and a foreign deity[66] and those who have abandoned that God for another—receive the same fate as those who do not even bother to inquire of God. The active worship of foreign deities may suggest a time frame early in the reign of Josiah, before his reform and purge of competing religious traditions. Additionally, the language, "remnant of Baal," may indicate that the purge is in progress or largely completed.[67] Zephaniah's combined references to Judah, Jerusalem, and Baal traditions in "this place" suggest that he delivered this prophecy in Jerusalem, perhaps in the temple complex. He may have prophesied regularly or only in Jerusalem. Prophesying in Jerusalem would not necessarily mean Zephaniah was in the service of either temple or monarchy since he would not have to be in the employment of either to declaim at the temple and neither he, nor his superscription, nor any other text makes that claim on his behalf.

Zephaniah 1:5-7 forms a bridge between the two parts of the first prophecy. The proclamation builds on the rationale for the impending doom and then shifts to descriptions of the day of reckoning. The prophecy slips into the third person for God in verse 6. Whether God or Zephaniah is speaking is unclear. Many more shifts in the speaker's voice will occur throughout the book. This shift may indicate that the prophet is expanding on the divine prophecy, including the seemingly overlooked worship of Milcom and those who have turned from God and no longer seek God through prophetic inquiry. To "inquire," דרש, of the deity means

64. Berlin, *Zephaniah*, 74.
65. The term הכמרים occurs in the canon only in 2 Kgs 23:5 and Hos 10:5 along with Zeph 1:4. Of those passages, 2 Kgs 23:5 is the most instructive: "[Josiah] deposed the idolatrous priests whom the kings of Judah had ordained to make offerings in the high places at the cities of Judah and around Jerusalem; those also who made offerings to Baal, to the sun, the moon, the constellations, and all the host of the heavens." Outside of the Scriptures, however, the term occurs widely in the ANE as a normative term for priest; see the *Chicago Assyrian Dictionary* (*CAD*) 8:532–33, 534–35.
66. I address the deity called "Milcom" in the Translation Matters on p. 145.
67. Sweeney, *Zephaniah*, 63.

to consult God through a prophet; the verb is professional language for qualified specialists just as "diagnosis" refers to a medical examination by a trained and credentialed professional. Thus, one component of Zephaniah's possible interpolation may be self-serving. Since he will later reject other prophets as being "reckless" and "faithless" or "treacherous" (see Zeph 3:4), I find it likely that Zephaniah means people are not inquiring of God through him, which might mean a loss of income.[68]

Zephaniah cries out to an unseen audience and thus marks the transition from the judgment in the preceding verses to the day of YHWH. His cry is onomatopoetic סה, *has!* "Silence!" in verse 7. The cry is familiar from Habakkuk 2:20: "Silence in God's presence all the earth!" The use of the third person suggests that Zephaniah is the one who is speaking and not God. The call for silence precedes the first mention of the day of YHWH in Zephaniah and prepares its hearers for what is to follow.

In Zephaniah 1:7 the day of YHWH begins ominously with a sacrifice in which God is the donor and the officiant. The ritual element is lacking in the Targum; there the slaughter is generic killing, קטל, rather than sacrifice, זבח, and instead of being consecrated, חקדיש, the guests are simply summoned, ערע. Since the common fate of guests condemned on the day of YHWH is ritual slaughter, it is small wonder that the targumic interpreters chose to come to a different conclusion when Judah was named.[69] The fact that the sacrificial animal is not named adds to the sense of impending doom for Judah. Will they escape harm just like Isaac once escaped his father's knife? Or will they be slaughtered as Jepthah slaughtered his daughter, without a word of protest from God?

Traditionally, according to the regulations in Leviticus, the one who offers the sacrifice as well as the one who performs the ritual partially consumed the sacrifice; however, when God is the officiant, a sword "consumes" the sacrifice.[70] In addition to preparing the sacrifice, God invites and consecrates guests who would normally eat some of the sacrifice as long as they were in the appropriate state of ritual purity. The guests are not further identified. Are they a remnant of Judah who have been found acceptable in the preceding judgment? Are they the foreign nations that God typically uses to execute judgment on Israel and Judah? The text withholds further description of the sacrifice. Many commentators break the text after verse 8, where a break occurs in the Peshitta but not in the MT.

---

68. I address Zephaniah's proclamation against other prophets in prophecy 5.
69. See Berlin, *Zephaniah*, 79.
70. See Isa 34:6; Jer 46:10; and Ezek 39:17.

## TRANSLATION MATTERS

Milcom/Malcom: Milcom appears in the NRSV in Zephaniah 1:5 with Baal and the hosts of heaven as provocations whose worship God will punish. *Malkom*, the vocalization which actually appears in the MT, Targum, and JPS is presumed to have been confused with *milkom*, Milcom, which appears in other passages. In some of those texts Milcom is clearly the name of a non-Israelite god. As a divine name Milcom is understood by some scholars to be an alternate form of Molech (see discussion below). Moloch is generally, though not universally, accepted as a Canaanite deity. All three names share the root מלך, "reign," hence βασιλέως, "king" in the LXX (Soph[71] 1:5/Zeph 1:5). Molech is the Qal active masculine singular participle, *molekh*, "he who reigns." The names *milcom*, *malcom*, and *molekh* do not occur outside of the canon, but the related names *m-l-k*, *malik*, *milki*, *miliki*, and the *mal(i)ku* appear in the region and wider ANE as the names of gods and other supernatural entities.[72] The Hebrew form מלכם can be vocalized and therefore translated in a number of different ways. Hence, a brief look at the relevant lexemes follows, beginning with *malkam*, the form that occurs in Zephaniah. מלכם, vocalized as *malkam* the MT *ketiv* in Zephaniah 1:5, occurs in a number of other places in the Hebrew Bible with a variety of context-derived meanings.

1. Malcam is a proper name in the Benjaminite genealogy in 1 Chronicles 8:9 where the traditional vocalization is maintained.

2. In 2 Samuel 12:30 and its duplicate, 1 Chronicles 20:2, David takes the crown of the otherwise unidentified *malkam* upon his subjugation of the Ammonites and crowns himself with it. The NRSV renders "Milcom" there, citing the LXX. Second Samuel 12:30 has Μελχολ and 1 Chronicles 20:2 has Μολχολ in the LXX, both variants of Milcom. It is also the case that the noun, "king," with an affixed third-person plural pronominal suffix is also spelled מלכם; therefore, the JPS and Targum piously translate that David took the crown of "their king" so David does not place an idol's crown on his head (though Rashi identifies the deity and relates "Malkam" to Molech). The identification of the Ammonite royal seat of Rabbah, the מלוכה, may have influenced the choice to render *malkom* as "their king" in Jewish tradition. The NRSV translation Milcom is likely based on the location of David's self-coronation in Ammon (see 2 Sam 12:26). According to multiple references in Kings, *milkom* is the god—alternately "abomination"[73]—of the Ammonites.

3. In a separate collection of texts—2 Samuel 20:2; Jeremiah 30:9; and Hosea 3:5—מלכם is vocalized as *malkam* and clearly means "their king," and in each case, the phrase refers to David.

---

71. The Greek texts uses a Hellenized version of the prophet's name in and as the title of the book, Sophonias.

72. George C. Heider, "Molech," *ABD*, 4:895.

73. The deity Milcom is described as a "detestable thing," שקץ," in 1 Kgs 11:5; a "god," אלהי, in 1 Kgs 11:33; and תועבה, an "abomination," in 2 Kgs 23:13.

4. Though vocalized as *malkam*, both NRSV and JPS interpret מלכם in Jeremiah 49:1 and 3 as the deity Milcom. The Targum has מלכהון, *malk'hon*, "their king." Both verses can be read with either the monarch or the deity as their subject without loss of meaning: either the Ammonite god or monarch has overrun and colonized Gad but will be sent packing with his priests and retinue. The priests in the third verse might seem to belong more easily to the god as "his priests." They could also be understood as "subject to," and therefore belonging to, the king.

5. In Zephaniah 1:5 מלכם is clearly a deity and not a monarch, god-kings notwithstanding. The context is profane worship in verse 4 and also in verse 5: Baal and his priests, those who bow down to the host of the heavens and those who bow down to and swear by God while swearing by *malkam* at the same time. Milcom, likely Molech (see discussion below), is the intended referent.

The choice to render מלכם as Milcom in Zephaniah 1:5 is influenced by the virtual certainty that the lexeme refers to an Ammonite deity in 1 Kings 11:5, 33 and 2 Kings 23:13 where it occurs in the company of other proscribed deities. Second Kings 23:13 is directly pertinent to Zephaniah, naming Milcom as one of the deities Josiah targets in his purge that frames Zephaniah's proclamations. That clarity does not extend to the corresponding passages in the LXX: in 3 Reigns 11:6 (= 1 Kgs 11:5) the name of the Ammonite god is missing. In 3 Reigns 11:33 (= 1 Kgs 11:33) the MT verb שחה, "worship," has been replaced with "worked for," ἐποίησεν, and the deity has been replaced with "their king." Finally, in 4 Reigns 23:13 (= 2 Kgs 23:13) the deity is clearly indicated by the context. Thus, the LXX has Μολχολ who corresponds to Milcom.

The identification of Milcom (whether vocalized *malkam* or *milkom*) with Molech, מלך, the Canaanite deity whom some Israelites also worshiped, is contested in biblical scholarship. Molech is a deity to whom some Israelites have apparently offered their children in human sacrifice, usually through fire based on the vociferous repeated prohibitions and castigations against such sacrifice in the canon. Molech appears nine times[74] in the Hebrew Bible and once in Acts 7:43, citing Amos 5:26 LXX. The association of Molech with Milcom is based in part on Kings: 1 Kings 11:7 identifies Molech as the שקץ,"detestable-thing" of the Ammonites; however, the LXX has Μελχομ, Milcom; 1 Kings 11:5 makes the same claim and uses the same language to identify Milcom as the שקץ of the Ammonites. The interplay between Molech and Milcom is furthered by the LXX use of Μολχολ/Μολοχ, the variants of Molech, for Molech and *milkam*. A significant difference between Milcom and Molech is that Molech normatively appears with the direct article as "the Molech," המלך, in Leviticus 20:5 and, למלך, *lammolekh*, in Leviticus 20:2-4 and Jeremiah 32:25. The definite article is not translated and does not help with the confusion between the terms.

---

74. See Lev 18:21; 20:2-5; 1 Kgs 11:7; 2 Kgs 23:10; Jer 32:35. In Isa 57:9 NRSV translates *lammelek* as Molech while JPS preserves "king," as do the Peshitta and Vulgate, while the Targum has "kingdom." The LXX, however, has τὴν πορνείαν σου, "your fornication."

Given that Molech and Milcom both stem from the same root, "king" or "one who rules," their confusion is understandable and explains the LXX preferential translation of ἄρχον, "ruler."[75] In two cases more royal persons substitute for the deity, "their king" in 3 Reigns 11:5 (= 1 Kgs 11:7) and "the king" in Jeremiah 39:35.[76] (The) Molech functions as a title, likely signaling the sovereignty of a deity whose proper name is not given in the passages in which it appears, much like Baal that came to represent Haddu/Adad. Further distinguishing Molech and Milcom is the association of the Molech with child sacrifice, passing over/ through (העביר) fire; the fire is not always articulated. Molech is also firmly connected with the Valley of Hinnom, (גי הנם, *Geh Hinnom*, more familiar to many in its Aramaic-derived form, Gehenna).[77]

The day of YHWH in Zephaniah 1:8-9 is declared to be a day of retribution on which punishment, signaled by the verb, פקד[78] occurs on the day of sacrifice.[79] This portrayal of the day is in keeping with the description that follows in Zephaniah 1:14-16. That day is a terrifying, dark, and ominous day. The day is presented in verse 8 by a synonym, "the day of God's sacrifice." The link between "punish" and "sacrifice" implies that being sacrificed is the punishment and further intimates that Judah is the sacrificial victim. In the middle of verse 8 the third person used in Zephaniah 1:5-7 gives way to the first person again. The first person continues through verse 9; the text returns to the third person in verses 10-12 and then switches again. On the day of sacrifice Zephaniah proclaims God will judge the monarchy. Those to be judged include court officials[80] and members of the royal family (the designation may

75. See Lev 18:21; 20:2-5.
76. The spelling of Molech in LXX Amos and Acts, Μολοχ, also occurs in 4 Rgs/2 Kgs 23:10 and Jer 39:35. Only one LXX verse corresponding to the MT preserves Moloch, 4 Rgs/2Kgs 23:10. Isa 57:9 lacks an equivalent expression in the LXX.
77. See Lev 18:21; 2 Kgs 23:10; Jer 32:35.
78. פקד contains within it the notions of visiting, assessing, and administering or overseeing whatever is necessary to redress what has been observed; in Zephaniah the sense is "punishment" or "retribution."
79. See a brief overview of the day of YHWH on p. 151.
80. The word שרים, "princes," here likely indicates officials if it is not a parallel articulation of royal offspring. Sweeney details a number of roles held by שרים throughout the canon: "military figures (Deut 20:9; 1 Kgs 2:5; 1 Chr 27:3; 2 Sam 24:2; 2 Kgs 9:5; etc.); religious leaders (Ezra 8:24, 29; 10:5; 2 Chr 35:14; 1 Chr 15:16, 22; etc.); judicial figures (Exod 2:14; 18:21; Deut 1:15; Hos 5:10; Mic 7:3; etc.); professional classes (Gen 37:36; 40:2); the magistrate or administrator of a city (Judg 9:30; Neh 7:2) or district (1 Kgs 20:14, 15; Esth 1:3; 8:9)" (see *Zephaniah*, 83).

also include officials). The infraction meriting adjudication is consorting with foreigners and adopting their cultural norms, i.e., their attire, הלבשים מלבוש. In view of the earlier mention of Baal in Zephaniah 1:4, the proscribed clothing could be ritual vestments for the service of Baal as in 2 Kings 10:22.

The persons meant by בני מלך, traditionally translated as "sons of the king," are not readily identifiable. A handful of texts exist in which men who are not identified as royal offspring in the Hebrew Scriptures are called "the son of the king," which raises the possibility that the title was either honorific or an appointment (see 1 Kgs 22:26-27; 2 Chr 18:25-26; 28:7; Jer 36:26; 38:6). Seals bearing בן מלך "son of the king," with personal names that do not match the identified royal male offspring of the kings of Judah also exist.[81] While the expression בני המלך, "sons/children of the king," may be an honorific one for high-ranking officials, here I am inclined to read the phrase as royal offspring, especially given the use of שרים to indicate "officials" in the same verse.

Virtually all contemporary translations render בני המלך as "the king's sons,"[82] ignoring the possibility, and arguably likelihood, of royal daughters who could be represented in the plural form.[83] Even with more than a dozen royal daughters in the canon,[84] no parity exists with respect to the number of offspring recorded by gender in the Bible. The gross imbalance

81. Gershon Brin, "The Title בן המלך and Its Parallels," *Annali dell'Istituto Orientale di Napoli* 29 (1965): 433–65.

82. The Bishop's and Geneva Bibles have "children."

83. I have argued previously that such plural expressions should be treated as common and inclusive expressions rather than masculine since they indicate the presence of only one male (theoretically) among a number of subjects that can be male or female. See Wilda Gafney, *Daughters of Miriam: Women Prophets in Ancient Israel* (Minneapolis: Fortress, 2007), 15, 164. In some texts, however, the form is used when no males are present, which one sees in some of Naomi's addresses to Ruth and Orpah; see Ruth 1:8-13.

84. Some of these Israelite and Judean royal daughters include Merab and Michal *banoth* Saul (1 Sam 14:49), Tamar *bat* David (2 Sam 13:1), David's daughters (2 Sam 5:13; 13:18; 19:5), Tamar *bat* Absalom (2 Kgs 14:27), Maacah *bat* Absalom (2 Chr 11:20-21), Taphat and Basemat *banoth* Solomon (2 Kgs 4:11, 15), Jehosheba *bat* Joram (2 Kgs 11:2), Ahab's daughter (2 Kgs 8:18), and Amaziah's daughter (2 Chr 25:18). Non-Israelite royal daughters include Maacah *bat* Talmai (2 Sam 3:3), Jezebel *bat* Ethbaal (1 Kgs 16:31), unnamed daughters in Ps 45:9 and Jer 41:10, and the daughters of one or more pharaohs (Exod 2:5 and 1 Chr 4:17). Unnamed daughters of kings, המלך/בת־מלך בנות, also appear in Ps 45:13 and Jer 43:6. In other places where the word "princess" appears, the NRSV translates נשים שרות as "royal women."

of female to male progeny in the Scriptures is an artifact of its producers' emphases and not a function of biology. To the degree that biblical portrayals of the monarchs of Israel and Judah correspond to actual persons, there are certainly unrecorded daughters and, arguably, unrecorded sons as well when they do not serve the interests of the narrative. The critique of the royal offspring is not rooted in or limited by gender, hence the LXX's choice of "king's house." Therefore, I prefer "children of the king" since women could have transgressed in whatever manner that has led to prophetic sanction. This translation is suitable no matter what the relationship the indicated persons have with the monarch.

The monarch and offspring and/or officials in question in Zephaniah 1:8 cannot be identified with certainty; some interpreters understand Josiah to be the monarch and the royal offspring to be his sons. Josiah's offspring are named in some detail because three of his four sons and one grandson succeeded him on his throne in short order. Multiple names are given for Josiah's sons. Those given in 1 Chronicles 3:14, where they are listed in apparent birth order, appear to include throne names: Johanan, Jehoiakim, Zedekiah, and Shallum.

Johanan, Josiah's firstborn son whose mother is unknown, was passed over for his throne. Second Kings 23:30 and its duplicate in 2 Chronicles 36:1 name Josiah's successor as Jehoahaz, Josiah's youngest son; his mother was Hamutal bat Jeremiah of Libnah. Both accounts specify that "the people" chose Jehoahaz. Questions arise as to whether or not Josiah had designated an heir, why the firstborn was passed over, and why the youngest was chosen. Jeremiah 22:11 names Shallum as Josiah's immediate successor. He is presumed to be the same person as Jehoahaz; in that case, Shallum is his throne name.[85]

According to the Chronicles genealogy, Pharaoh Neco imprisoned and deposed Jehoahaz/Shallum and chose his brother Eliakim, Josiah's second son, to follow on his father's throne. Eliakim was the son of Zebidah bat Pedaiah of Rumah. The double account in 2 Kings 23:34 and 2 Chronicles 36:4 records that Neco changed Eliakim's name to Jehoiakim.

Eliakim/Jehoiakim became subject to Nebuchadnezzar (2 Kgs 24:1) and was succeeded by his own son Jehoiachin with Nehushta bat Elnathan of Jerusalem (2 Kgs 24:6). Three months later Nebuchadnezzar besieged Jehoiachin (2 Kgs 24:10) who surrendered himself, the queen

85. Gary N. Knoppers, *I Chronicles 1–9*, AB 12 (New Haven: Yale University Press, 1974), 326.

mother Nehushta, his military officers, and palace officials to Nebuchadnezzar (2 Kgs 24:12).

After the fall of Jerusalem in 586 BCE, Nebuchadnezzar deposed and
imprisoned Josiah's grandson Jehoiachin and replaced him with his
uncle, Josiah's third son Mattaniah, whom Nebuchadnezzar renamed
Zedekiah (2 Kgs 24:17).[86] Mattaniah/Zedekiah, like Jehoahaz/Shallum,
was the son of Hamutal bat Jeremiah of Libnah. The vital statistics of
Josiah's sons and one grandson were recorded in some detail because
they ruled Judah successively though they were deployed by competing
imperial powers to occupy Judah's throne held in thrall.

To read Zephaniah's pronouncement as against Josiah's sons, given
the function of Jehoiakim and Zedekiah as Egyptian and Babylonian
proxies, would be tempting. Yet if Zephaniah's preaching is in support
of Josiah's reform begun when he was eighteen (2 Kgs 22:1-3), then for
his sons to be old enough to transgress as so described let alone to have
been enthroned would be impossible. Also unlikely is that the puppet
kings would be censured for the circumstances of their captivity and
subjugation. Another possibility could be that Zephaniah is critiquing the
young Josiah and/or his siblings. As expected, the canon does not mention any siblings for Josiah. Since there is no struggle for succession in his
generation (2 Kgs 21:23-24; 1 Chr 3:14), this possibility cannot be ruled
out. A final possibility is that the "king's children" is a broad reference
to royal relatives. In any case, either to identify the alleged transgressors
or to exclude women from their number is just not possible.

The last charge in this unit, "those who leap over the threshold, fill-
ing their lord's house with violence," in Zephaniah 1:9 is obscure. Carol
Dempsey reads it as a superstitious practice to avoid evil spirits.[87] The
LXX and Peshitta omit the leaping; Targum Jonathan interprets the leaping as a non-Israelite cultic practice, as do subsequent contemporary
interpreters. The notion is that the behavior is similar to the Philistine
practice of not stepping on the threshold of Dagan's temple (see 1 Sam
5:5); however, the Samuel passage does not mention "leaping." The
Targum identifies the transgression as "walking according to Philistine
customs" in verse 9. The identity of "their lord's house" in the same
verse is unclear; it could refer to the palace and regime or the temple
complex. In either case God will visit retribution upon them on the divinely appointed day.

86. Second Chronicles 36:10 identifies Zedekiah as "his brother," presumably Jehoiachin's brother.
87. Dempsey, *Amos, Hosea, Micah, Nahum, Zephaniah, Habakkuk*, 122.

*Excursus: The Day of YHWH*

The day of YHWH is a metanarrative that distinguishes prophetic discourse in the Hebrew Scriptures and continues in pseudepigraphal and apocryphal texts,[88] in the Christian Testament,[89] rabbinic literature,[90] and in the apostolic fathers.[91] The rubric endures in contemporary preaching, apocalyptic literature, film, and other media. The lack of references to the expression outside of the canon in the ancient world does not allow for determining how widely the expression figures in the *Sitz im Leben* of the Scriptures.

To the degree that Amos is accepted as the earliest example of Israel's prophets (excluding Jonah), Amos 5:18-20 may be the earliest use of the day of YHWH motif and formula in the biblical corpus. Amos's argument that the day will not be as expected—darkness not light, gloominess not brightness—suggests that a commonly held set of beliefs about the nature of the day and events/phenomena associated with it was in play. Amos's rhetoric expresses perplexity at why anyone would actually want the day of YHWH; clearly they must not understand this day as he understands it. The fact that the literary production of Zephaniah follows Amos (and Hosea) may mean that traditions about the day were influenced by Amos and Zephaniah or were a part of the broader cultural milieu or both. Micah, Isaiah, and Ezekiel are particularly close to Zephaniah in their day of YHWH discourses. Other references to the day[92] presume familiarity with the tradition. Key components of the day are judgment, a decisive war-ending battle that culminates in a new theo-monarchal order, re-creation that leads to a secondary function, and salvation of a remnant who may be characterized as faithful.

A composite of the day of YHWH across biblical texts and some of its synonyms results in the following portrait: The day of YHWH is an event that could be a single day or span a longer period of time. It is perpetually near at hand (Isa 13:6; Joel 1:15; 2:1, 11; 3:14, etc.) and comes with or brings world-ending destruction (Isa 13:9). Occasionally the day

88. See 1 Enoch 60:24; 2 Enoch 18:6; Apoc. Zeph. 12:6; Apoc. Dan. 14:13; Gos. James 1:2; 2:2; 17:1.

89. See 1 Cor 5:5; 2 Cor 1:14; 1 Thess 5:2; 2 Thess 2:2; 2 Pet 3:10.

90. See b. Šabb. 118a, Ḥag. 4b, Sanh. 98b, Gen. Rab. 8:2; 99:11, Lev. Rab. 26:7; Num. Rab. 4:11; Lam. Rab. 2:25; Ecc. Rab. 5:5; Zohar A 67b, 107a, and 217b; and Zohar C 54a.

91. See Barn. 15:4.

92. See Isa 13:6, 9; Jer 46:10; Ezek 13:5; 30:3; Joel 1:15; 2:1, 11, 31; 3:14; Amos 5:18, 20; Obad 15; Zeph 1:7, 14; Mal 4:5; 1 Cor 5:5; 2 Cor 1:14; 1 Thess 5:2; 2 Thess 2:2; 2 Pet 3:10.

of YHWH is a past event. The day is dark, cloudy or darker, gloomy, and ominous (Ezek 30:3; Joel 2:31; Amos 5:18, 20). The day targets sinners both in Israel and in foreign nations (Obad 15). Innocents may be swept up in the cataclysm; often the righteous survive scathed or unscathed. Some of that destruction is the consequence of battles with human and heavenly forces (Ezek 13:5). The day is accompanied by anger and fury (Isa 13:9). It is a day of retribution and vindication against the enemies of God and, to a lesser degree, those of Israel (Jer 46:10). In some cases that punishment will be directly reciprocal. Israel or portions of Israel— the powerful, the monarchy, individual rulers—may find themselves dispensed with as enemies of God. The day often includes a sacrifice at which God presides and a subsequent meal (Zeph 1:7). Neither the sacrificial beast nor the content of the feast beyond sacrificial flesh is identified. The day is great and terrible. It is bitter and terrifying and reduces warriors to tears. The day is apocalyptic; it extends from the heavens to the earth with the sun turning to darkness and the moon turning to blood (Joel 2:31). Even though the advent of the day cannot be determined, there is often a promise of a herald that will precede the day (Mal 4:5).

Study of the day must account for the number of expressions related to the day of YHWH: "the day of X," "(in/on) that day" and, "the day (when) X." This catalog not only demonstrates the deep roots of the concept in Israelite culture and prophetic rhetoric but also the concept's flexibility and adaptability. The most frequent of these eschatological expressions, ביום ההוא, "in/on that day," occurs more than a hundred times, nearly half of which are in Isaiah. It occurs repeatedly in Zephaniah (see 1:9-10, 15; 3:11, 16). In Zephaniah the word "day" itself is apocalyptic and signifies the portentous day of ultimate resolution, with the possible exception of the last use in 3:18. It occurs twenty times in varying configurations:

the day of YHWH (1:7, 14 [2x])
the day of God's sacrifice (1:8)
that day (1:9, 10, 15; 3:11, 16)
a day (1:15 [5x], 16)
the day of God's fury/wrath/anger (1:18; 2:2, 3)
the day when (3:8)
a day of festival (3:18)

In Zephaniah the day of YHWH is simultaneously at hand (1:7) and near and approaching fast (1:14), which corresponds with the use of the expression throughout the canon. The day of YHWH in Zephaniah is an awe-inducing day calling for silence (1:7), one on which God has prepared a sacrifice for guests who have been called and sanctified (1:8). It is a day of punishment and retribution (1:8-9) on which piercing cries and shattering sounds will be heard across Jerusalem (1:10). Among those cries are the bitter cries of warriors (1:14); there is nothing else they can do. Staccato descriptions in Zephaniah 1:15-16 yield a day of wrath, a day of distress and anguish, a day of ruin and devastation, a day of darkness and gloom, a day of clouds and thick darkness, and a day of trumpet blast and battle cry. The devastation of God's day in Zephaniah is absolute and catastrophic; it consumes the whole earth and its inhabitants (1:2-3, 18). Within the horror is a slim chance of respite for the humble and the righteous; it may be that God will hide them on that great day, though nothing is certain. The judgment of God will be formalized with legal proceedings; God will testify personally (3:8). After God's testimony, the nations and monarchies will have no opportunity for appeal. They will be sentenced to burn in the fires of God's fury. Yet, in spite of the world-consuming conflagration rhetoric, someone will survive (3:12, 20). She is subsequently identified as בת ציון, *Bat Zion*, Daughter (or the Daughter of) Zion.[93] Unexpectedly the day is transformed into one of restoration in the closing verses of Zephaniah. An unanswered question is whether the day of YHWH refers to a specific historical event; if so, as Adele Berlin argues, it would be the decline and fall of the Assyrian Empire.[94] Michael Ufok Udoekpo offers a more in-depth treatment of the day in his survey of the scholarship on the day of YHWH as a prelude to his study of select prophecies in Zephaniah.[95]

93. I will take up the translation and identification of בת ציון in the Translation Matters section of chapter 3. Contributing author Rabbah Arlene Berger and I will offer Christian and Jewish readings in the Contextual Hermeneutics section.

94. Berlin, *Zephaniah*, 94.

95. Udoekpo, *Re-Thinking the Day of YHWH*, 43–108.

## Zephaniah 1:10–2:15

# The Day of YHWH Is at Hand: Where You Gonna Run All on That Day?

### Prophecy 2 (Zeph 1:10-18)

Zephaniah's second prophecy begins with a description of the effect of the day on parts of Jerusalem. Shrieks, howls, wailing, and the sound of shattering ring out first at the Fish Gate in the northern wall of the city. Then the cacophony moves through the Second Quarter, the home of Zephaniah's contemporary, the prophet Huldah. The final outcry is wailing in the "Mortar"[1] neighborhood. The wailing, יְלָל, is often commanded by the prophets[2] as the suitable response to their words and God's; it will be spontaneous here. These are prosperous neighborhoods inhabited by merchants, and, according to rabbinic tradition, Torah scholars also inhabit the area. The devastation targets

---

1. Another rendering of this word is the "Hollow," מכתש; the Targum and Peshitta simply transliterate it as *Maktesh*.
2. For example, see Isa 13:6; Jer 4:8; Ezek 30:2; Joel 1:5; Zeph 11:2; etc.

<sup>10</sup>On that day, says the L<sc>ord</sc>,
a cry will be heard from the
Fish Gate,
a wail from the Second Quarter,
a loud crash from the hills.
<sup>11</sup>The inhabitants of the Mortar wail,
for all the traders have
perished;
all who weigh out silver are
cut off.
<sup>12</sup>At that time I will search
Jerusalem with lamps,
and I will punish the people
who rest complacently on their
dregs,

those who say in their hearts,
"The L<sc>ord</sc> will not do good,
nor will he do harm."
<sup>13</sup>Their wealth shall be plundered,
and their houses laid waste.
Though they build houses,
they shall not inhabit them;
though they plant vineyards,
they shall not drink wine from
them.

<sup>14</sup>The great day of the L<sc>ord</sc> is near,
near and hastening fast;
the sound of the day of the L<sc>ord</sc>
is bitter,
the warrior cries aloud there.

the wealthy and singles out the traders and merchants[3] and those who handle money (silver). God will personally roam the streets and search Jerusalem with lamps for those who say God is inept or at least indifferent.[4] The Targum, ever vigilant against anthropomorphic presentations of God, instead has God appointing searchers in verse 12.

This proclamation portrays a God who is present and active in the world of humanity. The text warns that God will plunder the homes and property of the wealthy and leave them desolate and uninhabited. Surprisingly, the poor are absent in Zephaniah, which is counter to general understandings of the Hebrew prophets' core message. The wealthy, however, are severely critiqued, which is consistent with other prophetic works. They are described as indolent, resting "on their dregs," שמיהם, otherwise known as fermented grape sediment. Consonantally שמיהם can also mean to "watch/observe them" and to "observe/keep them" (commandments, Sabbath, etc.), so the phrase has been alternately understood as "those who despise their commandments" (LXX) and "those

---

3. In Zeph 1:11, as in Isa 23:8, 9; Ezek 16:29; 17:4; Hos 12:7; Zech 14:21; Job 40:30; and Prov 31:24, עם כנען is "trades-people." The "weighing of silver" makes clear that עם כנען is not to be read as "Canaanites."

4. This graphic image of God is one of several images in Zephaniah where God is described in anthropomorphic terms. See 1:4, 12; 2:13; and 3:8.

<sup>15</sup>That day will be a day of wrath,
a day of distress and anguish,
a day of ruin and devastation,
a day of darkness and gloom,
a day of clouds and thick darkness,
<sup>16</sup>a day of trumpet blast and
battle cry
against the fortified cities
and against the lofty
battlements.

<sup>17</sup>I will bring such distress upon
people
that they shall walk like the
blind;

because they have sinned
against the LORD,
their blood shall be poured out
like dust,
and their flesh like dung.
<sup>18</sup>Neither their silver nor their gold
will be able to save them
on the day of the LORD's wrath;
in the fire of his passion
the whole earth shall be
consumed;
for a full, a terrible end
he will make of all the
inhabitants of the earth.

who despise their Watcher," here "Watcher" means God (Peshitta). The Targum has "those who are at ease because of their possessions." Verse 12 continues with the idea that the wealthy project their apathy and inertia onto God, imagining that God is equally, if not more, lethargic than they are. The passage uses the hendiadys "good" and "evil" to connote all action just as the same expression connotes the tree of all knowledge in Genesis 2:9. The wealthy are in effect saying, "God will do neither good nor evil," which means that "God won't [or doesn't] do anything."

Zephaniah ignores the claim that God is as shiftless as God's people and instead articulates the reversal of privileged fortunes in the passive voice. They will not act; they will be acted upon. The privileged will watch as everything they have built and acquired by any means will be destroyed. The language in Zephaniah 1:13 is strikingly similar to the Deuteronomistic curse in Deuteronomy 28:30, recapitulations of which appear in Amos 5:11 and Micah 6:15: they will build houses but not dwell in them and plant vineyards but not enjoy their fruit. This curse language is also fairly common throughout the ANE.[5] Zephaniah is distinct: here no outsider will enjoy what the community itself has planted and built, unlike other ANE texts.

---

5. James B. Pritchard, *Ancient Near Eastern Texts: Relating to the Old Testament* (Princeton: Princeton University Press, 1969), 300, 659.

The loss of wealth is juxtaposed with the reintroduction of the day of YHWH. In Zephaniah 1:7 the day was "at hand." Now in Zephaniah 1:14 the day is "near" and "coming fast." "Nearness" is a stock phrase that describes the day throughout the canon (see Isa 13:6; Ezek 30:3; Joel 1:15; 3:14; Obad 15). Translation of שם צרח גבור in Zephaniah 1:14 has been disputed and varies among the witnesses. The NRSV has "the warrior cries aloud there." The verb צרח, "cry aloud," occurs elsewhere only in Isaiah 43:13. The LXX interprets the phrase as describing the day as "bitter and harsh and has been made powerful." The LXX achieves this reading by interpreting צרח as הרצ, reading the *het* as a *heh* and translating it with σκληρά, "harsh." The LXX preserves the sense of strength that is at the root of גבור and applies it to the day as "powerful." Curiously, the Greek manuscript of the Twelve from Nahal Hever, 8HevXIIgr, corresponds more closely to the MT than to the LXX and records ἐπίσημος, "groan," in part.[6] The Peshitta maintains that the day is "bitter" and "strong." The Targum preserves the warriors crying out and provides their outcry: "[men/warriors] are being killed!" The Vulgate states that the day is bitter and a day of "tribulation" for the warrior. The confusion about bitterness, harshness, strength, and power gives way to concrete descriptions of the day itself in verse 15 and the first portion of verse 16. The language has a beautiful lyric quality because of the suffix -*ah* on all of the feminine nouns that describe the day.[7] Zephaniah 1:14-16 has been immortalized in the Gregorian arrangement of the Latin hymn *Dies Irae*. The repetition in verse 15 is particularly amenable to hymnody.

The cataclysm in Zephaniah occurs under layers of gloom; the day is יום ענן, "a day of clouds," in Zephaniah 1:15, just like it is described in Ezekiel 30:3; 34:12; and Joel 2:2. Three of the four verses share more language, ביום ענן וערפל, "a day of clouds and thick-darkness"; Ezekiel is the outlier. Joel shares, or perhaps copies, an entire phrase with or from Zephaniah, יום חשך ואפלה יום ענן וערפל, "a day of darkness and gloom, a day of clouds and thick-darkness." This thick-darkness is the common dwelling of God made visible to mortals in theophanous moments throughout the canon.[8] The שופר, *shofar*, ram's horn trumpet, and תרועה, *teruah*, a specific pattern blown on the *shofar*, both give the day a martial aspect. Rather than God as the Divine Warrior marching out to defend God's people,

---

6. Marvin A. Sweeney, *Zephaniah: A Commentary on the Book of Zephaniah*, ed. Paul D. Hanson, Hermeneia 36 (Minneapolis: Fortress, 2003), 98.

7. *yôm 'ebrâ hahû; yôm ṣārâ ûmṣûqâ, yôm šōâ ûmšô'â; yôm ḥōšek wa'ăpelâ, yôm 'ānān wa'ărāpel. yôm šōpār ûtrû'â . . .*

8. See Exod 20:21; Deut 4:11; 5:22; 2 Sam 22:10; 1 Kgs 8:12; Isa 60:2.

God is marching against them. Against such a warrior the "fortified cities" and "lofty battlements" of Judah and Jerusalem in Zephaniah 1:16 cannot stand. Those familiar with modern Hebrew will hear in the language of destruction and devastation in Zephaniah 1:15, ומשואה, the term that has come to designate the decimation of the Holocaust, the *Shoah*.

Zephaniah's first prophecy concludes with judgment on humankind because the people have sinned against God. The text does not specify the offense. Their fate will be gruesome; their blood and their innards, לחמם,[9] will be poured out like the waste of human bowels. The language is intentionally and shockingly graphic. Removal of blood and bowel evokes the ritual preparation of sacrificial animals, a nod to the sacrifice over which God presides in Zephaniah 1:8. The destruction is no longer limited to Jerusalem; the whole earth will be consumed and all who dwell on the earth will come to a terrible, horrifying end in verse 18. Cycling back to the wealthy "who weigh out silver" in Zephaniah 1:11, the prophecy concludes in verse 18 with the warning that no one will be able to buy his or her way out of this judgment—not with silver, not with gold. Ezekiel 7:19 duplicates Zephaniah 1:18, "their silver and gold will not be able to save them in the day of God's wrath." The only difference is that the phrase in Zephaniah begins with "[not] even," גם. The suggestion of justice that is for sale is likely a foreshadowing of the charges laid against corrupt officials in Zephaniah 3:3-4.

## Prophecy 3 (Zeph 2:1-3)

The end of Zephaniah 1 would seem to forestall any further revelation or discussion. The earth and her inhabitants will be consumed in the fires of God's wrath. The existence of a further prophecy is the first hint that all may not be lost. Indeed, some people may escape the divine wrath, and something of the earth may be left for these survivors to inhabit. Zephaniah speaks to an unidentified nation that seems to have survived the cataclysm. The word גוי used in 2:1 normally indicates any nation that is not Israel. The prophet is intentionally vague, even coy, not telling his hearers or readers whether the nation is Judah or not. The nation is לא נכסף, "undesirable" or "unashamed," depending on which of two identical roots was intended. Both meanings may have been intended. Since the root is the same as "silver," "worthless nation" may be the better

9. NRSV translates the word as "flesh"; the putative root לחום occurs only twice, here and in Job 20:23.

### Zephaniah 2:1-3

2:1Gather together, gather,
　O shameless nation,
2before you are driven away
　like the drifting chaff,
before there comes upon you
　the fierce anger of the Lord,
before there comes upon you

the day of the Lord's wrath.
3Seek the Lord, all you humble of
　the land,
who do his commands;
seek righteousness, seek humility;
　perhaps you may be hidden
on the day of the Lord's wrath.

choice.[10] The Targum preserves the sense of a lack of desire, configuring it as a "generation that does not desire to return to Torah" and making the proclamation explicitly about Judah. Other witnesses translate לא נכסף as "uneducated" (LXX), lacking "discipline" (Peshitta), and "unlovely" in the Vulgate, which becomes "unworthy to be loved" in Wycliffe, the Bishop's, Geneva, and Douay Bibles. King James preserves the literal "not desired." The Targum notwithstanding, the nation is not named. The prophet plays with the ambiguity. Is it Judah of 1:4, Jerusalem of 1:10-12, or any of the nations of "all the earth" destroyed in 1:18?

The mysterious nation is given the slim hope of a reprieve in Zephaniah 2:2-3. If they gather (for worship?), they may escape being driven away and dispersed. The "gathering" in Zephaniah 2:1 is odd; the word קשש means "gather-kindling" and is used of straw for bricks (Exod 5:7, 12) or twigs for burning (Num 15:32, 33; 1 Kgs 17:10, 12); it is not used to "gather" or assemble people apart from Zephaniah. If the gathering is for the purposes of worshiping God, then the mysterious nation might be Judah. The surviving people are "chaff [מץ] whose day has passed"[11] in 2:2. They are altogether insubstantial and imminently flammable. The end of the verse makes clear that these souls have not escaped the conflagration at all; rather, the prophet has backtracked. If the assembly of human kindling does as instructed, then they may escape; they may "be hidden" (2:4) on the day.

The key word in the third prophecy is "before," בטרם, in Zephaniah 2:2. If the kindling-people gather (2:1) *before* the "birth of the decree [announcing the day],"[12] *before* the furious anger of God and the day comes upon them, then they may just be hidden, put away in secret, תסתרו, and,

10. "Shame" proper, בשת, is regularly attributed to Israel and Judah (Jer 2:26; 3:24-25; 7:19; 11:13; 20:18; Hos 9:10; Mic 1:11), including subsequently in Zephaniah (3:5, 9).

11. NRSV renders the text as "drifting" chaff.

12. NRSV has "before you are driven away." The translation amends the verb unnecessarily.

thus, just might escape (2:3). The people who might survive are still not named, though everything in the text thus far seems to indicate that they must be Judah. In Zephaniah 2:3 God calls for the "humble of the land" to seek God. The עֲנָוִים, often translated as the "poor," "meek," or "humble," are a particular concern of God throughout the canon. That language continues in the Christian Testament, e.g., Matthew 5:5. Even if the "meek" are understood as the "humble poor," no divine or prophetic concern for the circumstances that render them so is present. Zephaniah does not target their exploitation directly.

Most often "the poor/meek/humble" appear without further delineation though the setting of the texts in which they occur—the Scriptures of ancient Israel—indicates they are to be understood as Israel/Judah.[13] Likewise, the command to "seek YHWH," is given to Israel and Judah. Virtually all who seek God in the canon are Israelite or Judean with the exception of the scene described in Zechariah 8:20-23 in which people of many cities and many nations seek God.[14] Zephaniah 2:3 builds the strongest case that the people is Judah without actually naming them: they are the meek of the earth who can be expected to seek God and know and perform just and righteous acts (suggesting knowledge of the unmentioned Torah). Zephaniah hints that the nation is Judah. He does not identify Judah outright at this point, and he does not articulate divine concern for the peoples of the larger world other than to judge and convict them. Zephaniah's God appears unconcerned for peoples of the wider world beyond Israel and Judah; this behavior is in accord with some prophetic texts but divergent from others.[15]

## Prophecy 4 (Zeph 2:4-15)

Placing Zephaniah 2:4 in the fourth prophecy reads against the Masoretic break after verse 3. Such a placement seems to run counter to the

13. See Isa 11:4; 29:19; 32:7; 61:1; Amos 2:7; 8:4; Pss 9:12, 18; 10:12, 17; 22:26; 25:9; 34:2; 37:11; 69:32; 76:9; 147:6; 149:4; Prov 3:34; 14:21; and 16:19.

14. In Zech 8:20-23 the multiethnic and multinational community begs the survivors of Judah to accompany them, saying, "We know God is with you." Most translations describe the Judean survivors as "Jews" anachronistically in this passage. The NETS and CEB are notable exceptions. In Zechariah what once was the monarchy of Judah is now the province of Yehud. Its citizens are properly speaking Yehudites. See the usage of Carol L. Meyers and Eric M. Meyers, *Haggai and Zechariah 1–8*, AB 25B (Garden City, NY: Doubleday, 1974), 440.

15. Compare Isa 2:2-4; 19:23-24; Mic 4:1-5; Zech 2:10-11; 8:22-23 with Isa 65:18-23; Ezek 37:21-27; Zech 2:10-12; 8:7-8.

⁴For Gaza shall be deserted,
and Ashkelon shall become a
desolation;
Ashdod's people shall be driven
out at noon,
and Ekron shall be uprooted.
⁵Ah, inhabitants of the seacoast,
you nation of the Cherethites!
The word of the LORD is against
you,
O Canaan, land of the Philistines;
and I will destroy you until no
inhabitant is left.
⁶And you, O seacoast, shall be
pastures,
meadows for shepherds
and folds for flocks.
⁷The seacoast shall become the
possession
of the remnant of the house of
Judah,
on which they shall pasture,

and in the houses of Ashkelon
they shall lie down at evening.
For the LORD their God will be
mindful of them
and restore their fortunes.

⁸I have heard the taunts of Moab
and the revilings of the
Ammonites,
how they have taunted my people
and made boasts against their
territory.
⁹Therefore, as I live, says the
LORD of hosts,
the God of Israel,
Moab shall become like Sodom
and the Ammonites like
Gomorrah,
a land possessed by nettles and
salt pits,
and a waste forever.
The remnant of my people shall
plunder them,

use of the הוי (woe!) particle that opens verse 5, which is traditionally
the start of a woe prophecy. The geographical vagueness of Zephaniah
2:1-3, however, in contrast with the specificity of verses 4-15 makes a case
for breaking the text between verses 3 and 4. Zephaniah 2:1-3 strongly
alludes to Judah without naming it, but the remainder of the chapter
explicitly identifies the foreign entities about which it prophesies.[16] The
foreign nations are the offspring of Cush and Canaan (Egypt is notably
absent), and therefore the children of Ham who represent city dwellers
as opposed to the nomadic children of Shem and sea-faring progeny of
Japheth.[17] The now unified collection of pronouncements against foreign
nations forms a discrete prophecy.

16. The text names Judah in Zeph 2:7 only as the beneficiary of the nations' despoliation.
17. Adele Berlin, *Zephaniah*, AB 25A (New Haven: Yale University Press, 1994), 122.
Berlin finds that Zephaniah is dependent on the family of nations tradition in Gen 10

and the survivors of my nation
shall possess them.
¹⁰This shall be their lot in return for
their pride,
because they scoffed and
boasted
against the people of the LORD
of hosts.
¹¹The LORD will be terrible against
them;
he will shrivel all the gods of
the earth,
and to him shall bow down,
each in its place,
all the coasts and islands of
the nations.

¹²You also, O Ethiopians,
shall be killed by my sword.

¹³And he will stretch out his hand
against the north,
and destroy Assyria;

and he will make Nineveh a
desolation,
a dry waste like the desert.
¹⁴Herds shall lie down in it,
every wild animal;
the desert owl and the screech
owl
shall lodge on its capitals;
the owl shall hoot at the window,
the raven croak on the
threshold;
for its cedar work will be laid
bare.
¹⁵Is this the exultant city
that lived secure,
that said to itself,
"I am, and there is no one
else"?
What a desolation it has become,
a lair for wild animals!
Everyone who passes by it
hisses and shakes the fist.

The כי conjunction that opens Zephaniah 2:4 links prophecies 3 and 4 by offering the fate of the foreign nations (prophecy 4) as motivation for the unnamed people in Zephaniah 2:1-3 (prophecy 3) to change their ways before the day arrives in flaming fury. In verse 5 Zephaniah addresses the כרתים, the Cherethites, understood by most to be Cretans with whom they share the same consonants. The LXX has Κρητῶν/Κρήτη here and in the following verse; the MT has "seacoast" again. In other

_____

in several places. Discussing Ham from the perspective of an African American biblical scholar has often meant wrestling with the misnamed "curse of Ham." The tradition that African peoples were cursed by God to perpetual slavery because Ham "saw" the nakedness of his drunken father Noah leaves sufficient ambiguity to allow for the possibility of something other than "seeing," i.e., sexual contact. In the episode in Gen 9:20-27 Noah curses Canaan and his descendants but not Ham, and therefore not Cush and his descendants, who have traditionally been identified with African peoples. The so-called curse of Ham featured prominently in some biblical and theological arguments in favor of American chattel enslavement of Africans and their descendants.

passages in the Hebrew Scriptures, Caphtor (also understood as Crete) is the place from which the Philistines emerge (see Gen 10:14; Deut 2:23; Jer 47:4; Amos 9:7; and 1 Chr 1:12). The Cherethites who served honorably as mercenaries for David—including as his personal guard and later served Solomon (2 Sam 20:23; 23:22-23; 1 Kgs 1:38)—have given no provocation for their destruction in Zephaniah or any other text. Zephaniah may be using the term כרתים, Cherethites, as a synonym for the Philistines, lumping them together due to their common Aegean origin. The choice to conflate the Philistines and Cherethites is likely also in service to a pun. "Cut off" is a homophone of Cherethites. The pun is even more explicit in the partial parallel in Ezekiel 25:16, הכרתי . . . כרתים, *hikhrati keretim*, "I will cut off . . . the Cherethites."

Oddly, Zephaniah identifies Canaan as the land of the Philistines in verse 5. He calls for their eradication and threatens to destroy every last inhabitant and leave nothing but pastureland in verse 6. Philistia, Israel's long-time nemesis with whom they unwillingly shared access to the sea, bears witness to God's power through the destruction and depopulation of her four chief cities: Ashdod, Ashkelon, Ekron, and Gaza. A set of artful, partially alliterative, and assonant puns that are almost impossible to translate articulates the outcome. The transliterations and suggested translations below give a sense of how they sound and what they mean:

*'azzâ 'ăzûbâ*, עזה עזובה, "Gaza will be godforsaken"

*'ašqəlôn lišmāmâ*, ואשקלון לשממה, "Ashkelon will be isolated"

*'ašdôd yəgārəšûâ*, אשדוד . . . יגרשו, "Ashdod will be dislodged"

*'eqrôn tē'āqēr*, ועקרון תעקר, "Ekron will be eradicated"

The fourth prophecy continues its focus on non-Israelite occupation of the seacoast (verses 6-7). Then, according to verse 7, the land will revert to Judah at long last. The Judeans will graze their flocks in the vacant lots that once held Philistine houses.

The mention of "the remnant [שארית] of the house of Judah" in Zephaniah 2:7 could indicate a post-Babylonian time frame just as it does in 2 Kings 19:30 (duplicated in Isa 37:31). The shorter form, "remnant of Judah," occurs regularly in Jeremiah, where it describes the survivors of the Babylonian decimation (Jer 40:11, 15; 42:15, 19; 43:5; 44:7, 12, 14, 28). Haggai uses "remnant of the people" (Hag 1:4; 2:2) and Zechariah just "remnant" (Zech 9:7). All of these citations are references to the Babylonian-administered province of Yehud, which is the surviving vestige of Judah after Nebuchadnezzar's invasion of Jerusalem and the sack of the temple. Given the temporal setting of Zephaniah, however, the expression could also refer to Judah, which survived the Assyrian decimation that reduced Israel from twelve tribes—eleven landed—to one with refugees from others, thus shrinking Israel's landmass by two-thirds. Moreover, since Sennacherib seized Judean land and handed it over to the Philistines to occupy and administer, Assyrian domination easily accounts for some of the framing of the text.[18] Finally, the expression may simply refer to those Judeans who have survived the day of YHWH.

The multiplicity of nouns and verbs with differing numbers and genders makes Zephaniah 2:7 difficult to sort out. The seacoast,[19] which is a masculine singular noun, will become the possession of the remnant (שארית), which is a feminine singular, of the house of Judah where "they" (עליהם) shall pasture (ירעון), both inclusive[20] plural, with the verb having a paragogic נ.[21] Grammatically, neither the remnant nor house of Judah can be the antecedent of the verb. The shepherds and flocks of verse 6 work as the antecedent grammatically and thematically: the shepherds of the remnant of the house of Judah shall pasture their flocks in the houses of Ashkelon. The shepherds and flocks can also be the subject of "they shall lay down," (ירבצון). Both verbs have a paragogic נ playing off the נ in Ashkelon. The shepherds and their flocks are less likely subjects for the last two plurals in Zephaniah 2:7; God will be mindful of them (יפקדם) and will restore their fortunes (שבותם). The remnant and house of Judah make more sense as beneficiaries of restoration than just the shepherds and their sheep, though the pastoralists and their flocks do function as a synonym for Judah.

Having dispensed with Israel's adversaries to the west, Zephaniah turns east and prophesies doom for Moab and Ammon. Now, however, God speaks in the first person (again). Verses 8-9 proscribe the legendary[22] fate of Sodom and Gomorrah for Ammon and Moab as retribution for mocking and taunting Judah and for making moves against their

---

18. Sweeney, *Zephaniah*, 130.

19. Here the term is חבל; חבל הים appears in the preceding verse.

20. I prefer "inclusive" to "masculine" since the form encompasses mixed-gender groups as well as plural masculine groupings. Some masculine/inclusive plurals are used with all-female subjects, which is repeatedly the case in the book of Ruth.

21. "Paragogic" refers to the practice of adding an extra letter at the end of a word in biblical Hebrew for euphony. The "n" sound, and likewise the "h" sound, is regarded as particularly mellifluous.

22. The tradition of the destruction of Sodom and Gomorrah pervades the Hebrew Scriptures, the Greek Deuterocanonical/Apocrypha, and the Christian Testament. The names function as an archetype of punitive destruction against wicked peoples.

border. A specific border conflict does not seem to be in mind; rather, the text evokes the broader period of the ninth to seventh centuries BCE, particularly after Assyrian annexation. The power that will ensure the fate of Moab and Ammon is the power of the God of celestial warriors.[23] The title opens verse 8 and closes verse 9. The promise of sure and certain vengeance is secured in verse 9 by the strongest oath in the Scriptures, חי אני, "as I live [exist eternally]." For humans to swear by the life of YHWH is slightly more common (thirty-five times in the HB, with nearly half occurring in the book of 1 Samuel) than for God to swear by the Divine self (twenty-three times, with most instances clustered in Ezekiel). The oath is made stronger by being presented as a prophetic proclamation through the use of the technical prophetic formula, יהוה נאם, "a prophetic-utterance of GOD."

God's oath in Zephaniah 2:9 is unbreakable and has an incontrovertible guarantee. The remnant of Judah will plunder, inherit, and occupy the depopulated lands of their long-time antagonists. Speaking in the first person, God describes the survivors as "the remnant of my people" and "survivors of my nation," a rare use of גוי for Israel or Judah.[24] The focus on Ammon and Moab (and Assyria, which follows) aims to restore Judah—itself the remnant of Israel—to the possession and control of the land that it lost in its decline from Solomonic glory.

In Zephaniah 2:11 the prophecy turns to unnamed gods evoking Baal and Milcom/Molech from 1:4-5. Rather than proscribe foreign worship again God plans to remove the temptation by removing, רזה, "shriveling" or "shrinking," all the gods of the land (or earth). The gods are "destroyed completely" in the LXX, where the phrase is rendered as ἐξολεθρεύσει. The targumic pious circumlocution "[objects of] worship," to avoid mentioning other gods in Judah, is unsurprising, but that they are merely "humbled" and not destroyed is surprising. Rather than gods, "kings" are destroyed in the Peshitta. In the MT some of the worshipers of other gods appear to survive their "shriveling" and submit to God. Those adherents are located on "all the islands [or coasts] of the nations." Their island location seems more like banishment than a holiday. The shift from landlocked Ammon and Moab to islands and seacoasts may be a reversion back to the Philistines who are decried at the beginning of the chapter. The portrait of Judah as henotheistic is in keeping with the

---

23. The phrase is traditionally translated as "Lord of hosts."
24. The possessive pronoun is missing from גוי in v. 9.

larger shape of the Hebrew Scriptures;[25] monotheism is secondary but becomes dominant, particularly in interpretation. This frank henotheism differentiates Zephaniah from Isaiah. Zephaniah and Isaiah share language and imagery, with Isaiah being militantly monotheistic.[26]

A single six-word line comprises a second-person proclamation that is directly addressed to the Nubians (Cushites) in Zephaniah 2:12. The first-person speaker is God. Contrary to the predictive slant of the NRSV, the prophecy is descriptive and interpretive. The Nubians are already "slain" since חלל is an adjective. "Shall be" is a verbal construction. (The same phenomenon occurs in Isa 7:14 with the young woman who is contemporaneously described as being pregnant, again an adjective, but translated as a verb, "shall conceive," in many translations.) The slain Nubians have been killed by the sword of God. Since the Kushite Empire fell to a successive Egyptian dynasty, Egypt is the sword of God in this metaphor. This description is well in keeping with other biblical accounts of God using foreign nations to discipline Israel and occasionally other nations (see 2 Kgs 17:22-23; Isa 10:5-6; 5:1; Hab 1:6).

The Nubians are not one of Israel's traditional enemies, i.e., the Egyptians, Canaanites of various sorts, Philistines, Assyrians, or Babylonians. The reference to Nubia seems to be out of place between acts of vengeance against Moab, Ammon, and Assyria, each of which dispossessed Israel to some degree at one time or another. The same cannot be said of Nubia/Cush except perhaps as mercenaries in the employment of Egypt, yet Egypt is not addressed. Though significant geopolitical overlap exists between Nubia and Egypt, the Scriptures do not use them interchangeably. Furthermore the form is odd insofar as it addresses the people, "Cushites," rather than the nation "Cush," as was the case for the others listed. The verse reads like an interpolation.[27] Where are

---

25. See Deut 32:8, where God divides the borders of the nations according to the number of foreign gods.

26. Examples include Isa 44:6: "I am the first and I am the last; besides me there is no god"; Isa 44:8: "Is there any god besides me? There is no other rock; I know not one"; and Isa 45:22: "I am God, and there is no other."

27. Some who read Zephaniah's Cushite heritage as problematic regard this verse as a sort of loyalty oath, i.e., Zephaniah is willing to critique his ancestor's people. Such a reading places a burden on Zephaniah that is not placed on the great many biblical characters with multiple heritages. That burden bears a striking resemblance to what is contemporarily called the "black tax." See Rodney Sadler's survey of the scholarship in *Can a Cushite Change His Skin? An Examination of Race, Ethnicity, and Othering in the Hebrew Bible* (New York: T & T Clark, 2005), 64–70.

the Nubians to whom Zephaniah is speaking directly? Certainly some Nubians have married and integrated into Judah. The bulk of the people of Nubia to whom Zephaniah is ostensibly prophesying are not present to hear their fate; they are in Nubia and in diaspora. This performance is for the benefit of Judah.

Just as scholars have questioned the inferences and implications of the name "Cushi" in Zephaniah's genealogy in Zephaniah 1:1, they have also questioned the identity and location of the כושים, Cushites or Nubians of Zephaniah 2:12, and כוש, Cush/Nubia in Zephaniah 3:10. Biblical "Cush" is the ancient African nation of Kush, which is congruent in part with ancient Ethiopia. Kush/Cush also incorporated parts of Egypt at various times, including the Nubian pharaohs of the Twenty-Fifth Dynasty (780–756 BCE). Some scholarly speculation also exists about a secondary Cushite nation outside of Africa. The reference in Habakkuk 3:7 to "Cushan" in parallel with "Midian" located on the Arabian Peninsula, and inclusion of the form "Cushan" as an element in the name of an Aramean monarch in Judges 3:8, 10, may point to a Cushite territory removed from the African continent. The references to Cush in Genesis 2:13 and 10:6-8 associate Cush with Mesopotamia and the legendary figure Nimrod. This Cush has been identified with the Kassites who migrated to Mesopotamia and ruled Babylon from the sixteenth to twelfth century BCE.[28] The JPS translation distinguishes Cush in Genesis from Cush in the Prophets broadly, transliterates the former as "Cush," and, with a few exceptions, translates it in the latter texts most frequently as "Nubia."[29] The traditions need not be in conflict. Geography in the early portion of Genesis is often figurative and etiological and does not easily correspond to ancient or modern maps, e.g., the Garden of Eden and its four rivers. At times, Kush reached the western edge of the Sinai Peninsula while Midian was just across the eastern fork of the Red Sea on the east side of the Sinai Peninsula, thus making the possibility of small colonies or outposts with Cushite and Midianite elements more than plausible.

28. John Huehnergard, "Languages," *ABD*, 4:165, and A. Kirk Grayson, "Mesopotamia, History Of," *ABD*, 4:761. See also Berlin, *Zephaniah*, 112–13, and Saddler, *Can a Cushite*, 18, for an overview of the range of identifications.

29. JPS translates every occurrence of Cush in Isaiah and Ezekiel as Nubia, with the exception of Isa 43:3 which it renders Ethiopia, and Ezek 38:5 in which it preserves "Cush." Use in the Writings is inconsistent, including disparate translations of the same expression in Esth 1:1 and 8:9: "one hundred and twenty-seven provinces from India to Nubia [1:1] / Ethiopia [8:9]."

Placement of the prophecy against the Cushites in Zephaniah 2 just before one against Assyria argues for reading the Cushites as the Kushite (Nubian) Empire that at one time seemed unstoppable when they dominated Egypt but which ultimately fell to Assyria. The rise of the Twenty-Sixth Egyptian Dynasty, founded by Psamatik (Psammetichus I) in 663 BCE, was not only the deathblow to Kush but also a death knell for Assyria in Zephaniah's interpretive prophecy. Psamatik's son Neco (I) would have been well-known to Zephaniah's audience as the Pharaoh who killed their beloved monarch Josiah (2 Kgs 23:29). Read in this light, Zephaniah's address to the people, Cushites, rather than the place, Nubia/Kush, reflects the erasure of the political entity and emphasizes the surviving remnant, an object lesson for Zephaniah's own people.

Zephaniah's fourth prophecy ends with a proclamation of Assyria's fall. Asshur, אשור, is both the Assyrian capital Asshur, which represents the larger nation, and the nation of Assyria itself. Neither Zephaniah nor his audience would be quick to forget the lessons of Assyria's conquest of Samaria and devastation of Israel in 722 BCE. Even though Zephaniah most certainly postdates the fall of Kush, the larger collection of proclamations likely straddles the fall of Nineveh in 612 BCE, making the imperfect verb forms in Zephaniah 2:13-15 that describe the fall of Assyria as predictive a credible reading. Zephaniah's description of the destruction of Nineveh and Assyria repeats the fate of the four great cities of Philistia in Zephaniah 2:4 and is resonant with Isaiah's indictment of Edom in chapter 34. Edom escapes notice in Zephaniah. Zephaniah's edict against Assyria (Zeph 2:13-15) and Isaiah's against Edom (Isa 34:5-7) both refer to God's sacrifice. In each instance, a day of reckoning occurs. In Isaiah 34:8 the day is called the "day of vengeance." The significant differences between the two collections are their relative lengths—seventeen verses in Isaiah versus three in Zephaniah—and the inclusion of a supernatural bestiary in Isaiah, including Lilith and goat-demons. Unlike Isaiah, none of Zephaniah's coterie is transmundane.

According to Zephaniah 2:14, a panoply of wild and domestic animals will inhabit what was once Assyria. The language is idiosyncratic— "every [wild] animal of a nation" in 2:14—and obscure. The menagerie in Zephaniah 2, like the one in Isaiah 34, includes words whose meanings are disputed. Is the קאת in Zephaniah 2:14 a "desert owl" (NRSV), "vulture" (RSV), "jackdaw" (JPS), "cormorant" (KJV), "hawk" (*DCH*), "pelican" (BDB), or "goose" (*HALOT*)?[30] Similarly, the קפד, ("screech

---

30. Most of these lexicons offer several of the possibilities represented here.

owl," NRSV) might actually be a hedgehog (*DCH, HALOT*).[31] Both terms occur in Isaiah 34:11 with equally varied translations among biblical editions. In any case, the prophecy is that the land peopled by Assyria and protected by one of the ancient world's most bloodthirsty armies will become the habitat of Judean flocks. Perhaps to the delight of the Judeans, especially those affiliated with the temple, Asshur will also become the haunt of various winged and footed unclean animals.

The prophecy shifts from describing the fall of Assyria in Zephaniah 2:13-14 to taunting her in 2:15: "Is this the city?"[32] Verse 15 is a transitional verse in the MT and begins the third chapter in the LXX. The city is not named but represents Assyria and is presumed to be Nineveh. The identification of the unnamed city in Zephaniah 2:15 as Nineveh is not universally accepted and rests heavily on the mention of Nineveh in Zephaniah 2:13. One can reasonably conclude that Nineveh represents Assyria in the Hebrew Bible.

The unnamed city is called a desolation. Verse 14 says that flocks/herds will lie down in "her." In Zephaniah 2:15, the feminine grammar could refer to any city: "Is this [זאת] the city," "the exultant one [העליזה]," "she who dwelt [היושבת]," "she who said [האמרה]," "in her heart [בלבבה]," and "she has become a horror [היתה שמה]." The ruin of Assyria will culminate in passers-by taunting her demise. Assyria, who thought so much of herself, that she was "the end all and be all" (2:15), will be brought to nothing. In pronouncing this judgment Zephaniah attributes language to Assyria that is suspiciously similar to God's monotheistic assertion in Isaiah 45:22 and mocks Assyria's hubris.[33]

The LXX reading of Zephaniah 2:15 as the beginning of chapter 3 makes the verse the introduction to the decree against the city God chastises in 3:1-7. Arguably that city is not Nineveh. That the city is most certainly Jerusalem will become clear because God is within its midst and because of its judges, prophets, and priests, all characteristic of Judah (Zeph 3:3-5). The proclamation will build to that identification. The ambiguous transition between the two cities and their respective proclamations is deliberate. Nineveh's fate is a warning to Jerusalem who must wonder if Zephaniah 2:14-15 pertains to her.

---

31. The identification of the hooting owl and croaking raven in Zeph 2:14 are more problematic. I address them in the Translation Matters section.

32. No interrogatory is present to identify a question in Greek. NETS has "This the city."

33. See Isa 45:22, אני אל אין עוד, and Zeph 2:15, אני ואפסי עוד איך.

## TRANSLATION MATTERS

The owl hooting at the window in Zephaniah 2:14 is simply a "voice singing," קוֹל יְשׁוֹרֵר, and not an "owl"; the suggested emendation in the *BHS*, כוס, requires changing two out of three radicals, which is a dubious proposition. None of the other sources have an owl for the "voice": the LXX and Peshitta have "wild animals," θηρία, and the corresponding *chywwt'*; the Targum has עוֹפָא, a generic bird, and the Vulgate follows the MT with a "voice singing."

The NRSV's choice of "raven" in the following phrase in Zephaniah 2:15 is slightly more comprehensible if one hears the text rather than reads it. The lexeme in the MT, *ḥoreb*, חרב, "desolation" is a close homophone of the raven, *'oreb*, ערב, and is closer still when *ayin* is pronounced with a strong guttural click. For example, words like עזה, *Azah*, and עמרה, *Amorah*, are transliterated with a hard "g" sound, i.e., "Gaza" and "Gomorrah." The two phrases form a partial parallel: a "voice singing in the window" and something else on the "threshold." The "something else" lacks a verb and thus the parallel is incomplete. The NRSV creates a fuller parallel by supplying two sonorous birds.

# Zephaniah 3:1-20

# *Daughter Zion,*
# *Daughter Jerusalem:*
# *God's Daughter, Safely Home*

## Prophecy 5 (Zeph 3:1-13)

Zephaniah 3 is the beginning of a new pronouncement as indicated by the ס break.[1] The first word of the chapter and prophecy is "woe." The proclamation is in two parts: the woe prophecy to an unnamed city followed by a first-person message to an audience whose identity is explicitly made clear in Zephaniah 3:14. The first line of the woe prophecy addresses the unnamed city directly and describes her as soiled, having been defiled, and actively oppressing someone unnamed. Without the following verses, the city could be Nineveh from the previous prophecy; that reading must also be presumed initially. The scholarship is divided on whether and how much of Zephaniah 3:1-13 pertains to Judah and Jerusalem. Why is the prophet prophesying to and

---

1. In the MT individual passages are delineated with a soft break marked with a ס and a hard break indicated by a פ, most often at the end of a verse.

*Zephaniah 3:1-13*

3:1Ah, soiled, defiled
oppressing city!
2It has listened to no voice;
it has accepted no correction.
It has not trusted in the LORD;
it has not drawn near to its God.

3The officials within it
are roaring lions;
its judges are evening wolves
that leave nothing until the
morning.
4Its prophets are reckless,
faithless persons;
its priests have profaned what is
sacred,
they have done violence to the
law.
5The LORD within it is righteous;
he does no wrong.
Every morning he renders his
judgment,
each dawn without fail;

but the unjust knows no shame.

6I have cut off nations;
their battlements are in ruins;
I have laid waste their streets
so that no one walks in them;
their cities have been made
desolate,
without people, without
inhabitants.
7I said, "Surely the city will fear me,
it will accept correction;
it will not lose sight
of all that I have brought upon
it."
But they were the more eager
to make all their deeds corrupt.

8Therefore wait for me, says the
LORD,
for the day when I arise as a
witness.
For my decision is to gather nations,
to assemble kingdoms,

against cities without naming them? What purpose does that rhetorical strategy serve? A preponderance of scholarship finds repeated reference to characteristic elements relating to Jerusalem throughout the passage and reads the whole in that light. From this perspective the proclamation builds suspense while leading up to the dramatic revelation.

Each of the three initial descriptions of the city in Zephaniah 3:1—"soiled," "defiled," and "oppressing"—has homophones with radically different meanings as evidenced by contemporary translations and multiple ancient textual witnesses. Translation and interpretation choices can yield the harsh critique of NRSV and JPS or a more tender portrait as in the LXX, Peshitta, and, to some degree, the Targum. The harsh critique is based on continuity with the preceding verses on Nineveh. The tender reading is clearly seen as more fitting for Jerusalem in the eyes of other translators and interpreters. Each term may well be a double entendre, with both (or all) meanings intended. The slant of the text reflects the

to pour out upon them my
indignation,
all the heat of my anger;
for in the fire of my passion
all the earth shall be consumed.
⁹At that time I will change the
speech of the peoples
to a pure speech,
that all of them may call on the
name of the LORD
and serve him with one accord.
¹⁰From beyond the rivers of Ethiopia
my suppliants, my scattered
ones,
shall bring my offering.

¹¹On that day you shall not be put
to shame
because of all the deeds by
which you have rebelled
against me;

for then I will remove from your
midst
your proudly exultant ones,
and you shall no longer be
haughty
in my holy mountain.
¹²For I will leave in the midst of
you
a people humble and lowly.
They shall seek refuge in the
name of the LORD—
¹³the remnant of Israel;
they shall do no wrong
and utter no lies,
nor shall a deceitful tongue
be found in their mouths.
Then they will pasture and lie
down,
and no one shall make them
afraid.

translator's understanding of the identification of the city and whether God is castigating (NRSV), critiquing (Targum, Vulgate), or compliment-ing (LXX/NETS, Peshitta) the city.

The city is first, מראה, which NRSV and JPS take the feminine singular Qal participle of the verb as מרא, "soil." The unpointed verb, however, could also be מרה, "to rebel," or even a nominal form of ירא, "fearful," i.e., "wonderful," which accounts for "distinguished" in the NETS and "well-known" in the Peshitta. The LXX seems to read the verb as ירא; its translation ἐπιφανής, "splendid," otherwise occurs only in texts with נוראה, the Niphal participle of ירא, "wonderful" or, perhaps better, "awesome."[2] The least likely option is ראה, "to see," though if the prophet was inten-tionally invoking layers of meaning, the phrase might have the sense that the frightful city will become wondrous to behold.

2. See Judg 13:6; Joel 2:11; Hab 1:7. See also Mal 1:14 and 1 Chr 17:21 where ἐπιφανὲς translates נראה, maintaining the pattern.

The second description, נגאלה, can be "defiled" (NRSV) or "polluted" (JPS) if it is the Niphal participle of גאל (II) or it can be "redeemed" if the root is גאל (I). The LXX's ἀπολελυτρωμένη, Vulgate's *redempta*, and Targum's מתפרקא (from פרק, "redeem" or "release") all concur on redemption. Taking seriously both roots suggests that the unnamed city that has been defiled shall be redeemed, which makes both interpretations applicable.

Finally, the city is היונה, which NRSV and JPS both interpret as "oppressing," reading the verb as ינה, as in "You shall not wrong or oppress a resident alien" in Exodus 22:21. The feminine singular Qal participle of ינה, יונה (*yonah*) is a homophone for the name of the prophet Jonah. The Peshitta identifies the city as "the city of Jonah." (What is not clear is if the text has in mind Gath-hepher, identified as Jonah's city in 2 Kgs 14:25.) The word יונה is also a homophone of the feminine singular noun "dove," and the LXX and Vulgate translate the city as a dove. The city is characterized as a *provocatrix* in the Vulgate and similarly in the Targum as דמסגיא לארגזא, "provoking anger." The range of possible interpretations reflects the ambiguity of the text. I suggest the ambiguity is intentional.

Because of the ambiguity, determining if the city is Nineveh continued from the previous verses or Jerusalem is difficult. All of the sources agree that the city, whether darling dove or vexing virago, receives a harsh prophetic word in the following verses. The description in the second verse strongly indicates that the city is Jerusalem. The stubborn city has "listened to no voice" and refused "correction." That correction, מוסר, "discipline" or "instruction," harks back to Deuteronomy 11:2 and features prominently in Proverbs (e.g., Prov 1:8; 3:11; 8:10, 33, etc.). Furthermore, the term מוסר is not used for non-Israelite nations except when God uses Israel's chastisement as an object lesson in Ezekiel 5:15. To this point, the first half of Zephaniah 3:2 is duplicated and expanded in Jeremiah 7:28, where clearly it refers to Israel and Judah. In addition, the primary charge, namely, that the city has failed to trust in God, is not regularly a charge for a foreign city. The claim that God is the god of the city is particular to Jerusalem. Texts with universalizing language claim the whole earth as God's or describe God winning a nation or city over. They do not single out individual non-Israelite peoples as belonging to God.[3] The context of the interpreter, however, shapes interpretation, and, as Sweeney notes, the Syrian church reads 3:1-7 in relation to

---

3. See Isa 19:19-22, where God makes God's self known to the Egyptians so as to be worshiped there, and Amos 9:7, where God compares Israel to the Nubians, Philistines, and Arameans in terms of divine care and attention visited upon them.

Nineveh.[4] The Targum clarifies that the city has failed to listen to the voice of the prophets. This reading strengthens the interpretation of the city as Jerusalem.

The next few verses, specifically Zephaniah 3:3-5, pertain even more strongly to Jerusalem. The administrative and religious offices are familiar from Israelite bureaucracy: officials/chiefs/rulers (שרים) and judges (שפטים) in verse 3, and prophets (נביאים) and priests (כהנים) in verse 4. All of those officials have failed in some way. Most significant, the civil and religious leaders are indicted for having "done violence" to (or, better, "violated" since the preposition is lacking) the Torah. The officials and judges are predatory, but, unlike ravening animals, they do not even leave scraps behind. Curiously, the prophet does not mention the people whom they plunder. This point is in keeping with the previous focus on the wealthy without any mention of the poor. Likewise, the city is "oppressing" in 3:1, but no one is described as being oppressed.

In Zephaniah 3:4, Zephaniah critiques his prophetic colleagues for being "reckless" and "treacherous," אנשי בגדות (contra NRSV's "faithless"). His language, "men of treachery," using the more exclusive איש, "man," over against the inclusive אדם, "human," excludes or erases female prophets,[5] including his contemporary Huldah. What I find unlikely is that Zephaniah did not know any women prophets. That he would not be aware of the prophet who served his monarch, Josiah, is hard to imagine. Given the many similarities, allusions, and likely quotes from Isaiah, I contend he would have also been aware of the woman prophet with whom Isaiah fathered at least one of his children.[6] Harder to imagine is the notion that Zephaniah (or his redactor) would be unaware that more women prophets lived in ancient Israel than the few individually identified[7] in the canon. The exclusion of Huldah may be deliberate;

---

4. Marvin A. Sweeney, *Zephaniah: A Commentary on the Book of Zephaniah*, ed. Paul D. Hanson, Hermeneia 36 (Minneapolis: Fortress, 2003), 161.

5. I address this point extensively in Wilda Gafney, *Daughters of Miriam: Women Prophets in Ancient Israel* (Minneapolis: Fortress, 2007).

6. Maher Shalal Hash Baz in Isa 8:1-4 is the son of the two prophets. The mother of Isaiah's son Shear Yashub (Isa 7:3) is unknown. Whether Isaiah has other children is unclear; see Isa 8:18. Some scholars argue that Immanu-El in Isa 7:14 may well be Isaiah's son as well, given his predilection for prophetic names and the cluster of the three names in the unit on the Syro-Ephramitic crisis in Isa 7–8.

7. Women who are explicitly identified as prophets include Miriam (Exod 2:1-10; 6:20 [LXX]; 15:20-21; Num 12:1-16; 21:1; 26; 59; Deut 24:9; 1 Chr 6:3 [5:29 MT]; Mic 6:4); Deborah (Judg 4:4-16; 5:1-31); Huldah (2 Kgs 22:8-20; 2 Chr 34:14-28); an unnamed

he may consider her to be faithful as he considers himself to be. It is hard to imagine Zephaniah so critiquing the prophet who validated some portion of the Torah and its commandments and led to the first recorded observance of Passover outside of the book of Exodus (see 2 Kgs 23:21-23). The expression "treacherous men" may also be generic and inclusive in spite of its apparent gender-exclusive language. The word אִישׁ is sometimes generic for "person."[8] If inclusive, the expression is likely rhetorical excess.

Not surprising is the fact that Zephaniah does not name any individual prophets in his critique. Rarely do Israelite prophets name their contemporaries or former prophets even when quoting them.[9] Consider that Moses is named only five times in the Prophets, which includes naming him with Miriam in Micah (Mic 6:4; see also Isa 63:11-12; Jer 15:1; and Mal 4:4 while Mal 4:5 mentions Elijah). The resort to Micah and his prophecies as a defense for the preaching of Jeremiah in Jeremiah 29:16-19 is one of the most striking exceptions. The derided prophets in Zephaniah 3:4 are paired with equally disreputable priests whom Zephaniah accuses of "profaning the holy" and "doing violence to the Torah" in the second half of verse 4. If the couplet is taken to refer to an alliance between those priests and prophets, then it may be possible to exclude Jeremiah from their ranks on the grounds that he was an outsider to the Jerusalem priesthood, his own priestly lineage notwithstanding.[10]

---

woman (Isa 8:1-4); a women-only guild (Ezek 13:17-23); Noadiah (Neh 6:15); and the Daughters of Heman (1 Chr 25:1-8). Women prophets are also represented in plural expressions, i.e., "prophets"; see Gafney, *Daughters of Miriam*, 160–64.

8. See Num 14:15, where אִישׁ represents each person in Israel; 2 Kgs 14:6 and Jer 31:30, where אִישׁ represents any person who sins; Job 38:26, where אִישׁ represents humanity; and Neh 8:1, where אִישׁ represents every returnee, later specified to include women in Neh 8:2.

9. Isaiah (9:15), Jeremiah (2:8), Ezekiel (13:2-4, 16-19), Micah (3:11), Zephaniah (3:4), and Zechariah (13:1-4) all castigate other prophets to some degree. Many more examples can be found through biblical literature; in some texts prophetic censure becomes a regular theme.

10. Jeremiah was an Abiatharian priest from the ill-named Anathoth in Benjamin. None of those circumstances would commend him to the Jerusalem temple establishment. Abiathar, a priest during the reign of David, supported Adonijah instead of Solomon to succeed David and was banished to Anathoth by Solomon (1 Kgs 2:26). I say Anathoth was ill-named because its root is Anat, the Canaanite goddess of war. Finally, the tribe of Benjamin is portrayed extremely negatively in the Hebrew Bible, from the gang-raping men of Gibeah in Judg 19 to Saul the failed Benjaminite mon-

The larger proclamation intimates that Jerusalem is its context without naming the city; prophets, priests, and Torah are hallmarks of Jerusalem. Though Jerusalem is not named in Zephaniah 3:2-5, the religious descriptions fit her: YHWH is her God and Torah is her sacred trust. Verse 5 locates God within the city, בקרבה, "in her midst," which is a clear reference to Jerusalem, God's particular habitation. That image will be expanded in the poem that comprises the second portion of the chapter. In Zephaniah 3:15 God is also in the midst of Jerusalem. In the NRSV a space exists between Zephaniah 3:2 and 3. The MT contains no corresponding break. That editorial space highlights the ambiguity of Zephaniah 3:1, which could pertain to the Assyrian city in the previous chapter, based on its content. The whole unit, however, appears to apply its harsh judgment to Jerusalem.

The most serious critique is reserved for the priests who stand accused of profaning that which is sacred, חללו־קדש, and doing violence to Torah, חמסו התורה. The sancta are likely the sacred donations whose profanation is prohibited in Leviticus 22:15, which uses the same language.[11] Profanation of the offerings is equivalent to profaning the holy name in Leviticus 22:2, where profanation is someone other than the appropriate members of a priest's household eating meat from sacrificial animals.[12] The Torah in Zephaniah 3:4 is not the Torah, a canonical scroll, or "the law" per NRSV; rather, it is teaching and legal rulings issued by priests, all of which are encompassed by the word. The charges in Zephaniah 3:4 are largely repeated and elaborated in Ezekiel 22:23-28. The absence of any critique for the king in Zephaniah is notable and consistent with the prophet or his editors backing the reforms of Josiah. Unlike the officials, priests, and prophets who have failed at the basic work of justice, God is righteous and faithfully renders justice each day.

The declaration of divine righteousness in Zephaniah 3:5 prefaces a description of the awful but just power of God that destroys nations and

---

arch. Disdain for his heritage may explain the less than gracious reception Jeremiah receives from temple and palace according his own account.

11. See Lev 22:15: ולא יחללו את־קדשו; Zephaniah 3:4: חללו־קדש.

12. An example of offering portions permitted to members of a priest's household is the breast and right thigh of well-being, שלם, sacrifices in Lev 7:31-36. Those who were permitted to eat of the donation were priests and their offspring, including daughters (whether unmarried, widowed, or divorced who lived in their father's household) and slaves but not servants who received a wage (see Lev 22:10-13). Those who were prohibited included an otherwise appropriate member of a priest's household who was taboo and thus prohibited from the assembly (see Lev 22:4-7).

cities in verse 6. In the second part of prophecy 5, specifically in 3:6-13, God speaks in the first person to an unnamed audience that is gradually revealed to be Jerusalem. One clearly sees now that God has punished not just Israel's enemies but also Israel and Judah. That punishment was the decimation of the Northern monarchy, subsequent vassalage of Judah, and virtual occupation of Jerusalem under Assyrian hegemony. In verse 6, a divine address begins with a list of God's credentials and qualifications that elevates the prophetic performance to a crescendo. God has not only cut off nations but also destroyed and depopulated them. God has already done what Zephaniah prophesied in 2:13-15 and can certainly do it again. Now God prophesies and speaks directly to an unnamed subject— NRSV supplies "the city" in verse 7—"surely you [fem. sing.] will reverence [תיראי] me and you [fem. sing.] will accept [תקחי] discipline/instruction [מוסר]."[13] The subject is no longer a mystery. God speaks to Jerusalem, who represents the Judean people.

In Zephaniah 3:7, God offers the people divine instruction. "Instruction," מוסר, is not offered to non-Israelite peoples in the Hebrew Scriptures. The use of מוסר signifies to the hearer and reader that this text pertains to Judah, the remnant of Israel who has survived a previous divine decimation. Instruction is, along with a mother's *torah*, part of the upbringing and education of a child (Prov 1:8; 13:1). The elements "reverence" or "fear" of God and "instruction" go together in Proverbs 1:7 and 15:33. "Instruction" for Israelites is what many African Americans would call "home training," a complex ethical and social code passed down intergenerationally, primarily from parent to child. Accepting divine instruction is linked to Judah's survival in Zephaniah 3:7 in the MT, ולא יכרת מעונה, that "her dwelling not be cut off." The NRSV, however, reads with the LXX and Peshitta against the MT: "it [the city] will not lose sight" of all that God has done. The Targum agrees with the MT, לא יפסוק מרורהון, "their dwelling will not cease/be cut off," though the MT's third feminine singular becomes third inclusive plural in the Targum. The Vulgate simply reproduces the MT.

In verse 7 God's proclamation becomes self-reflective and retrospective. The revelation of God's inner thoughts reveals a deity who is not omniscient in Zephaniah's rhetoric. God thought that the demonstration of divine power would have proved instructive, but it was not so. In-

---

13. The combination of ירא and מוסר here further suggests that ירא is the root of the disputed form מראה in 3:1.

stead, "they" doubled down on their corruption in spite of God's power displayed in their own history. The address has shifted from a feminine singular recipient, the city, to an inclusive plural recipient community, specifically to the inhabitants of Judah and Jerusalem.

Zephaniah 3:8 begins with "therefore," which connects the judgment in verses 9-13 with the conclusions at the end of verse 7. The city has failed to show reverence for God who will now display even more awe-inspiring power. The anthropomorphic declaration that God will rise communicated that all of God's dread power will be focused on Jerusalem and Judah. But for what purpose? The MT has the word לעד pointed as "for prey," but the NRSV follows the LXX and Peshitta in reading it as "[for] a witness." The JPS has an "accuser." The Vulgate has chosen the highly problematic *in die resurrectionis meae*, "in the day of my resurrection." I see no reason to amend the text. God has arisen to prey on the nations.

The image of God rising is meant to provoke terror and awe. The phrase "Rise, O GOD" was the opening of the ancient war chant attributed to Moses in Numbers 10:35. In Zephaniah 3:8-13, one sees that God will judge the whole world. The day of YHWH is now a day of reckoning in the judicial sense. It is the "ruling" of God, משפט, normally "justice," to gather nations and monarchies together for punishment (Zeph 3:8). This punishment will be a purge that will destroy "all the earth/land" in the fury and flames of God's wrath, indignation, and jealousy. God's "jealousy," preferable to NRSV's "passion," fuels the inferno and points back to the worship of Baal and Milcom/Molech in Zephaniah 1:4-5 and 2:11.[14] While monarchies and nations—presumably Gentile—are initially the focus of the divine indignation and fury, the flames will eventually consume the whole earth. Rhetorically, Judah and Jerusalem are included.

In spite of Zephaniah's many prophecies of total destruction not only does a remnant remain in Judah (2:7) and Israel (3:12-13) but also peoples in other nations survive (3:9, 20). Immediately after the conflagration, God will tend to the survivors left in and beyond Israel. Starting with the peoples outside of Israel, God transforms the speech of the nations (see 3:9) and reverses the aftereffects of the tower of Babel in Genesis 11:1-8 that resulted in cacophonous human language. The reason for this new

---

14. Jealousy is one of God's traditional responses to idolatry, particularly when expressed as abrogation of a marital or other covenant; see Exod 20:4-6; 34:13-15; Deut 4:23-24; 5:8-10; 6:14-15; and Josh 24:19-20.

linguistic unity is so that people from all nations would be able to call on the name of God. True universalizing language is rare in the canon. Zephaniah's language is joined by Isaiah's famous feast for all peoples (25:6), Jeremiah's gathering of all nations in God's presence in Jerusalem (3:17), and Micah's vision of all peoples walking together, each in the name of their individual gods (Micah 4:5). Conversely, the destruction of all nations is nearly ubiquitous in the canon. Zephaniah's language, לקרא יהוה בשם, "to call on the name of GOD," is worship language.[15] It is the opposite of what the Torah describes as God calling Israel out of the nations to be God's people and to worship God (Deut 7:6-7; 10:15; and 14:2). In verse 8, God is calling nations together not only for destruction but also to call on the most holy Name of God and to serve God in unity, שכם אחד, with one accord, literally "a single shoulder [put to the same work]" (v. 9).

The new universal language will be "plain," "pure," or "clean," ברורה, so that all the survivors from whatever nation will be able to serve God harmoniously. The newly transformed speech of the peoples will most likely be the Judean language, (biblical) Hebrew, the language in which God was accustomed to receiving worship. If so, then the language of the Judean survivors will not be changed. If Hebrew is indeed being portrayed as a "pure" language, uniquely suited for worship, this presages the rabbinic notion of Hebrew as לשון קדושה, *leshon haqodesh*, "the holy tongue." The passage may also serve as both an incentive and a rebuke for diaspora Judeans who need to return to their mother tongue.

A particular community of worshipers will come from these nations gathered in Zephaniah 3:8, and they will bring offerings to God in verse 10. These nations will come from "beyond the rivers of Nubia [Cush]."[16] Reading Kush as the nation "beyond the rivers of Nubia" would make the rivers the two tributaries of the Nile that divide in the city of Khartoum. Alternately, the scope of the passage may call for reading the nations as the legendary nation associated with the Garden of Eden in Genesis 2:13. The phrase from which those "worshipers" are derived, עתרי בת־פוצי, "my supplicants, my scattered ones" (NRSV), is greatly contested in antiquity and modernity. The LXX and Peshitta omit the phrase entirely. Berlin offers a range of possibilities from the scholarship,[17] and

---

15. See 1 Kgs 18:24-25; 2 Kgs 5:11; Pss 63:4; 79:6; 80:18; 105:1; 116:13, 17; and Isa 12:4.

16. The same expression occurs in Isa 18:1. At the end of that unit the people of Cush bring gifts to God (Isa 18:7).

17. Adele Berlin, *Zephaniah*, AB 25A (New Haven: Yale University Press, 1994), 134–35.

I address this range in the Translation Matters section. Reading Zephaniah 3:10 as pertaining to the return of exiled Judeans would require a later dating for this text and for the book as a whole than is traditionally argued, later than the Josianic period to which the book is assigned. Undoubtedly some postexilic readers read Zephaniah this way. Given the reference to "peoples" in the preceding verse, however, to read Zephaniah 3:10 as pertaining to foreign supplicants makes sense.

### TRANSLATION MATTERS

"My supplicants, daughter of my scattered [ones]," עתרי בת־פוצי

In Zephaniah 3:10 the expression the NRSV translates as "my supplicants, my scattered ones," עתרי בת־פוצי, baffles translators and was omitted from the LXX and Peshitta.[18] The first part is rather straightforward: JPS, NRSV, and the Vulgate read עתרי as a nominal form of the verb עתר, "entreat," with the root well attested in the Hebrew Scriptures as a synonym in the Qal for "praying" (Gen 25:21; Exod 8:8-9; Judg 13:8) and in the Niphal for God "heeding" those entreaties (2 Sam 21:14; Isa 19:22; Ezra 8:23). The second part is the most vexing, resulting in JPS's partial transliteration "in Fair Puzi" as though it were a personal name, adding the preposition. The JPS regularly translates "daughter" cities as "Fair X" cities, i.e., "Fair Zion" and "Fair Jerusalem" in Zephaniah 3:14 and, in other texts, "virgin daughter" cities as "Fair Maiden X" cities, i.e., "Fair Maiden Sidon" (Isa 23:12), "Fair Maiden Babylon" (Isa 47:1), etc. The בת, "daughter," in בת־פוצי is without dispute. פוצי appears to be from פוץ, "scatter" or "disperse;" the expression would then be "daughter of my scattered ones." The expression likely functions as a euphemistic expression for those in the diaspora, e.g., "children of the dispersion." The use of "daughter" here suggests a singular or collective entity and one that is equal parts vulnerable and valuable as is Bat Zion, Daughter (of) Zion. As פוץ is used for both Israelites and other peoples, it cannot be definitively determined which community in diaspora is meant here.[19]

In Zephaniah 3:11 the passage shifts to direct speech as God assures a feminine singular entity, the unnamed "you" of verse 7, that she will not be neglected as God receives these alien devotees into the fold. Most scholars, both ancient and contemporary interpreters, understand Jerusalem to be the addressee. The remainder of this section addresses the

18. The Targum has instead גלות . . . דאיתגליאה, "the exiles . . . in which they have been exiled."

19. For example, see Gen 11:8 for the scattering of the nations after the tower of Babel episode and Deut 4:27 for the scattering of Israel.

survivors first in a direct address (vv. 11-13) and then in third person
with the shift coming in the middle of verse 12. God calms the apparent
fears of the unnamed addressee. In spite of her rebellion, she will not
be put to shame. Instead, God will purge her numbers of those who are
still proudly exulting (possibly over the fate of others) even at the end
of the world (v. 11). That will put an end to "haughtiness" on God's
holy mountain, a new location introduced in the text. Given the Judean
context, the mountain is more likely to be Jerusalem, stylized as Mount
Zion, than Sinai, Horeb, or any other location.[20]

According to Zephaniah 3:12, the people who remain will be עני,
"humble," "poor," or, in other contexts, "afflicted." Throughout Zephaniah and the larger prophetic tradition, pride and haughtiness are associated with wealth, and humility is associated with poverty. The assertion
that the remnant will be humble-poor speaks more to their spiritual
condition than to their material possessions, though Zephaniah's rhetoric
does not allow space for riches to survive the day of YHWH. The humble-
poor remnant are also the "needy-poor," דל. Hebrew has a number of
words for the poor. Many emphasize different aspects of privation, including its causes and consequences. The combination of עני and דל occurs in a handful of texts. The exact expression עני ודל is duplicated only
in Isaiah 26:6.

In Zephaniah 3:13, the survivors are identified as the remnant of Israel, שארית ישראל. Israel has been named previously only with reference
to God in Zephaniah 2:9 where God is the God of Israel. The verbs
that follow and serve the feminine singular שארית, "remnant," do not
correspond with remnant in gender or number. They are third-person
inclusive plural (hence, "they" in the NRSV). JPS, the Targum, Peshitta,
and the Vulgate take the remnant as the subject of the verbs in spite of the
gender and number mismatch; the LXX omits the phrase. The conduct
of the surviving remnant is markedly different from the conduct of the
corrupt officials, priests, and prophets in Zephaniah 3:3-4 and the city in
3:7. The now purified remnant is as docile as sheep. They do not speak
anything amiss but pasture and lie down without fear. This description
circles back to Zephaniah 2:7 in which the remnant of the house of Judah
takes possession of the Philistine coast where they pasture and lie down
in the plundered houses of Ashkelon. The prophecy concludes with a

---

20. The prosaic description of Jerusalem and Mount Zion is common in the Psalms
and Isaiah; see 2 Kgs 19:31; Pss 48:2, 11; 74:2; 78:68; 125:1; Isa 4:5; 8:18; 10:12, 32; 16:1;
18:7; 24:23; 29:8; 31:4; 37:32; Joel 2:32; Obad 1:17, 21; and Mic 4:7.

bold assertion: the remnant does not have to fear anyone ever again. The surety for this fearlessness is the name of God who is their safe haven and the refuge of the humble, needy poor who make up the remnant (2:12).

The idea of the divine name functioning as a virtual entity is particularly characteristic of Deuteronomy, where God chooses a place for the divine name to dwell (Deut 12:5, 11; 14:23; 16:2, 6, 11; 26:2). The name of God is also the source for blessing (Deut 21:5; 2 Sam 6:18) and cursing (2 Kgs 2:24). It is the source of authority for oaths (1 Sam 20:42; 1 Kgs 22:13) and also divine service (Deut 18:5, 7, 22; 1 Kgs 18:32). The Name is the armament that David brought with him while Goliath carried spear and javelin (1 Sam 17:45). Finally, this name is a place of refuge in the psalms (Ps 124:8). The security guaranteed in and by the name of God sets the stage for the final prophecy, a call to jubilation.

## Prophecy 6 (Zeph 3:14-20)

The sixth prophecy concludes the book. It is addressed to בת ציון, *Bat Tzion*, Daughter Zion, and בת ירושלם, *Bat Yerushalayim*, Daughter Jerusalem (Zeph 3:14). Zion is a traditional name for Jerusalem and the larger land and people throughout the Bible, inclusive of the Deuterocanonical/Apocryphal writings. The expressions בת ציון and בת ירושלם can also be read as "daughter *of* Zion" and "daughter *of* Jerusalem," referring to a woman (or girl) from the city. The expressions also serve as a reference to the city. "Daughter [of] Jerusalem" is a rarer formulation and occurs only seven times in the canon[21] versus twenty-six occurrences of "Daughter [of] Zion."[22] In all but one case, namely, in Lamentations 2:15, Daughter [of] Jerusalem occurs in parallel with Daughter [of] Zion. I address the larger use of the expressions in the Translation Matters section.

In keeping with the grammatical and cultural gender of cities, God through the prophet addresses Zion/Jerusalem with feminine grammar. Three of the imperatives in Zephaniah 3:14 are feminine singular: רני, "sing," שמחי, "rejoice," and ועלזי, "exult." The verb הריעו, "shout," in verse 14 is inclusive plural, addressed to Israel as a whole. The prophecy then uses the feminine forms in verses 15-19 until the final verse, verse 20, where it uses the inclusive second-person plural to address the whole community.

21. See 2 Kgs 19:21; Isa 37:22; Lam 2:13, 15; Mic 4:8; Zeph 3:14; and Zech 9:9.
22. See 2 Kgs 19:21; Ps 9:14; Isa 1:8; 10:32; 16:1; 37:22; 52:2; 62:11; Jer 4:31; 6:2, 23; Lam 1:6; 2:1, 4, 8, 10, 13, 18; 4:22; Mic 1:13; 4:8, 10, 13; Zeph 3:14; and Zech 2:10; 9:9.

*Zephaniah 3:14-20*

¹⁴Sing aloud, O daughter Zion;
   shout, O Israel!
Rejoice and exult with all your
      heart,
   O daughter Jerusalem!
¹⁵The LORD has taken away the
      judgments against you,
   he has turned away your
      enemies.
The king of Israel, the LORD, is in
      your midst;
   you shall fear disaster no more.

¹⁶On that day it shall be said to
   Jerusalem:
Do not fear, O Zion;
   do not let your hands grow weak.
¹⁷The LORD, your God, is in your
      midst,
   a warrior who gives victory;
he will rejoice over you with
      gladness,
he will renew you in his love;
he will exult over you with loud
      singing

The day of YHWH has been a terrifying one up to this point. Now it is a day of comfort and consolation. "On that day," Zion will have no reason to fear ever again (v. 16). After the destruction of the day and the preservation of a remnant, the time has come to celebrate. The directives to make merry in the imperative evoke the image of a people stunned by all that they have been through. Their praise is not spontaneous. It is solicited and does not occur in the text. Zephaniah explains why she, Zion/Jerusalem, should rejoice—because God has taken away the judgments against her. The judicial language harks back to 1:2-6, 18; 3:8. She has not been found innocent; rather, the case against her has been dismissed; the charges have been vacated; and/or the sentence has been suspended. The discharge (הסיר) of judgment and redirection (פנה) of Jerusalem's enemies are presented with synonyms, both of which mean "turn [away]." The turning away of Jerusalem's enemies is a likely reference to the end of Judah's subjugation by Assyria, which could also be read with reference to Babylon. Nevertheless, the primary reason Zion, Jerusalem, and Israel should celebrate is the presence of their sovereign in their midst, more specifically, in "her" midst.

"In your [fem. sing.] midst" is repeated in Zephaniah 3:15 and 17. In the former reference, God is the sovereign ruler of Israel; in the latter, God is Jerusalem's God. The emphasis on the presence of God is in contrast to the intimation that God has been absent from Jerusalem, a situation that opens the door for Israel's enemies to overwhelm her. This reading is supported by the nature of God's presence, גבור יושיע, "as a warrior who saves/delivers" in Zephaniah 3:17. The divine warrior is a comforting presence here because the warrior rejoices over Jerusalem, עליך ישיש, instead of threatening her. In verse 17 God responds to Jerusalem

<sup>18</sup>as on a day of festival.
I will remove disaster from you,
   so that you will not bear
    reproach for it.
<sup>19</sup>I will deal with all your oppressors
   at that time.
And I will save the lame
   and gather the outcast,
and I will change their shame into
    praise

and renown in all the earth.
<sup>20</sup>At that time I will bring you home,
   at the time when I gather you;
for I will make you renowned and
    praised
   among all the peoples of the
    earth,
when I restore your fortunes
   before your eyes, says the
    LORD.

out of love. The nature of that response is disputed. NRSV translates יחריש באהבתו as "[God] will renew you in [God's] love," emending חרש to חדש and reading with the LXX (καινιεῖ, "affection") and with the Peshitta (*chwb'*, "love").[23] I find with Berlin (and the Vulgate), the verb in the MT is likely חרש (II) "remain silent/be deaf" rather than its homophone חרש (I), "plow."[24] The sense is that God refrains from mentioning and/or hearing of Jerusalem's sins any further. This reading is also preferable because it does not require emendation to make sense of it. Marvin Sweeney's choice to read the verb as חרש (I), "he plows with his love," is highly sexually suggestive in a way that the text generally avoids with God and Israel, even in the marriage metaphor. The deity, seemingly intentionally, lacks an explicit phallus with which to "plow."[25] "Plowing" is sexually suggestive in the Hebrew Bible as in the case when Samson accuses the Philistines of "plowing with [his] heifer" (Judg 14:18). The framers of the Hebrew Bible may well have refrained from any mention of divine "plowing," given the popularity of the Sumerian epic poem, the Court-ship of Inanna, in which the goddess famously asks, "Who will plow my vulva?" and then passionately urges on her suitor: "Plow my vulva!"

23. The Peshitta has "renew in love, *chwb'*."
24. Berlin, *Zephaniah*, 145.
25. References to an implicit divine phallus in the Hebrew Scriptures are conjectural. For example, Gershon Hepner argues for reading קשת, "bow," as "phallus" in *Legal Friction: Law, Narrative, and Identity Politics in Biblical Israel* (New York: Lang, 2010), 143–45. The bow is associated with young men and their vigor and the enduring vigor older men (Job 29:20), overlapping with virility. Emphasis on the "tautness" (Gen 49:24) of the bow may well be a double entendre; however, in each text the "bow" can also be read merely as a bow.

### TRANSLATION MATTERS

*Bat Zion/Yerushalyim,* Daughter (of) Zion/Jerusalem, בת ציון/ירושלם:

Daughter Zion/Jerusalem is a personification of the city as woman. The depiction of Zion and Jerusalem as female reflects Hebrew grammatical gender and social conventions in the wider ancient world in which cities are nearly universally feminine. Correspondingly, both cities and their inhabitants are regularly personified as women in the Hebrew Bible. In the Hebrew Bible cities are "daughter" cities, often virginal, therefore marriageable and presumably youthful like Jerusalem/Zion (2 Kgs 19:21/Isa 37:22; Jer 14:17; Lam 1:15; 2:13), Babel (Isa 47:1; Zech 2:10 [2:14 MT]), Tarshish (Isa 23:10),[26] Sidon (Isa 23:12), Dibon (Jer 48:18), Edom (Lam 4:21, 22) and Tyre (Ps 45:12 [45:13 MT]).[27] In other texts Zion and Jerusalem are further personified as a woman or girl of indeterminate age indicated by daughter language without the virginal descriptor.[28] The expressions בתולה ישראל, "Virgin Israel";[29] בת עמי, "My Daughter-People"; and יושבת ציון, "she-who-dwells (in) Zion," are related.[30]

The formula *bat Zion/Jerusalem* is the same one that identifies a woman's (or girl's) heritage, i.e., Dinah bat Leah (Gen 34:1). In *bat PN* expressions בת is in construct and the proper name is absolute, forming a construct chain indicating the possessive, normally requiring "of" in translation, i.e., "Dinah, [the] daughter of Leah." Therefore, the grammar of *bat Zion/Jerusalem* also allows the expression to be read as "daughter of" Zion or Jerusalem signifying an individual woman. In Zephaniah it is relatively clear that Daughter Zion and Daughter Jerusalem refer to the city; however, in other texts there is the possibility that a character long interpreted as a personified city may in fact be a woman, a daughter of Zion or Jerusalem.

In Isaiah 40:9 מבשרת ציון/מבשרת ירושלם has been traditionally understood as both "Zion/Jerusalem, she who proclaims good news" and "she who proclaims good news *to* Zion/Jerusalem." If the מבשרת, "she-who-proclaims-good-news," is not

---

26. This verse is difficult, but the NRSV's choice of "ships of Tarshish" for "daughter Tarshish" is inexplicable. The RSV is preferable to the NRSV here: "Overflow your land like the Nile, O daughter of Tarshish; there is no restraint any more."

27. In Ps 45:12 (45:13 MT) בת צר signifies a woman, not a city. The NRSV, however, translates it as "people of Tyre" and obscures the fact that the psalm is addressing a daughter of Tyre, a royal woman marrying into Israel. The only person who fits that description is Jezebel; see "Tyrian lass" in the JPS.

28. See Ps 9:14; Isa 1:8; 10:32; 16:1; 52:2; 62:11; Jer 4:31; 6:2, 23; Lam 1:6; 2:1, 4, 8, 10, 18; 4:22; Mic 1:13; 4:8, 10, 13; Zeph 3:14; Zech 2:10; 9:9.

29. ישראל בתולה can mean either "Virgin Israel" or "virgin of Israel" as in Deut 22:19.

30. Tikva Frymer-Kensky helpfully reviews these tropes in *In the Wake of the Goddesses: Women, Culture, and the Biblical Transformation of Pagan Myth* (New York: Free Press, 1992), 168–78. Though she omits Zephaniah, Christl M. Maier addresses the use of gender to characterize Jerusalem in exilic and postexilic periods of crisis in *Daughter Zion, Mother Zion: Gender, Space, and the Sacred in Ancient Israel* (Minneapolis: Fortress, 2008).

the city, then she is most likely a prophet sent to the city. Translations that render Zion/Jerusalem as the preacher-prophet in this passage include the Geneva and Bishop's Bibles, KJV, RSV, NRSV, and CEB. Those that present an unidentified preacher to Zion and Jerusalem are the NETS, Vulgate, Douay, and JPS. None of the texts that present a preacher-prophet proclaiming to the city reveal the feminine gender of the speaker.[31] Using a similar argument, Mayer I. Gruber argues for the presence of one or more female prophets in conflict in Micah 7. He focuses on the dialogue in verses 8-10 where one female subject calls another her enemy using the feminine form of the noun איבתי, "my enemy," which establishes the gender of the second woman. The gender of the first woman, the speaker, is confirmed when she recalls her enemy mocking her and her God using the feminine form of the second-person singular pronoun, אלהיך, "your God."[32] These texts serve as a reminder to explore the possibility that *Bat Zion* and *Bat Yerushalayim* are women, perhaps prophets in the texts in which they occur, rather than reflexively adopting the traditional city-personification without reflection.

Zephaniah 3:18 is difficult to interpret, which results in wide-ranging translations with varied sequencing of the phrases. The opening phrase of verse 18 in the NRSV, "as on a day of festival," is attached to its translation of verse 17. Many modern translations, like the NRSV and CEB, carry a note that the Hebrew of verse 18 is uncertain. What is certain is that a shift in the speaker occurs from Zephaniah 3:17, where the prophet speaks of God in the third person. In Zephaniah 3:18-19 the voice switches to first person, where God addresses Zion directly.

In the midst of and in spite of the joy evoked in Zephaniah 3:17, some people are suffering some ill or "disaster," נוגי (Zeph 3:18). How this suffering is related to the liturgy of the temple introduced by the next word, ממועד, is unclear. As written, the MT has "I will remove from the [day of] festival." In verse 18 God promises to gather someone (those experiencing disaster?) from the midst of Jerusalem and continues to speak to her in the second-person feminine singular. The syntax of the verse does not supply an object for the gathering.

In Zephaniah 3:19 God promises retribution to all those who have oppressed Judah and Jerusalem. The proclamation soars, promising

31. A similar phenomenon occurs with the translation of המבשרות צבא רב in Ps 68:11 (68:12 MT): "The women who proclaim the good news are a mighty army." Only the JPS renders the women present.

32. Mayer I. Gruber, "Women's Voices in the Book of Micah," *lectio difficilior*, no. 1 (2007); http://www.lectio.unibe.ch/07_1/mayer_gruber_womens_voices.htm.

restoration to the people of Israel. God will gather all of the dispersed exiles, referred to as "lame" and "outcast." Their lameness is parallel to their forcible exile, which suggests an image of exile as disabling. The next step in restoration is the transformation of their shame (from occupation and deportation) to praise, תהלה, most commonly translated as "psalm." The restoration is complete in verse 20 when God restores Israel to its land. In verse 20 a final change in address occurs: using the first person God speaks to Zion/Jerusalem/Israel as a collective in the second-person plural:

> I will bring you all home
> I will gather you all
> I will make you all renowned
> I will restore the fortunes of you all
> before the eyes of you all

Zephaniah ends on a note of triumph, which is the inverse of its beginning: "I will utterly sweep away everything from the face of the earth." The day of YHWH has moved from sacrifice (1:8) and punishment (1:9), wailing (1:10) and bitter cries (1:14), wrath, distress, anguish, ruin, devastation, darkness, gloom, clouds, thick darkness, and battle cry (all in 1:15) to wrath and more wrath (1:18; 2:2-3). God's wrath moves from the whole earth and all people (1:18) to specific nations (2:1-14), to a specific city, perhaps two (2:15–3:5). There is a crescendo of wrath in 3:8 in which God rises to prey on the peoples on whom God is pouring all of God's wrath and jealousy. The "all" in Zephaniah 3:8 is significant. Having poured out all, God's wrath is spent. Wrath, however, is not the last word. From the crucible of God's wrath, God transforms and restores those who have been spared. God changes their language so that they may call on the most holy name. God welcomes supplicants from the uttermost parts of the earth (3:9-10). The day of YHWH becomes a day of restoration in Zephaniah 3:11-20, an end to shame (v. 11), an end to fear (v. 16), a day of festival (v. 17), the ingathering of outcasts (v. 19), and the restoration of Zion's fortunes (v. 20). The promise addressed to Daughter Jerusalem and Daughter Zion (3:14) expands to the whole people (3:19-20).

# Contextual Hermeneutics

# *A Rabbi and a Priest, Daughters of Zion*

## A Jewish Reading of *Bat Zion* and *Bat Yerushalayim*

I am fascinated by the way the same words and phrases are inter-preted by different religions. An expression that is full of meaning for those of one faith can be fairly ordinary for another. That is my experi-ence with the phrase Bat Zion. Dr. Gafney has written beautifully on a Mariological reading linking Bat Zion to the Virgin Mary. My exploration of the term in my tradition found Bat Zion is treated as most any other phrase in the Hebrew Bible; there is a simple meaning and then there are embellishments. As is often the case, there is no universally accepted understanding of Bat Zion within Judaism.

*Parshanut* (traditional Jewish interpretation and commentary) and Midrash (classical and contemporary exegesis) are fairly straightforward, understanding Bat Zion as a daughter—someone who lives in—the city of Zion/Jerusalem. I observed that Bat Zion is used in the Prophets when good news or redemption is referenced. When the people are being casti-gated, the phrase Bat Jerusalem is employed. So what does this all mean?

I read with the larger tradition that Zion/Jerusalem refers to the physical city of Jerusalem: the land, the Jerusalem stone that makes up the buildings and the streets, the Western Wall that remains of the temple. In the time of biblical Israel, when the city was under siege, then destroyed, and the Israelites went into exile, the Shekinah, God's presence on earth, went into exile with them. Letting them know and feel that God was always with them wherever they were.

Bat Zion, similar to the role of the Shekinah, is a place that can never be taken away. Zion/Jerusalem remains a physical place that Jews yearn to return to, while her daughter, Bat Zion/Shekinah, spiritually travels with the people to wherever they go. Bat Zion is the part of Jerusalem the city that stays with the Jews no matter where they are.

I personally have always considered myself a Bat Zion, a daughter of Zion. As an intensely involved Jew, even though I do not live in Israel, since childhood a part of me has always resided in Jerusalem, the holy city. I took up spiritual residence there long ago. I never feel complete spiritually unless I am there. It is as if there is a hole in my soul that is filled only when I enter Jerusalem and am reunited with the part of my soul that resides there. Then I am truly a Bat Zion.

*Rabbah Arlene Goldstein Berger*

## A Christian Reading of *Bat Zion* and *Bat Yerushalayim*

The Daughter Zion/Jerusalem poem has a special association with the Virgin Mary in many Christian denominations. It is read on Gaudete Sunday in Orthodox, Catholic, Anglican, Episcopalian, Lutheran, and some Presbyterian, Methodist, and other churches that follow the lectionary. Gaudete (or "Rejoicing") Sunday is the Third Sunday of Advent, making it a week and some days prior to Christmas. The name comes from the Latin for "[God] will rejoice" in Zephaniah 3:17, Sophonias 3:17 in the Vulgate: *gaudebit*. When I read and hear Zephaniah 3:14-20 religiously as a Christian, I experience it through a Mariological lens. The use of this passage during Advent when the Church is reliving the end of the Virgin's holy pregnancy suggests that the Church and lectionary framers share and encourage this imagination.

My reading turns on the fluidity of the meaning of בת־ציון between Daughter Zion and Daughter of Zion; it is a hermeneutics of imagination. As I, a modern woman for whom the Hebrew Bible is Scripture, seek to find myself in the text and hear it addressed to me, I have often asked how ancient women heard the text and wondered if they listened to hear it to speak to them individually or collectively. One of the ways in which I listen to the text as a woman is to read it or hear it read aloud in Hebrew and listen to the places where the Divine speaks to a feminine singular entity, like Daughter Zion or the Daughter of Zion,[1] especially when that address is in the second-person feminine singular. I have been particularly drawn to the "fear nots," אל תיראי[2] and לא תיראי.[3] Both expressions occur in Zephaniah's prophecy to *Bat Zion*, in 3:15-16.

In this Mariological reading I imagine the Blessed Virgin[4] listening for God and hearing herself addressed in the feminine grammar of her Scriptures during her unprecedented and miraculous pregnancy. I imagine the Virgin hearing/reading Scripture much as people do today, as though it were directly addressed to her and interpreting it with regard to her singular situation:

> Sing Miryam, thou Daughter of Zion! Rejoice in the miracle of your
> pregnancy!
> GOD has taken judgments against you daughter.
> You will not be condemned for being pregnant before your marriage.
> The sovereign of Israel, GOD—whose holy Name may not be spoken—
> God is in your midst, daughter—in the midst of your woman's body.
> Fear not evil any longer, daughter.
> Fear not, Daughter of Zion.
> GOD—whose Name is holy—is in your midst, daughter.
> God rejoices over you with gladness, renews you in love
> exults over you with loud singing as on a day of festival.
> I will not permit you to suffer,[5] be stoned nor bear reproach.
> At the appointed time, I will save the lame and gather the outcast
> (through this pregnancy).
> At the appointed time, I will bring you all home and restore all of your
> fortunes before your eyes (through this pregnancy).

1. Having had a renewal of my faith in the African Methodist Episcopal Zion Church, often simply called "Zion," and having been licensed to preach, first ordained, commissioned as an Army Reserve chaplain, and appointed a pastor in that community, I consider myself a daughter of Zion.

2. Gen 21:17; Isa 40:9; 41:14; 54:4; Zeph 3:16. In addition to this list in Isa 41:14 God addresses Jacob as a תולעת, a feminine singular "worm," and uses the feminine imperative to speak to her/him/it. Added to this list is Boaz's declaration to Ruth: "And now, my daughter, do not be afraid, I will do for you all that you ask, for all the assembly of my people know that you are a warrior-hearted woman." (The root חיל is translated as "worthy," "virtuous," "noble," "fine," "capable," etc., here and in Prov 31:10 is a warrior, his strength, occasionally wealth, or the whole army itself; see Gen 34:29; Exod 14:4; Deut 3:18; Judg 6:12; Prov 31:3.)

3. Isa 54:14; 57:11; Zeph 3:15.

4. Since this is an explicitly religious reading I am using the religious language of my Episcopal tradition.

5. The NRSV has "bear reproach," נוגי.

I imagine the Blessed Virgin being comforted by the words of God through Zephaniah during her peculiar pregnancy. Individualized, personal readings of Scripture can bring great comfort and strengthen the faith of a religious reader. Imaginative, midrashic, readings of the Scripture are long-standing practices of Jewish and Christian religious readers, both critical and uncritical (or pre-critical) reader-response criticism. As a scholar I hope that religious readers can separate their (our) readings from the context of the text and what we can know about its original use and intent. As a religious practitioner I hope there is room at the table for all of our readings.

*Wilda C. M. Gafney*

# Conclusion

# *Post-Apocalyptic Afterword*

Zephaniah's prophecy begins with no less than the end of the world. The rhetoric is horrifying, and intentionally so. Zephaniah uses the rhetoric of horror to "scare [Judah and Jerusalem] straight."[1] Amy Kalmanofsky's analysis of the horror rhetoric in Jeremiah is helpful in theorizing the intent and impact of the prophecies of Zephaniah. Kalmanofsky argues that horror rhetoric in the Bible is designed to elicit an emotional response from the reader consisting of fear and disgust (the classic responses to any genre of horror literature)[2] and shame (a particular characteristic of biblical horror literature).[3] Indeed, shamelessness is one of the charges leveled against the nameless nation in Zephaniah 2:1, and Zephaniah links fear and shame in prophecy 5 (Zeph 3:7, 11). Removal of fear and shame are key components of the Daughter Zion proclamation in prophecy 6 (Zeph 3:15, 19).

Kalmanofsky argues that two types of horror exist, specifically, direct and indirect. Direct horror is a response to the terrifying or terrorizing entity (God or enemy nations). Indirect horror is a response to the terror

---

1. Amy Kalmanofsky, *Terror All Around: The Rhetoric of Horror in the Book of Jeremiah* (New York: T & T Clark, 2008), 1.
2. Ibid., 3, 9.
3. Ibid., 12, 14.

wrought by the terrifying or terrorizing agent, such as dispossession, destruction, exile, or becoming the object of hissing, etc. For Kalmanofsky "dismay," חתת,[4] in Jeremiah indicates direct horror in response to God's actions against people and land, Judean and foreign (Jer 8:9; 14:4; 23:4; 50:2, etc.). While the term חתת does not occur in Zephaniah, צרה, "distress" as a response to the day of YHWH in Zephaniah 1:15, and צרר, also translated as "distress" in 1:17, function similarly. Kalmanofsky uses שמם to indicate indirect horror; she points to combinations of the nominal and verbal forms where the devastation of a person or people is in response to the devastation of the land.[5] Both forms occur in Zephaniah, שממה, "devastation" in Zephaniah 2:4, 9, and 13, and שמם, "be desolate" ("in ruins," NRSV) in 3:6.

One of the distinguishing characteristics of horror is the figure of the monster. Building on the work of Noël Carroll,[6] Kalmanofsky argues that monsters are found wherever characters are horrified: "Horrified characters react to horrible figures."[7] In Zephaniah, as in Kalmanofsky's analysis of Jeremiah, "God is the single most significant and direct threat to the stability and survival of the Israelite people."[8] The day of YHWH is the means through which God horrifies God's people in Zephaniah. Corresponding to the typology of Carroll and Kalmanofsky, horrified characters respond to God's threats and actions: people wail in Zephaniah 1:10; a warrior cries in 1:14; and people walk staggeringly as though they were blind in 1:17. These characters and their responses indicate the presence of a monstrous figure who horrifies them, God. The horror that God wreaks and threatens to wreak serves a singular purpose: to terrify and shame the people of Judah and perhaps the wider world into turning back to God: "Seek God, all you humble of the land, who do God's commands; seek righteousness, seek humility; perhaps you may be hidden on the day of GOD's wrath" (Zeph 2:3).

Zephaniah's God is wrathful on behalf of her people. This God seems like a monster about to devour everything in its path. God in Zephaniah is like the bear robbed of her cubs in Hosea 13:8 and Proverbs 17:12. This image of God is potentially comforting: God will avenge her people, and

---

4. Also translated as "break down" in the NRSV.

5. Kalmanofsky, *Terror All Around*, 31, 36.

6. Noël Carroll, *The Philosophy of Horror or Paradoxes of the Heart* (New York: Routledge, 1990).

7. Kalmanofsky, *Terror All Around*, 46.

8. Ibid., 51.

their enemies will finally get what is coming to them. This God is like an action hero in a movie playing for a cheering crowd and blowing up villains with little regard for collateral damage.

The recent proliferation of superhero movies with characters that sometimes do as much harm as good suggests that people are hungry for stories of superhuman avengers to set the world to rights. Strikingly, those heroes are often deeply flawed, even anti-heroes—immoral or amoral characters—who perform heroic or even moral deeds often while leaving carnage in their wake. In Zephaniah God is both monster and hero.

The book of Zephaniah gives voice to the sense that more wrong exists with the world than can be patched and repaired, and more than a hero or antihero can set out to right by defeating a monstrous villain. The sense is that the universe would be better off if the earth were scrubbed clean, down to its mantle or core, and if God began the work of creation again. Accordingly, the scope of the destruction is monstrous and indiscriminate, decimating whole nations and cities. Yet in spite of all that is wrong with the world, the dread warrior chooses restraint in Zephaniah 3:12 to save some lives, hoping, predicting, or prophesying that they will in turn seek God.

In many post-apocalyptic movies a small band of survivors is left to make a new life and a new world from the remnant of the old. In similar fashion, the book of Zephaniah ends with a promise of rebuilding and restoration. The mother bear has put her claws away and tends to her cubs.

# Nahum Works Cited

Abegg, Martin, Peter Flint, and Eugene Ulrich. *The Dead Sea Scrolls Bible: The Oldest Known Bible Translated for the First Time into English*. San Francisco: HarperCollins, 1999.

Bassett, Frederick W. "Noah's Nakedness and the Curse of Canaan: A Case of Incest?" *VT* 21 (1971): 232–37.

Baumann, Gerlinde. "Nahum: The Just God as Sexual Predator." In *Feminist Biblical Interpretation: A Compendium of Critical Commentary on the Books of the Bible and Related Literature*, edited by Luise Schottroff and Marie-Theres Wacker, with the cooperation of Claudia Janssen and Beate Wehn, American edition edited by Martin Rumscheidt, translated by Lisa E. Dahill, et al., 433–42. Grand Rapids: Eerdmans, 2012.

Ben Zvi, Ehud. "The Concept of Prophetic Books and Its Historical Setting." In *The Production of Prophecy: Constructing Prophecy and Prophets in Yehud*, edited by Diana V. Edelman and Ehud Ben Zvi, 73–90. London: Equinox, 2009.

Bridgeman, Valerie. "Nahum." In *Africana Bible*, edited by Hugh Page Jr., et al., 194–96. Minneapolis: Fortress, 2010.

Brown, Francis, S. R. Driver, and Charles A. Briggs, eds. *The Brown-Driver-Briggs Hebrew and English Lexicon*. Oxford: Clarendon, 1906.

Butler, Judith. *Bodies That Matter: On the Discursive Limits of "Sex."* New York: Routledge, 1993.

Carden, Michael. "The Book of the Twelve Minor Prophets." In *The Queer Bible Commentary*, edited by Deryn Guest, 432–87. London: SCM, 2006.

Christensen, Duane L. *Nahum: A New Translation with Introduction and Commentary*. AYB 24F. New Haven: Yale University Press, 2009.

Clines, David J. A., ed. *The Dictionary of Classical Hebrew*. Sheffield: Sheffield Phoenix, 2011.

Dempsey, Carol J. *Amos, Hosea, Micah, Nahum, Zephaniah, Habakkuk*. New College-ville Bible Commentary 15. Collegeville, MN: Liturgical Press, 2013.

Embry, Bradley. "The 'Naked Narrative' from Noah to Leviticus: Reassessing Voyeurism in the Account of Noah's Nakedness in Genesis 9.22-24." *JSOT* 35 (2011): 417–33.

Frymer-Kensky, Tikva. *In the Wake of the Goddesses: Women, Culture, and the Biblical Transformation of Pagan Myth*. New York: Free Press, 1992.

Gaebelein, Frank E. *The Expositor's Bible Commentary: Daniel, Minor Prophets*. Vol. 7. Grand Rapids: Zondervan, 1985.

Gafney, Wilda. *Daughters of Miriam: Women Prophets in Ancient Israel*. Minneapolis: Fortress, 2007.

———. "A Womanist Midrash on Zipporah." In *I Found God in Me: A Womanist Reader*, edited by Mitzi Smith, 131–57. Eugene, OR: Cascade, 2014.

García-Treto, Francisco O. "Nahum." In *The New Interpreter's Bible: General Articles and Introduction, Commentary, and Reflections for Each Book of the Bible, Including the Apocryphal/Deuterocanonical Books*. Nashville: Abingdon, 1994.

Gesenius, Wilhelm. *Gesenius' Hebrew Grammar*. Edited by E. Kautzsch and A. E. Cowley. Oxford: Clarendon, 1910.

Gordon, Pamela, and Harold Washington. "Rape as a Military Metaphor in the Hebrew Bible." In *A Feminist Companion to the Latter Prophets*, edited by Athalya Brenner, 308–25. FCB 8. Sheffield: Sheffield Academic, 1995.

Grayson, Albert Kirk. "History and Culture of Assyria." In *The Anchor Yale Bible Dictionary*, edited by David Noel Freedman, 4:732–55. New Haven: Yale University Press, 2008.

Hallo, William W., and K. Lawson Younger Jr., eds. *The Context of Scripture*. Vols. 1–3. Leiden: Brill, 2003.

Harris, R. Laird, Gleason L. Archer, and Bruce K. Waltke, eds. *Theological Wordbook of the Old Testament*. Chicago: Moody Press, 1980.

Harris, Rivkah. "Women: Royal Women." In *The Anchor Yale Bible Dictionary*, edited by David Noel Freedman, 6:950. New Haven: Yale University Press, 2008.

Koehler, Ludwig, Walter Baumgartner, and M. E. J. Richardson, eds. *The Hebrew and Aramaic Lexicon of the Old Testament*. Leiden: Brill, 2000.

Lanner, Laurel. *"Who Will Lament Her?" The Feminine and the Fantastic in the Book of Nahum*. Vol. 11. New York: T & T Clark, 2006.

Lemaire, André. "Education: Ancient Israel." In *The Anchor Yale Bible Dictionary*, edited by David Noel Freedman, 2:305–11. New Haven: Yale University Press, 2008.

Lewis, Theodore J. "Amon (Diety)." In *The Anchor Yale Bible Dictionary*, edited by David Noel Freedman, 1:197. New Haven: Yale University Press, 2008.

Magdalene, F. Rachel. "Ancient Near Eastern Treaty-Curses and the Ultimate Texts of Terror: A Study of the Language of Divine Sexual Abuse in the Prophetic Corpus." In *A Feminist Companion to the Latter Prophets*, edited by Athalya Brenner, 326–52. FCB 8. Sheffield: Sheffield Academic, 1995.

Marsman, Hennie J. *Women in Ugarit and Israel: Their Social and Religious Position in the Context of the Ancient Near East*. Leiden: Brill, 2003.

Melville, Sarah C. "Neo-Assyrian Royal Women and Male Identity: Status as a Social Tool." *JAOS* 124 (2004): 37–57.

O'Brien, Julia M. *Nahum*. Readings: A New Biblical Commentary. London: Black, 2002.

Parpola, Simo. *Assyrian Prophecies*. State Archives of Assyria. Vol. 9. Helsinki: Helsinki University Press, 1997.

Pietersma, Albert, and Benjamin G. Wright, eds. *A New English Translation of the Septuagint*. Oxford: Oxford University Press, 2007.

Pinker, Aron. "Descent of the Goddess Ishtar to the Netherworld and Nahum II 8." *VT* 55 (2005): 89–100.

Raheb, Mitri. *Faith in the Face of Empire: The Bible through Palestinian Eyes*. New York: Orbis Books, 2014.

Reade, Julian. "The Evolution of Assyrian Imperial Architecture: Political Implications and Uncertainties." *Mesopotamia: rivista di archeologia, epigrafia e storia orientale antica* 46 (2011): 109–25.

———. "The Ishtar Temple at Nineveh." *Iraq* 67, *Nineveh. Papers of the 49th Rencontre Assyriologique Internationale, Part Two* (Spring 2005): 347–90.

Rosenberg, A. J. *Twelve Prophets: A New English Translation*. Vol. 1. New York: Judaica Press, 1991.

Sanderson, Judith. "Nahum." In *The Women's Bible Commentary*, edited by Carol A. Newsom and Sharon H. Ringe, 232–36. London: SPCK, 1992.

Shao, Joseph, and Rosa Shao. *Joel, Nahum and Malachi*. Asia Bible Commentary Series. Manila: Asia Theological Association, 2013.

Teutsch, David A., and Betsy Platkin Teutsch. *Kol Haneshemah: Shabbat Vehagim*. 3rd ed. Elkins Park, PA: Reconstructionist Press, 2000.

Thistlethwaite, Susan. "'You May Enjoy the Spoil of Your Enemies': Rape as a Biblical Metaphor for War." *Semeia* 61 (1993): 59–75.

Van der Woude, Adam S. "The Book of Nahum: A Letter Written In Exile." *OtSt* 20 (1977): 108–26.

Weems, Renita J. *Battered Love: Marriage, Sex, and Violence in the Hebrew Prophets*. Minneapolis: Fortress, 1995.

# Habakkuk Works Cited

Alexander, Michelle. *The New Jim Crow: Mass Incarceration in the Age of Colorblindness*. New York: New Press, 2012.

Anderson, Francis I. *Habakkuk: A New Translation with Introduction and Commentary*. AB 25. New Haven: Yale University Press, 1974.

Ben Zvi, Ehud. "Habakkuk." In *The Jewish Study Bible*, edited by Adele Berlin and Mark Zvi Brettler. Oxford: Oxford University Press, 2004.

Cannon, Katie Geneva. "Womanist Interpretation and Preaching in the Black Church." In *I Found God in Me: A Womanist Reader*, edited by Mitzi Smith, 56–67. Eugene: OR, Cascade, 2014.

Carruthers, Iva E. "Called to Be the Salt of the Earth: Black and Womanist Theologies—Which Way Forward?" In *Walk Together Children: Black Church and Womanist Theologies, Church and Theological Education*, edited by Dwight N. and Linda E. Thomas, 297–317. Eugene, OR: Cascade Books, 2010.

Clines, David J. A., ed. *The Dictionary of Classical Hebrew*. Sheffield: Sheffield Phoenix, 2011.

Coggins, Richard, and Jin H. Han. *Six Minor Prophets through the Centuries: Nahum, Habakkuk, Zephaniah, Haggai, Zechariah, Malachi*. New York: Wiley & Sons, 2011.

Cook, Stephen. "Habakkuk 3, Gender, and War." *lectio difficilior*, no. 1 (2009); http://www.lectio.unibe.ch/09_1/steve_cook_habakkuk_3.html.

Cross, Frank Moore. *Canaanite Myth and Hebrew Epic: Essays in the History of the Religion of Israel*. Cambridge: Harvard University Press, 1976.

Floyd-Thomas, Stacey M. *Black Church Studies: An Introduction*. Nashville: Abingdon, 2007.

Gafney, Wilda. *Daughters of Miriam: Women Prophets in Ancient Israel*. Minneapolis: Fortress, 2007.

Ginsburg, Christian D. *Introduction to the Massoretico-Critical Edition of the Hebrew Bible*. New York: Ktav, 1966.

Hallo, William W., and K. Lawson Younger Jr., eds. *The Context of Scripture*. Vols. 1–3. Leiden: Brill, 2003.

Kirk-Duggan, Cheryl. "African-American Spirituals: Confronting and Exorcising Evil through Song." In *A Troubling in My Soul: Womanist Perspectives on Evil and Suffering*, edited by Emilie Townes, 150–71. Bishop Henry McNeal Turner Studies in North American Black Religion. Vol. 8. Maryknoll, NY: Orbis Books, 2015.

Levine, Baruch. *Leviticus: The Traditional Hebrew Text with the New JPS Translation*. The JPS Torah Commentary. Edited by Chaim Potok, Nahum M. Sarna, Jacob Milgrom, and Jeffrey H. Tigay. Philadelphia: Jewish Publication Society, 1989.

O'Brien, Julia M. *Nahum, Habakkuk, Zephaniah, Haggai, Zechariah, Malachi*. AOTC. Nashville: Abingdon, 2004.

Roberts, J. J. M. *Nahum, Habakkuk and Zephaniah: A Commentary*. Louisville: Westminster John Knox, 1991.

Sweeney, Marvin A. "Habakkuk, Book of." In *The Anchor Yale Bible Dictionary*, edited by David Noel Freedman, 3:1–5. New Haven: Yale University Press, 2008.

Walker, Alice. *In Search of Our Mothers' Gardens: Womanist Prose*. San Diego: Harcourt Brace Jovanovich, 1983.

# Zephaniah Works Cited

Avigad, Nahman. "The King's Daughter and the Lyre." *IEJ* 28 (1978): 147–51.

Berlin, Adele. *Zephaniah*. AB 25A. New Haven: Yale University Press, 1974.

Blenkinsopp, Joseph. *A History of Prophecy in Israel*. Louisville: Westminster John Knox, 1996.

———. *Isaiah 1–39*. AB 19. New Haven: Yale University Press, 1974.

Brin, Gershon. "The Title בן המלך and Its Parallels." *Annali dell'Istituto Orientale di Napoli* 29 (1965): 433–65.

Carroll, Noël. *The Philosophy of Horror or Paradoxes of the Heart*. New York: Routledge, 1990.

Clines, David J. A., ed. *The Dictionary of Classical Hebrew*. Sheffield: Sheffield Phoenix, 2011.

Cogan, Mordechai, and Hayim Tadmor. *II Kings*. AB 11. Garden City, NY: Doubleday, 1988.

Dempsey, Carol J. *Amos, Hosea, Micah, Nahum, Zephaniah, Habakkuk*. New Collegeville Bible Commentary 15. Collegeville, MN: Liturgical Press, 2013.

Frymer-Kensky, Tikva. *In the Wake of the Goddesses: Women, Culture, and the Biblical Transformation of Pagan Myth*. New York: Free Press, 1992.

Gafney, Wilda. *Daughters of Miriam: Women Prophets in Ancient Israel*. Minneapolis: Fortress, 2007.

———. "It Does Matter If You're Black or White, Too Black or Too White, but Mestizo Is Just Right." In *Re-Presenting Texts: Jewish and Black Biblical Interpretation*, edited by W. David Nelson and Rivka Ulmer, 53–64. Society of Biblical Literature Consultation on Midrash. Piscataway, NJ: Gorgias, 2013.

———. *Womanist Midrash: A Reintroduction to the Women of the Torah and of the Throne*. Louisville: Westminster John Knox, 2017.

Gruber, Mayer I. "Women's Voices in the Book of Micah." *lectio difficilior*, no. 1 (2007); http://www.lectio.unibe.ch/07_1/mayer_gruber_womens_voices.htm.

Hallo, William W., and K. Lawson Younger Jr., eds., *The Context of Scripture*. Vols. 1–3. Leiden: Brill, 2003.

Heffelfinger, Katie M. "Zephaniah." In *Women's Bible Commentary*, edited by Carol A. Newsom, Sharon H. Ringe, and Jacqueline E. Lapsley, 335–38. 3rd ed. Louisville: Westminster John Knox, 2012.

Hepner, Gershon. *Legal Friction: Law, Narrative, and Identity Politics in Biblical Israel*. New York: Lang, 2010.

Kalmanofsky, Amy. *Terror All Around: The Rhetoric of Horror in the Book of Jeremiah*. New York: T & T Clark, 2008.

Knoppers, Gary N. *I Chronicles 1–9*. AB 12. New Haven: Yale University Press, 1974.

Liddell, H. G., and Robert Scott, eds. *An Intermediate Greek-English Lexicon*. New Haven: Yale University Press, 1996.

Maier, Christl M. *Daughter Zion, Mother Zion: Gender, Space, and the Sacred in Ancient Israel*. Minneapolis: Fortress, 2008.

McCarter, P. Kyle Jr. *II Samuel*. AB 9. New Haven: Yale University Press, 1974.

Meyers, Carol L., and Eric M. Meyers. *Haggai and Zechariah 1–8*. AB 25B. Garden City, NY: Doubleday, 1974.

Pietersma, Albert, and Benjamin G. Wright. *A New English Translation of the Septuagint: And the Other Greek Translations Traditionally Included Under That Title*. New York: Oxford University Press, 2007.

Pritchard, James B. *Ancient Near Eastern Texts: Relating to the Old Testament*. Princeton: Princeton University Press, 1969.

Rice, Gene. "The African Roots of the Prophet Zephaniah." *JRT* 36 (1979): 21–31.

Sadler, Rodney Steven. *Can a Cushite Change His Skin? An Examination of Race, Ethnicity, and Othering in the Hebrew Bible*. New York: T & T Clark, 2005.

Sanderson, Judith E. "Zephaniah." In *The Women's Bible Commentary*, edited by Carol A. Newsom and Sharon H. Ringe, 335–38. Louisville: Westminster John Knox, 1998.

Strong, Augustus H. *Strong's Greek Dictionary of the New Testament*. Accordance electronic edition, version 2.6. Altamonte Springs: OakTree Software, 1999.

Sweeney, Marvin A. *Zephaniah: A Commentary on the Book of Zephaniah*. Edited by Paul D. Hanson. Hermeneia 36. Minneapolis: Fortress, 2003.

Udoekpo, Michael Ufok. *Re-Thinking the Day of YHWH and Restoration of Fortunes in the Prophet Zephaniah: An Exegetical and Theological Study of 1:14-18; 3:14-20*. Bern: Lang, 2010.

Thayer, Joseph H. *Greek-English Lexicon of the New Testament*. Accordance electronic edition, version 1.6. Altamonte Springs: OakTree Software, 2004.

# Index of Scripture References
# and Other Ancient Writings

# Index of Subjects

of Jerusalem/Zion, 32, 125, 153,
183, 185, 188–93; *see also* Bat
Zion
daughters (unrecorded), 149
David, 135, 145, 164, 185
as author or dedicatee, 108–9
children of, 134, 135n36
daughters of, 148n84
Dempsey, Carol, 4, 150
desolation, 40, 162–63, 170–71
devastation, 29, 40, 153, 155, 157, 159,
169, 196
divine glory/Shekinah, 100–101, 106,
111
divine jealousy. *See* God
divine phallus, 187n25
divine tenderness. *See* God
divine warrior, 17, 62, 100, 106–7,
109–13, 114, 158, 159, 186

Egypt, 7, 47, 51, 53, 56–57, 77, 112,
129, 130n11, 167–69
Assyria and, 14n8
decline of, 139
fall of Thebes and, 56
Eliakim, 149; *see also* Jehoiakim
empire, 9n32
addiction and, 102
beloved community, 9n32
construction of, 100
critique of, 103
as demonic, 9n32
as enemy, 15
evil, 9
oppression of, 9n32
power abuse of, 100
violence of, 16
Esarhaddon, 23, 42
Esharra-hamat, 42
exile, 37
effects of, 29, 47
language of, 37–38, 190
rhetoric of (sexualized), 38–39
Shekinah in, 32, 192

"fear not," 184–86, 193
figs, 47, 58, 113
fruit, 42, 108, 113
cursed, 157
forbidden, 101
uncircumcised, 101
Frymer-Kensky, Tikva, 30, 188

Gafney, Wilda C. M., 43, 130, 135, 148,
177, 178, 191, 194
García-Treto, Francisco O., 61–62, 64
Gath-hepher, 176
Gedaliah, 134
Ginsburg, Christian D., 88
God
anger and, 3, 6, 18, 21, 89, 106, 107,
112, 152, 160, 175, 176
anointed by, 112
anthropomorphized, 21, 124, 156,
181
attributes of, 21, 22, 26, 93, 100
awe, 86, 88, 100, 106, 181
battering, 64–65
as Commander of Heaven's
Armies, 44
control of, 26
as Creator, 36, 88, 99, 119, 197
as destroyer, 79, 127, 140, 157, 160,
162, 163, 164, 166, 179–81, 197
earth and, 18, 100, 103, 107, 111,
124, 141, 153, 157, 159–60, 175,
176, 181, 190, 192, 197
faithfulness of, 92, 93, 179
good and evil, 26
hybridized, 22
jealousy of, 17–20, 181, 190
maleness of, 51n13, 62, 64
as monster, 196–97
name, 18, 20, 185
nationalistic gods and, 64
plundering, 156
portraits of, 21, 64, 118, 151
power of, 6, 8, 17, 21, 22, 39, 61,
70–71, 106, 111, 119, 158, 164,
166, 179–81

Haddu, 110, 142, 147
Ham, 53n18
  African American discussion of,
    163n17
  children of, 162
  misnamed curse of, 163
Hamutal bat Jeremiah of Libnah, 149,
  150
Hezekiah, 16, 17, 41 43, 128, 129, 134–38
  genealogies of, 136–37
  identity of, 137–38
Hilkiah, 138, 176
Holy One, 78–79, 86, 103, 106, 111,
  117–20
honeymooning
  language of, 9n30
hope, 22, 35–36, 58
host(s), 100n7, 110; *see also* armies
  divine, 37
  of heavens, 143, 145, 146
  Lord of, 44, 46, 96, 162, 163, 166n23
house
  as dynasty, 96, 99, 107, 112
  of Judah, 162, 164, 165, 184
  king's, 149
  Lord's, 150
  priest's, 179
Huldah, 124, 155, 177
human trafficking, 39n40
humble of the land, 160–61, 196
humble-poor, 184–85

identity
  African/Nubian, 131–32
  ethnic, 65, 99, 130, 133
  God's, 109
  Israelite, 83, 132
  prophetic, 109
idol, 97, 103, 139, 141–42, 145
  terms for, 103
  worth of, 103
idolatry, 142, 181
  of priests, 143

Inanna, 30, 31n13, 187
instruction, 176, 180
  liturgical, 108–15
  vision, 91
intermarriage, 132–33
intoxicants, 98n5, 100, 101, 102; *see
  also* wealth, wine, wrath
Ishtar, 7, 8n25, 22, 26n3, 30, 31, 38, 39,
  42, 51; *see also* Asshur
  conflation with Asshur, 30–31; *see
    also* Nabu and Marduk/Bel
  conflation with Nineveh, 20, 37n34
  descent myth of, 38
  Holy Spirit and, 31n13
  as mother aspect of Asshur, 7n22,
    31n13
  in Nahum, 7
  Nineveh and, 37n34, 51
  as prostitute, 48
  rape of, 63
  subjugation of, 30
  as transgressive, 64

Jacob, 27, 35
  Israel and, 10, 62
  as synonym for Judah, 35
  as worm, 193
Jehoahaz, 42, 149, 150
Jehoiachin, 149–50
Jehoiakim, 149–50; *see also* Eliakim
Jeremiah (book), 195–96
  Baruch as author, 91n37
  as scroll, 3n4
Jeremiah (prophet), 8, 178n10
Jerusalem, 25, 124, 170, 173–76,
  179–92
  absence of, in Nahum, 25
  commerce in, 33
  as daughter, 191
  daughter of, 185, 188; *see also* Zion
  day of Lord and, 155–61
  fall of, 77, 98, 150
  God's jealousy of, 20

women, 55
*See also* Ashurbanipal, Asshur-
  nadin-sumi, Esarhaddon,
  Esharra-hamat, Libali-sharrat,
  Naqia, Sennacherib, Shadditu,
  Sherua-etirat
locusts, 48, 58
logosprosodic analysis, 6n13
loins, 28, 29, 34, 40n2
love, 160
  absence of, in Nahum, 21
  divine, 6, 21, 63, 64, 186–87, 193
  punishment and, 53
  women's, 89–90
lynching, 63

Magdalene, F. Rachel, 55, 58
Marduk (Bel), 31
marriage
  abduction, 132
  forced, 55, 132
  language of, 8n28
  metaphor, 54, 187
  rape-, 133
Marsman, Hennie J., 43
Masoretic break, 11, 77n6m 96, 98,
  126
master, 39n40, 94n44, 110n7, 142
  sorcerer, 46
mastery, 37, 94, 94n44
Mattaniah (Zedekiah), 150
messiah, 39, 92
  coming of, 92n39
  -king, 112
Milcom (Malcom), 125, 141–47, 166,
  181
mistress, 38, 39n40, 46, 94n44
monster(s), 70, 196–97
  God as, 197
Moses, 178
  access to God, 100
  hiding of, 127
  horns of, 110

naming of, 178
plural heritage of, 132
visions of God by, 111
Mot, 92; *see also* Baal

Nabu, 30, 31
Nahum (book)
  Assyrian Empire and, 9, 12, 16–17,
    55
  audience of, 5, 6, 8, 10, 19, 27, 35,
    36, 42
  author(s) of, 4, 19
  authorship periods of, 5–6
  as book/scroll, 3, 13
  as epistle, 14
  gendered rhetoric of, 7, 11n37, 12
  God depiction in, 3, 17–22, 26, 36,
    44, 53, 61–64; see also God
  as good news, 61
  Hebrew of, 11
  language of, 6, 7
  liturgical absence of, 61
  love in, 21
  misogyny in, 62–63; *see also*
    Nineveh
  as oracle, 13
  as postcolonial literature, 12
  proclamations of, 11, 39
  pronouns in, 11
  prophecies of, 11, 39
  as prophecy, 4n5, 10, 13, 27, 35
  rhetoric of, 12, 15, 48, 61, 63
  sexual violence in, 8, 50–56, 61, 62;
    *see also* Nineveh, rape, sexual
    violence
  subject of, 6, 8, 11n38, 12
  violence in, 8, 62–63, 64
Nahum (person)
  as character, 4, 5, 14n4
  dating of, 10n36
  gender of, 4n7, 19
  name of, 10, 14, 21n36
  prophethood of, 14, 27

## General Editor

Barbara E. Reid, OP, is a Dominican Sister of Grand Rapids, Michigan. She holds a PhD in biblical studies from The Catholic University of America and is vice president and academic dean and professor of New Testament studies at Catholic Theological Union, Chicago. Her most recent publications are *Wisdom's Feast: An Invitation to Feminist Interpretation of the Scriptures* (2016) and *Abiding Word: Sunday Reflections on Year A, B, C* (3 vols.; 2011, 2012, 2013). She served as president of the Catholic Biblical Association in 2014–2015.

## Volume Editor

Carol J. Dempsey, OP, PhD, is professor of theology (biblical studies) at the University of Portland, Oregon. Her primary research interest is in prophetic literature as it relates to the ancient and contemporary world. Her recent publications include *The Bible and Literature* (Orbis Books, 2015) and *Amos, Hosea, Micah, Nahum, Habakkuk, and Zephaniah: A Commentary* (Liturgical Press, 2013) and numerous articles related to prophets, gender studies, ethics, and environmental concerns. She is a member of the Dominican Order of Caldwell, New Jersey.

## Author

The Rev. Dr. Wilda (Wil) Gafney is an associate professor of Hebrew Bible at Brite Divinity School where she prepares students undertaking a first master's degree in religion, seeking to serve in a variety of social and ecclesial settings, and students seeking the PhD in Hebrew biblical studies. She is the recipient of the Catherine Saylor Hill Faculty Excellence award. Dr. Gafney is the author of *Daughters of Miriam: Women Prophets in Ancient Israel* (2007) and *Womanist Midrash: A Reintroduction to the Women of the Torah and the Throne* (2017).